THE COMPENSATIONS OF WAR

THE COMPENSATIONS OF WAR

The Diary of an Ambulance Driver during the Great War

By Guy Emerson Bowerman, Jr.
Edited by Mark C. Carnes

University of Texas Press
Austin

Cover illustration by Sue Durban

Copyright © 1983 by the University of Texas Press
All rights reserved
Printed in the United States of America

First edition, 1983

Requests for permission to reproduce material
from this work should be sent to:
Permissions
University of Texas Press
Box 7819
Austin, Texas 78712

Library of Congress Cataloging in Publication Data

Bowerman, Guy Emerson, 1896–1947.
The compensations of war.

Includes bibliographical references.
1. Bowerman, Guy Emerson, 1896–1947. 2. World War, 1914–1918—Medical care—France. 3. World War, 1914–1918—Personal narratives, American. 4. World War, 1914–1918—Campaigns—France. 5. France—History—German occupation, 1914–1918. 6. Ambulance drivers—United States—Biography. 7. Ambulance drivers—France—Biography. I. Carnes, Mark C. (Mark Christopher), 1950–   . II. Title.
D629.F8B693   1983   940.4'7573   82-23846
ISBN 0-292-71074-7

For "M"

Contents

Introduction
ix

Diary
1

Maps
167

Appendix 1
Complete Roster of S.S.U. 585 from
August 7, 1917, to April 23, 1919
173

Appendix 2
Station List, Section 585
175

Glossary
177

Introduction

"St. Anthony's Boy Not Yet 21 Years Volunteers." So read the headline of the August 23, 1917, *Teton-Peak Chronicle*, published in eastern Idaho. Guy Emerson Bowerman, Jr., a twenty-year-old Yale freshman, had just arrived in France after enlisting in the United States Army Ambulance Service. Too young for the upcoming draft, Bowerman had enlisted from "purely patriotic motives and a desire to serve his country." His photograph showed "splendid physical development and a clear cut appearance which warrants us in saying that he will give a good account of himself." The editor joined the "entire community" in wishing him well in France.

There was good reason for the community to take particular note of Bowerman. His father, Guy Bowerman, Sr., founder of the Idaho State Bank, organizer of the Idaho State Bankers Association, and member of the executive council of the American Bankers Association in New York, was an economic leader in a farming community dependent on credit. Moreover, young Bowerman had for some time dated Marguerite Comstock of nearby Rexburg, daughter of the founder of the First National Bank of Rexburg. In a Mormon region, the eventual marriage of this Protestant couple no doubt seemed a foregone conclusion, thereby uniting two of the major banking firms in the region.

Bowerman had received a better education than most boys from rural Idaho. Rather than attend the provincial schools in the area, he was sent to East Side High School in Salt Lake City, where he was able to meet students of diverse backgrounds. After graduation he went to a preparatory school in Mercersburg, Pennsylvania, for one year and, in September 1916, to Yale. He was not a serious student his first year of college, and he became increasingly distracted by events in Europe.

When Congress declared war on the Central Powers in April 1917, Bowerman immediately made plans to join the air corps. But his parents, despite a patriotic enthusiasm for the war, insisted that their only child display his valor more sensibly. Bowerman chafed at this parental interference in what was perhaps the most important decision of his life, but he yielded to their wishes. He took solace in the fact that the ambulance corps were departing almost immediately. He commenced training on June 28, 1917, and boarded a troopship for France within five weeks.

Bowerman served as an ambulance driver in France and Belgium for a year and a half. He received the Croix de Guerre for conspicuous bravery and devotion to duty after having volunteered to evacuate wounded men during an especially severe bombardment. He was assigned to the army of occupation in Germany for two months, and then to France before being sent home. In the spring of 1919 he returned to Idaho and became engaged to Marguerite (referred to as "M" in the diary). Granted a year's credit for his service abroad, Bowerman matriculated that fall as a junior at Yale. Yale did not then allow married students, so Bowerman quit school after his junior year, married his childhood sweetheart, and went to work as a teller at the Columbia Trust Bank of Salt Lake City. On January 1, 1921, he and his wife moved to California, where he worked as a teller in the Security First National Bank of Los Angeles. Several years later Bowerman and his father organized an independent bank in Los Angeles, which they sold to the Security First National Bank. Bowerman, Jr., was made branch manager of that bank. In 1931 he worked as a bank examiner for the Federal Reserve. Always impatient with close supervision, Bowerman longed to be his own boss. In 1936 he purchased a small Los Angeles exporting firm, which he managed until his death in 1947. He also operated family interests in lumbering in eastern Idaho. He and Marguerite had three children, Suzanne, Guy Emerson, and Joanne.

Bowerman began keeping a diary as soon as he arrived at the training camp outside Allentown, Pennsylvania, in June 1917, and he continued it throughout the war. While stationed in Belgium and France after the armistice, he recopied the diary and, in doing so, added a number of details and observations that he had not had time to put into the original version. This second version, which is the one reproduced here, is more complete, as well as more legible, than its predecessor. (The original version has been donated to the Yale University libraries; the version reproduced here is in the possession of Joanne Bowerman Wiley.)

The diary is interesting for many reasons; one was Bowerman's attention to the details that often are missing from the generals' accounts or the secondary literature on the war. Malcolm Cowley has commented on the "spectatorial" attitude that pervaded the ambulance service, and Bowerman was acutely conscious of his role as observer. Every word, every sight, every movement seemed to hold portent, and he copied them all down faithfully, occasionally lamenting his inability to decipher their meaning. After his troopship had been attacked by submarines, for example, he pondered the theatrical aspects of the event.

> What a queer world this is! I bet there were a couple hundred men on board who had read, in open mouthed awe and admiration, stories of sea battles in our previous wars. Here they were holding box seats at a modern sea fight . . . and they seemed to enjoy it immensely . . . (Aug. 20, 1917)

Later in the war he watched as a passing infantry column was shattered by an artillery barrage; as the men began to scurry across the open field Bowerman thought the sight "so unnatural that one cannot help but believe that he is at a movie" (July 18, 1918). When the great German offensives of 1918 brought him into the war as never before, Bowerman confessed that he had not enlisted because of a love of France or a hatred of Germany, but because it was "a duty to be accepted gladly because thru its performance we should see new sights and experience thrills and strange sensations." Now, he reflected, "we are no longer supernumeraries in a show we are part of the cast itself" (May 30, 1918).

Ambulance drivers were well placed to chronicle the war. They were usually assigned either to *postes de secours* (dressing stations) near the front lines or to evacuation centers that collected the wounded from the *postes* and sent them by large ambulances or trains to army hospitals. The handful of drivers at each *poste* were almost entirely unfettered by supervision. Bowerman's section, attached to a French division, was probably more independent than those sections that were part of the American army. Section 585 was nominally under the supervision of the Médecin Divisionnaire—a position roughly equivalent to the division surgeon of the American army. Bowerman's M.D., known by the men as "the Old Man," delegated routine decisions to two lieutenants, one French (Lieut. Jamon, often spelled Jamou or Jamoux in the diary) and the other American (Lieut. John R. Abbot). It appears that the American lieutenant was pretty much left on his own, and he in turn seemed reluctant to impose on his men. Thus Bowerman was free to spend time exploring trenches or abandoned chateaux, chatting with French soldiers, or otherwise soaking up as much information as possible about the war.

Moreover, Bowerman saw the war from several different vantage points. Shortly after his section arrived at St. Nazaire it was attached to the 128th French infantry division, which held a quiet portion of the front stretching from Verdun to Nancy. Known as "Les Loups des Bois le Prêtre" (The Wolves of Bois le Prêtre) for its defense of a woods near Toul in 1914, the division fought in important battles at Verdun from 1914 through 1917. After especially bloody conflicts near Verdun in July and October 1917, the 128th was sent for recuperation in the Lorraine. It was here that Bowerman's section joined it. During this period he told of camp life and his desire to see what war was really like.

During the German spring offensive of 1918, when the French center buckled and German troops advanced to within thirty-five miles of Paris, the 128th took up a defensive position in the forest at Villers-Cotterêts. The heavy casualties, the confusion, and the pervasive sense of despair caused Bowerman to contemplate the meaning of war and his response to it. But he had relatively little time to brood, or to make entries in the diary, because he was busy taking care of wounded. The initial success of the German offensive probably hastened Germany's demise; the German forces, stretched thin by the advance and depleted by enormous losses, were vulnerable to the combined French and English counterattack of July 18. "Les Loups" took part in that and a succession of battles that thrust the Germans out of France and Belgium.

In August, Bowerman came down with dysentery and was himself evacuated to a hospital in Toulouse. After several weeks he was able to return to his unit; in Paris he eluded his staff escort and hastened back to the ambulance section, which was about to be transferred to the northern front to work with the combined French, English, Belgian, and American forces that pursued the Germans across the plains of Belgium. Bowerman, who had longed to witness a war of movement, was dismayed that the muddy Belgian roads were impassable, leaving him and the Allied armies stalled in huge traffic jams. Twice in November his unit received word of an armistice; the first time, however, the announcement was punctuated by the explosion of a shell nearby. Bowerman had already come to distrust military communiqués, and even a week after the armistice he remained skeptical about the prospects for peace.

The diary is absorbing for reasons apart from Bowerman's conscious attempt to record the war and his extensive travels along various fronts. Innocently snobbish, ingenuously wholesome, yet mature enough to write unsparingly of his failings and fears, Bowerman is himself interesting. He was aware of his personal development during the war; on the anniversary of his having taken up the diary he reflected that the war had changed "everything connected with me and my life."

> Here I am living a story such as would have held me enthralled as a boy, and—I think nothing of it! The whole business is unromantic, too close at hand for a man of my capacity to grasp the "heroics" of it. It seems that I have never known any other life but this . . . it is just as if we'd been born again in another world and this war was a perfectly natural mode of life. Thus are we able to adapt ourselves . . . (June 28, 1918)

Bowerman's views of social rank were broadened by the war. "A gentleman will never get ahead in the Army," he noted on the troopship when personal belongings disappeared (Aug. 12, 1917). Later he was relieved that his unit was "composed of men who are or at least have been gentlemen. I can't imagine how these days would pass in the company of men with whom you had nothing in common," he stated (Oct. 27–Nov. 2, 1917). Gradually, however, "true human values," learned from "all manners and breeds of men," displaced his earlier conceptions (June 28, 1918). The most striking example of this change occurred while he was driving an overloaded ambulance and a severely wounded Senegalese, suffering silently in the front seat, toppled against Bowerman's shoulder. "I had never supposed that I would like to have my coat stained with a nigger's blood," he wrote, "but if I could have eased that fine fellow one jot of pain I would gladly have had my whole uniform wet with it" (July 18, 1918).

Bowerman's original notions of war, like those of most Americans, were naïve. From the army recruiting posters he had "learned to imagine" that war consisted of "batteries galloping into position in the wheat fields." He was unprepared for a war in which men cowered in mud-filled trenches before machine-made death. "It is the unnaturalness of being killed by a huge screaming thundering shell that gives one fear and horror of dying. Not the fear of *death*, but the manner of death" (July 19, 1918). Similarly, his attitude towards the "Boches," though consistently condemnatory, became more complex during the course of the war. On seeing his first wounded German prisoner, Bowerman envisioned him raping Belgian women and mutilating their children (Jan. 15, 1918). Several months later Bowerman came across a child who had been killed in an air raid; "the baby killers lived up to their rep," he commented (May 12, 1918). Yet later, when French stretcher-bearers ignored a wounded German's cries for water, Bowerman, who generally emulated the French in all things, incurred their scorn by coming to his aid (June 3, 1918). A week before the armistice, as the Germans were being chased through Belgium, Bowerman happened upon an open letter written in French by a German soldier seeking forgiveness for the war. Bowerman's initial reaction was cynical, yet he finally conceded that perhaps this soldier was a "gentle, God fearing person who realized that the Germans were unwelcome guests and not God sent overlords of a benighted race" (Nov. 4, 1918).

Perhaps the most profound change came in Bowerman's definition of courage. Like many in war before him, he had hoped to measure up. "Everyone is keen to know how he'll act in a tight place," he wrote following the torpedo attack on his ship. "What you fear is that when the test comes you'll show fear" (Aug. 20, 1917). During artillery barrages he furtively glanced at the faces of his companions and "secretly rejoiced" that they shared his fear. "It would be terrible to be the only one afraid" (March 11, 1918). Once he panicked while leading an ambulance convoy through a town during a bombardment; his mistake prolonged the convoy's exposure and he was mortified (May 27, 1918). Several weeks later he made amends by offering to evacuate wounded across a bridge that was being subjected to a fierce artillery barrage. He prayed to "have the guts to go thru with it" and drove quickly toward the bridge. Shells were bursting on both sides of the road.

> I saw them but somehow they didn't seem to register on my brain. I saw them & that was all. The road surely had been & was being shelled. Shell holes, branches & wires littered the road. Despite this I had had from the time I said my prayer the most peculiar feeling almost of abstraction, the shells didn't worry me in the least because something inside me kept saying "you're safe"; "they won't hit you"; "don't be

afraid." As we dashed along the road I recall how it seemed that I was merely driving along a country road at home. A most peculiar feeling and I believe I have failed to express just exactly what it was. (June 14, 1918)

The pages at the end of the diary are mostly blank; but on nearly ten of them Bowerman had begun to write a story. The first-person narrator, Harry, enters an *abri* and listens intently as another ambulance driver discourses on the meaning of bravery. "Most people think that bravery consists of not being afraid," he says, but "bravery is being afraid but carrying on just the same." The man without fear is certainly courageous, he concedes, but "he is not as brave as the man who conquers his imagination." The dialogue devolves into a disquisition by the veteran, but the story ends in mid-sentence. Perhaps Bowerman realized that his fictional account was merely a rehash of the ideas and events of the diary. Several years later he spoke to a publisher in Los Angeles about the diary; nothing came of the conversation, but Bowerman seemed convinced that his message was worth repeating.

Bowerman was not the first American ambulance driver to attempt a fictional version of his wartime experiences. Malcolm Cowley, himself a volunteer ambulance driver, included John Dos Passos, Ernest Hemingway, Julian Green, William Seabrook, E. E. Cummings, Slater Brown, Harry Crosby, Sidney Howard, Louis Bromfield, Robert Hillyer, and Dashiell Hammett as members of the literary generation of ambulance and camion drivers shaped by the war. Many remained in Paris after the war, part of what Gertrude Stein termed the "lost generation." A sense of rootlessness, of being cut adrift from cultural traditions and wandering in search of others, was their distinguishing characteristic. "All our roots were dead now," Cowley recalled.

> We were fed, lodged, clothed by strangers, commanded by strangers, infected with the poison of irresponsibility—the poison of travel, too, for we had learned that problems could be left behind us merely by moving elsewhere—and the poison of danger, excitement, that made our old life seem intolerable.[1]

These novelists who afterward wrote about the war underscored its disjunctive role: war changed men in such a way that they could

---

1. Malcolm Cowley, *Exile's Return* (New York: Viking, 1972), p. 38 (originally published in 1934).

never be made whole. Hemingway's one-dimensional heroes (like Hemingway himself) are inexplicably drawn to war and seem most comfortable there. In *A Farewell to Arms* it is obvious that ambulance driver Frederic Henry does not belong in a hospital or, for that matter, in Switzerland after the rout at Caporetto—"In civilian clothes I felt a Masquerader." Although he might distance himself physically from war, it remains with him.

> I realized it was over for me. But I did not have the feeling that it was really over. I had the feeling of a boy who thinks of what is happening at a certain hour at the schoolhouse from which he has played truant.[2]

It is impossible to imagine Frederic Henry living a life apart from war. The driver in Cummings' autobiographical novel on the war escapes from the war but not from its hold. Because of incautious remarks about the war he is thrust into a detention center where he passes the time with a collection of people who had proven similarly unsuited to the war. Yet the "misfits" in *The Enormous Room* (1922) are clearly less unhinged than the society that had endorsed the carnage. The implicit message was that jailors and captives should have exchanged places. The main characters of Dos Passos' best novel on the First World War, *Three Soldiers* (1921), find different—and equally disillusioning—ways out of war. A materialistic immigrant, a sensual optimist, and an aesthete are meant to represent American society, and war produces changes in each that prevent his reconciliation with society. The immigrant's hopes for advancement are repeatedly disappointed. The optimist is goaded into murdering an officer. The aesthete, like Frederic Henry, deserts and is arrested by military police.

The soldier's existence is discontinuous for the simple reason that wars eventually come to an end. Despite elation at having accomplished their purpose (or relief at having managed to survive), soldiers usually experience some disillusionment at the end of the war. Gone are the camaraderie, the sense of collective purpose, and the reassuringly explicit identity war confers upon its participants. Perhaps soldiers are always wary of returning to a society that has granted them sanction to commit acts of violence. War is inherently a disjunctive—even disillusioning—experience. What distinguished the Great War from its predecessors, however, was the extent to which war became associated with the *expectation* of disillusionment.

2. Ernest Hemingway, *A Farewell to Arms* (New York, 1929), Chapter 34.

Compare the hopeful conclusion in Stephen Crane's *The Red Badge of Courage* (1894) to the somber endings of the post–World War I books on war. Paul Fussell goes so far as to regard the Great War as the seminal event of twentieth-century Western culture.

> I am saying that there seems to be one dominating form of modern understanding; that it is essentially ironic; and that it originates largely in the application of mind and memory to the events of the Great War.[3]

Historian Eric J. Leed has proposed an explanation of why the Great War proved so disillusioning for European soldiers. The reality of the war frustrated attempts to render it meaningful. Those who came seeking emotional release found themselves huddled in trenches or participating in absurd assaults which only demonstrated the insignificance of the individual human will. Those who thought war an antidote to the poisons of industrial society learned that machines and technology subjugated more completely during war than ever in peace. Irrevocably separated from their past, soldiers were trapped in a psychological "no man's land," equipped with knowledge that would be useless in the society to which they were to return. Some escaped into themselves, victims of war-induced neurosis; but most European soldiers, Leed argues, returned from the Great War profoundly disillusioned.[4]

In some respects Bowerman's experiences paralleled those depicted by the novelists and those of the European soldiers. Upon seeing star shells for the first time he pronounced them "very pretty" and reminded himself to look up a passage in Walter Scott about "fiery crosses" (Oct. 9, 1917). Somewhat later he watched the "wonderful sight" of artillery firing at airplanes. "The bursting shells were beautiful to see—big red blotches of flame way up in the heavens" (Nov. 13, 1917). But when pinned down by a heavy barrage, he was momentarily disillusioned: "I have said before," he wrote of the incident, "that bursting bombs are beautiful and I wish now to denounce myself as a liar—a monstrous liar. Bursting bombs are the ugliest things on God's green earth" (July 22, 1918). On another occasion Bowerman was awakened in the middle of the night and his section was sent to transfer wounded from incoming trains. The trains were late and the ambulance drivers grumpy, so Bowerman

---

3. Paul Fussell, *The Great War and Modern Memory* (London: Oxford University Press, 1975), p. 3.
4. Eric J. Leed, *No Man's Land: Combat and Identity in World War I* (London: Cambridge University Press, 1979).

entertained them with a routine of singing and dancing. Then the trains arrived and the doors swung open, releasing the "sickening smells" of the wounded. Bowerman became ill (Oct. 15, 1917). When the armistice came, moreover, Bowerman was curiously quiet. He sensed that the war had somehow made him unsuited for a life of peace; his words anticipated Frederic Henry.

> Here we were, men made for war, men born to war, men whose life is filled from beginning to end with war and we felt secretly in our hearts that there could be no other life. (Nov. 17, 1918)[5]

Part of the significance of Bowerman's diary, however, is that his overall assessment of the personal value of the war was not diminished by its horrors or its ironies. Though occasionally disillusioned by certain incidents, he was totally absorbed in the wonder and challenge of what he called "this splendid spectacle." He once wrote that he would not have traded his war experiences for any five years of his life. "Admitting that war is a terrible thing," he stated, "it still has its compensations for those who live" (June 28, 1918).

For the section history of the war Bowerman wrote a humorous article, entitled "Pinard," which extolled the merits of the cheap table wine issued to French soldiers.[6] Upon returning home he made an effort to lead life to the fullest; occasionally he demonstrated his driving prowess to nervous friends and relatives, and at times he spoke longingly of the camaraderie and adventure he had discovered in the trenches of France. He was eager to tell his wife and children about the war, and he encouraged them to read the diary. When the succeeding generation of young Americans was called on to fight in Europe, Bowerman talked to an officer at the recruiting office. But even then he was suffering from the cancer that would result in his death in 1947. A doctor thought it possible that his illness could be traced to a mustard gas incident in 1918.

Both versions of Bowerman's war diary were carefully preserved by his wife, who is my aunt. My mother, née Jennie Claire Com-

---

5. Another possible indication of disillusionment is the verse with which Bowerman began his aborted story:
"Down thru the ages it has been the same
Young men earning the old man's gain.
Young men sow while the greybeards reap
Young men find but they never keep."
6. George J. Shively, ed., *Record of S.S.U. 585* (N.p.: E. L. Hildreth & Co., 1920).

stock, read the diaries in utter fascination on a visit to her sister in 1978. She brought back the earlier version and pleaded for me to take a look at it. Then a graduate student in history, I thought I had better things to do than struggle through a mud-splattered, decaying manuscript written by a relative I had never known. But she was persistent, and I finally agreed to glance at the diary, fully expecting to put it down after a few pages. This proved impossible.

As noted above, the diary reproduced here is the recopied and amplified version prepared by Bowerman in 1919. Insofar as possible I have tried to keep the flavor of the manuscript. I have in most cases retained Bowerman's errors in spelling, grammar, and punctuation. He tended to use a private shorthand, condensing "thought" to "thot," for instance, but this poses no real obstacle to the reader. There was no need to clutter the diary with very many footnotes. Bowerman was writing for an audience—perhaps Marguerite, perhaps his descendants, perhaps the reading public—and he usually offered explanations of the terms or provided sufficient context to make the meaning clear. Nevertheless, some French words have been translated (in brackets) where they first appear; frequently used French and military terms are listed in a glossary. I put "[illeg.]" when I could not make any sense of Bowerman's handwriting and "[?]" when I was uncertain of the accuracy of my transcription. Names of people and places are given in Bowerman's spelling, with the correct name, when known, provided in brackets on first reference.

DIARY

Guy Emerson Bonorman JUNIOR

G.E.Bonorman Jr.
S.S.U. 585
Convois Auto.
Par B.C.M. Paris

Section
Sanitaire
Unis
5
85

BOOK ONE

June 28. Enlisted at New Haven. Sworn in by Major Stiles, U.S.A. It's a funny feeling when you hold up your right hand to take the oath, you swear away your body to your government; lose your identity and become a cog. Well I'm in the thing for better or for worse, soit!

July 5. Leave for Allentown Pa. at 11. Lunch in New York at McAlpin; last square meal? Leave New York 3:15 arrive Allentown 7:15. Met by trucks and crowds of soldiers whose shout is eternally, "Where are you from, boys?" First army mess a terrible thing consisting of liver and onions. Ye Shades of '76 is this the price of democracy? To bed at 9:30 in a horse-stall. Oh well remember the Nativity.

July 6. Volunteer for a detail, loafing around is too disagreeable. Juggle *new* garbage cans; help build barracks. Lots of presperation. To town for dinner and I feed not wisely but too well. Call up Trexler, who takes us for a ride. Puncture, visions of guard house as we must be in by 9:00. Fears useless, to bed at 9:30.

July 7. Mess no better. Morning free but a detail in afternoon brings some job not! Mess at camp. After mess take in Central Park & had a fair time. Home at 11 as we have an Honor Pass.

[July] 8. Up at 6. Drew detail but no work. Keen ball game but we lose. War almost begins in U.S. Big crowd of visitors in afternoon. Walk up town where I run across Dad and, later, Mother with whom I have dinner.* To bed early as I'm very tired.

[July] 9. Rise at usual time. Raining. Detailed for ditch digging with Cunningham. Depth of ditch 10 ft. Oh boy! Dinner with family. To bed early.

[July] 10. Still raining. No detail but drill in morning. In afternoon I write letters and sleep. Dinner with folks, after that to a show then to bed to shiver half the night with cold.

July 11 to Aug. 7. More rain. Lecture by Captain on military etiquet.

---

*Bowerman's parents were living in New York City. Bowerman, Sr., had recently been appointed secretary of the American Bankers Association.

Five men chosen for auto school. I have no luck. "Oaky," Kelly, Bill and I have opportunity to transfer to section #85.* This seems advisable as #85 is a Yale Section while #113 is Yale in name only. Also I am having trouble with Sergt. Stiles. Bill and I decide to join #85 while "Oakey" and Kelly go to the Fordham Unit Section #51. Spend some time in "casuals" again while quarters are being arranged for us with #85. Eat with family whenever possible and spend most of my spare time with them. Finally established in #85. Seem to be a fine crowd tho I only know a few at first. "Pete"; Campbell and Flint. Johnstone is 1st sergt.; Peters 2nd sergt. Hubbard 3rd sergt. and Lundgren, corporal. Ferguson 1st Lieut. Quarters are sheds but fairly comfortable. Drill nearly all the time and my training at East Side stands me in good stead. The long hikes in the hot sun trim off the superfluous flesh and put us in good condition. We hope to go across soon. Rumors begin[?] to appear to the effect that we are due to leave. Are they true? is the question. Lieut. Wharton replaces Lieut. Ferguson and orders to get ready follow tho no definite date of departure is set. Steve and I are on provost duty in Central Park. Sergt. of the Guard is an extremely blood thirsty person and threatens to shoot a half dozen at least. Steve manages to get passes to the amusements and we see the whole show. The man in charge of the ferris wheel went the limit of hospitality. Every time we'd wave for him to stop the thing he thot the waves expressed our joy and desire for more. Consequently we rode till we nearly died.

All men are obliged to stay around quarters as orders to leave may come at any moment. I manage a "leave" to see the folks. They take the news well. I feel very sorry for Mother. Due to numerous false starts I say goodby three times before I really left. However the last time came much easier because of the practise. Said my final goodby to the family in the little YWCA guest house. Dad tried his best to conceal his emotion and was almost successful. Mother did not succeed quite so well tho she behaved splendidly. Kissed Mother for the last time, shook Dad's hand and my last words to them were "I'll see you again in two years"

---

*Section 85 was later renumbered 585 when a system of notation was installed assigning each branch of the service different numerals, the ambulance series beginning with 500.

as I raced to the quarters being late already. I hope that's a true prophecy.

August 7. Left camp last night at 12:30 with a great show of secrecy. Roll call by flash-light; orders given in low voice; commands to be quite and not to talk. The only result was to create excitement which tho fairly well suppressed still showed itself in word and action. Short mess then we march off to entrain just outside the camp. Number of people to see us off. Mother and Dad were not there which pleased me. After the usual considerable fuss attendant upon a movement of this kind we are all on board and start on the first lap of our journey to France, 12 sections strong!

[*August*] 7. Arrive in Jersey City at 5:00 a.m. after a most tiring ride. Now on the ferry. There is considerable delay but we are accustomed to that now. Finally go on board the San Jacinto, which before our entry into the war had been a South American fruit steamer but was now poorly fitted up as a transport. Our bunks were below the water line, one deck below what had formerly been the steerage. It had been the central hold of the vessel but by the liberal use of gas pipe bunks to accommodate 300 men had been arranged. These bunks were rectangles formed of piping with canvas slung between. They were in three tiers and the passageways barely permitted one man. The only air and light came through the hatchway and the former was greatly contaminated by the odors of the mess hall, kitchen, latrines and showers which were placed in different corners on the deck above ours. The salon was of course reserved for the officers and field-clerks and even the meager deck space was generally forbidden to us except for short moments. Formerly fitted to carry 250 passengers, the San Jac, as she was familiary called, offered small comfort and convenience to the 1100 men with their impedimentia! The inevitable question when a man was shown his bunk was—Can they expect *men* to live here? Following out the fruitless plan of secrecy which the govt. had adopted, like a man caught in a lie but sticking to his story, everyone was ordered below as we dropped down to the lower harbor. Houlihan and I are put on K.P. where we're further initiated into the horrors of transporting troops. When one sliced the mouldy bread cock-roaches would scurry out from under the loaf only to meet a soldier's death by being severed in twain with the bread-knife. Needless to say "Hap" and

I did not eat bread that day. We laid in the lower harbor till 8 p.m. watching the lights of the ferry boats and of the city which many of us were going to look upon for the last time. Shortly after eight a tug brought some officers and men who had missed the boat and we all hurriedly scribbled cards to our friends who would not hear from us again for some time. I wrote a note to Mother and to Marguerite. Finally the tug drew away and our last link with America was cut. On to France! Our convoy consisted of five transports, three destroyers and a battle-cruiser, the "Montanan." Remainder of day quite uneventful. Reported for mess at 4:30 and went below at 9 to sleep my first night on one of Uncle Sam's transports. Slept well tho air was rotten; damp and heavy.

August. Wed. 8. Up at 6 and have a fair mess. On guard duty in our quarters below. After sleeping all night the air is even more putrid and hotter than the fiery furnace. My guard runs one hour on, one off so I get enough air on deck in one hour to last me an hour below. Free distribution of tobacco and cigarette papers. Bill gives me his issue. Now 10:10 and I am on duty I hope my relief is prompt. Just had "Abandon ship" drill which proves conclusively that if anything does happen we have small chance of getting out. Our hold is crowded to capacity and the only means of getting out are two flights of narrow, steep and slippery stairs which lead up to the mess deck. A sharp turn here and you mount another flight to the main deck. Still another flight remains before you reach the promenade on the port side, forward of which is our station and our life belts. Once on the main deck there is another way to reach our station thru two narrow doors into the salon then up the stairs to the promenade. As a consequence of this drill we have christened our habitation the "Rat-Trap." Poor Bill is laid low with sea sickness and occaisons much laughter, there is always something extremely funny in seeing a big hunk laid low by such a disease. Poker to break the monotony of the afternoon. If this keeps up it will break more than the monotony. I hope to retrieve my losses tomorrow. As we retire a large rat is seen, "ho ho and a bottle of rum." All the atmosphere of "Treasure Island." Night uneventful and I have a fine sleep.

Thurs. [August] 9. 7:10 A.M. bunk all made and am waiting for morning mess. Fine weather and a smooth sea thank the Lord! If these conditions only prevail I may be able to get my sea legs painlessly. Our friend Detail who like the poor is with us always in the army has shunned me so far this day here's hoping he's completely down on me. Fire drill and poker do much to break up the afternoon tho the latter is by far the most exciting. I played with Durant, Weber, Googins, Tremaine, Green, Lynch and Houlihan and recover losses with interest. Exercise on promenade deck at 3 P.M. consisting of calisthentics and a marathon. I find that I'm not in the best of condition for long distance running. Take a salt water shower with salt water soap far from satisfactory but manage to get clean. Few men are suffering from the sea.

Friday. (August) 10. Wonderful weather continues. Life boats are swung out which makes us wonder if we are in the danger zone yet. Last night our convoy took a new formation. At sunset they close in close together to permit them to run fast and not lose sight of each other as we run without lights. No smoking is allowed after sun set as even the glow of a cigarette is said to show many miles on the sea. In the morning the convoy spreads out and the destroyers chase around looking for trouble. The mess this morning was fair. It isn't the food that sickens one it is being forced to eat it in such a dirty, filthy, sloppy, smelly place as this mess hall is. Many have bribed the officer's stewards and are living on officer's mess. I'll stick to the regular diet for that idea does not appeal to me.

First touch of sickness caused by a heavy ground swell. Try the calisthentics but my "pep" is gone. The sun is setting in a bank of clouds while a crowd of us lean on the railing aft smoking our last fag for the night. Marcellus says that those clouds mean bad weather. I hope he's mistaken, this boat is bad enough now and a storm would make it a perfect hell. Marcellus is perhaps the most interesting member of our crew. Born in New York to parents who were far from the best, he was successively newsboy, sailor on a wind jammer, mechanic and traveling salesman. His education has been his own extensive reading and [as] is usually the case with such a type he is well versed in many things. Considering his early environment and training he is exceptionally clean cut and decent. He is our head mechanic. A school of porpoises is sighted but I miss seeing them, usual luck! Learn why they named a certain card game "Rummy" when I play it with Hap and Bal. Some of the fellows are playing "Bridge." I can't see that it is such a "brainy" game. Three days on the way to France with at least nine more to go and probably eleven. We are running N. by E. at about 10 knots. (Reckoned by Marcellus). We have received orders not to throw anything overboard as it is known that a ship can be followed by its waste. To quote Major Jones' lecture today—"When our ship toured the world one ship was left by the fleet at Honolulu to get mail and didn't have to use a compass till it caught up with the fleet again." Our speed is being changed every little while and our course also. Tho this increases the distance it lessens the danger so will not grumble at the length of the voyage. No fire drill today so we need not be surprised if we're turned out in the night. Need a good sleep so I'm off to bed. Had a horrible dream last night, dreamed I tried to kill Father in a quarrel. Good old Dad. What impossible things dreams are. My beard is fierce I must shave tomorrow.

Sat. August 11. A good sleep last night and I feel fine. Gil must have been wrong for the weather is as good as one could ask for. Latest reports or rumors rather, have it that we will dock next Thursday. That's only five days more but I shan't be disappointed if we don't get in for nine more. The captain is supposed to open sealed orders the 6th day out. Another reports says that we are 600 miles South and 900 miles East of New York. This makes the distance covered about 1100 miles. The army is to rumors what a slough is to mosquitoes. I've heard more rumors since June 28 than I ever heard before in my life. One soon ceases to believe in anything. 4:30 P.M. We sight a ship and a destroyer hurries over for a "look-see." First she stands across the steamer's bow, then circles around her and finally draws alongside, evidently satisfied that she isn't a German raider or a mother ship for "subs." During all this the 1200 men on board crowd forward to view what they earnestly hope will be a sea battle. A thousand dark purposes are given to the vessel and when she proves herself a harmless self respecting oil tanker and is God sped on her way the disgust of the men is great. They had hoped that at least she might be a German raider. In the Army some special phrase is singled out and used on every possible occaison. The phrase just now happens to be "You can't stay here." The sentence originated with the officers and guards when they rouse some sleeping doughboy in order that his deck space may be used for countless formations or because he occupies a spot forbidden by the rules. 1200 men on a boat fitted to carry 250 passengers doesn't give much space per man. A little rain and the promise of a storm tonight.

Sun. Aug. 12. Another promise broken. Weather remains fine and sea is smooth as a pond. Wash day and everyone rolls up their sleeves. When we go to hang them out we learn that "wash day" on a transport doesn't necessarily mean "drying day" so we take the wet clothes off the line and stow them away in quarters. I suppose they'll rot. Detailed to search for our Post Exchange box of candy cigarettes and tobacco in the forward hold. We could not find our box and Sergt. Johnny refused to take someone else's tho it is perfectly evident that someone else took ours. Such is the fault of good breeding. A gentleman will never get ahead in the Army, it is necessary to take what you can when you can. The Section is bitterly disappointed as we are very much in need of chocolate and candy as we don't get enough sugar in our food. Crabbing is rampant and the spirit of mutiny runs thru Section 585.* Durant, Tremaine, Green, Wassom [Wasem] and Van Doran [Van Doren] find me easy pickings in a poker game. Oh well unlucky at cards lucky in love. Censorship regulations are posted. They are very strict. Among other things we are forbidden to mention casualties; to mail letters in civilian mail boxes and to talk "shop" with civilians. No drill today. Fine supper and I eat a huge meal during which I overheard an engineer arguing that the world is not round (seriously too) and (ye gods bear witness) quoting Scripture to prove his contentions. I could believe anything of the crew, they certainly are a hard lot.

Mon. Aug. 13. Thank Heaven this isn't Friday! After a good sleep and an early mess I start the daily routine of killing time. I believe I can get away with sleeping in the salon at least it's worth trying. The ancient Roman scribe who said "Tempus fugit" surely never included among his travels an ocean voyage on an imperial transport. Spend the evening in the Music Room listening to a Harvard man with a natural or possibly acquired taste for high brow music, play and sing. I would have greatly preferred "jaz" because real music makes me homesick.

Had our first fire drill today and we find that we can evacuate

---

* Section 85 was renumbered 585 while stationed at Nancy, more than three months after this entry. Bowerman apparently forgot this chronology when he recopied the diary.

the Rat-Trap, get into our life belts ready to take to the brine in six minutes. That leaves a margin of four minutes provided it takes ten to sink. Seems to me I've heard of ships sinking in five but that's just a minute too soon so this old tub will have to keep afloat for at least seven. Saw a large turtle as he swam peacefully by, he must have been several hundred years old at least. Maybe he swam by the French ships as they brought Lafayette and soldiers to America. He's the first turtle I ever saw and I was impressed with his size, why he'd make soup enough for an army. One of our convoy, the Henderson, broke down this afternoon and we all had to stop and wait for her. They finally got her running but we chafed at the delay as we don't want to spend all eternity on this junket.

We're in the danger zone now and I'm going to be real "cagey" tonight. I'm going to include my trousers in my night apparel. This will give me a head start on the others who will, I believe, stop to put theirs on. A minute's head start may mean the difference between "the fields of France" and "Davy Jones' Locker" and I much prefer to have my bones whiten on some field than to have fish playing tag in and out through my massive frame. Huge meal this noon. I feel like a stuffed pig. This voyage surely hasn't put my appetite to the bad.

Tues. Aug. 14. My plan for a bed last night worked beautifully and I can testify that cushions in a ship's salon certainly approximate more nearly the old Osterman than a sheet of canvas, stretched between two iron rails. That canvas is not only cold & hard but it's too short. I had to get up at 5 in order not to be seen by the guard but the beauties of the morning fully compensated and I had a fine half hour promenade. I ordered two pies at 75¢ per pie yesterday but today I'm told that there will be no more profiteering in pie. The cook was caught. No detail. We are now really in the submarine zone and from now on our trip is liable to be interfered with. No one seems to be at all anxious in fact everyone expresses the fervent hope that we'll see "one of them there XX*!—?? things" as a Massachusetts farmer put it. We have been out a week now and with all our zig-zagging we must have covered considerable ground or rather water. The memorandum for today reads—"Men who have been sleeping outside their quarters either on the decks or with friends in the staterooms will cease to do so. All deck space is needed to bring up ammunition for the guns in case of a night attack."

Wed. Aug. 15. Slept well, but was awakened at two by the astounding fact that it was cold in "Hell" (new name for the Rat Trap) we must be out of the Gulf Stream. More unique dreams. Breakfast in first mess. (We seat in three messes and the sections take turns on first mess.) The California section very graciously offers to share their Post Exchange box with us and after considerable debate amongst ourselves we accept. One can't imagine how fine that chocolate tastes to men who get practically no sugar in their food. No detail so I play cards but meet with indifferent success. Very foggy this morning and one ship gets separated from the convoy. It returned to line about nine. Meet an oil-tanker and the destroyers fill up with fuel. The formation of the convoy is changed now, the ships follow each other in a line. The battle cruiser Montanan leads and the destroyers chase around on all sides like sheepdogs watching a band of sheep. At sunset one destroyer makes a complete circuit of the convoy and then the ships all close in. "General quarters" were sounded at 6 bells (3 P.M.) and we assembled at our station forward on the port side of the promenade deck. We will have a good seat if any "show" is put on. It's a long jump to the water but I imagine that if we do have to jump the water will come to meet us a good way if we only wait for it. My luck at cards continues the same, that is to say rotten! Our course is being altered more frequently now and we turn at nearly right angles. We are driving along at a good clip. Seven days out, seven days more? 4:15—"Captain" Holbrook has just completed a successful minor operation on an engineer's knee and has assumed even more importance—in his own eyes. Precotious youth! Going below for my mess kit.

Thurs. Aug. 16. Joy dethrones Deep Gloom! The assistant engineer assured four of us who were shooting an "after-hours" smoke in his condensing room, that we would land in four days. (Sunday). We drove hard all last night but are running slow today as we expect to meet our new convoy. They should be here at 12:50 and report comes from the decks that they are already in sight. Foggy, rainy, cold and utterly disagreeable all morning. The engineer tells us that our stop the other day was to wait for the oil-tanker which had been delayed. He has offered to take some of us through the engine room and the stoking hold. I hope he doesn't forget as I am anxious to see them. More poker this morning and I get ahead of the game with some phenomenal "hands." Four sixes, four fives, five queens and a straight flush. I am writing in the condensing room where it is warm, the air is good and I can smoke. Think I shall bundle up a bit and go on deck. I have mastered the ocean time system finally and can now yell out "four bells" with the best of 'em.

Friday Aug. 17. There was much confusion below last night due to the presence of a young tidal wave which threatened to sweep away the lower bunks. After futile efforts to discover the reason for its being by all the engineers on board, a number of ambitious but unseamanlike lieutenants and a goodly body of even more ambitious and less seamanlike privates, the crowd finally managed to get to sleep. Every time the boat rolled the wave swept the lower bunks causing a roar from their occupants— somewhat the sound of an angry surf crashing against a rock bound coast.

Sat. Aug. 18. Cold during the night and a rough sea. We could hear the waves crash against the ship's sides in a line with our heads (we are below the water line or nearly so) and wondered why the plates didn't give way and let the flood in on us. It is easy to understand now how a ship can be battered to pieces. The convoy rumor was unfounded and we have still to meet them. The rain has stopped but it's cold and the old tub is rolling to beat the cars [?]. P.M.—The convoy of six destroyers appears and the battle cruiser and two destroyers start back for the U.S.A. Wish I were aboard. Smith the asst. engineer makes good his offer and shows us the engine room and the stoke hole, explaining the different apparatus as we went along. It is all very interesting especially the drive shaft in the long tunnel. The stoking room was not quite so bad as I had imagined but it was too hot for me to work in. The stokers are mostly Portugese and are quite inhuman looking brutes I ever saw. Little wonder considering the life they lead. Poor devils, they have little chance of getting out alive if a torpedo hits us amidships.

Sunday Aug. 19. Just before noon we sighted ten ships in a fleet; transports with convoy. Just after lunch the expected and almost hoped for happened. Six blasts sounded from our boat and we hurried to our positions anxious to see the "sub." A destroyer left the convoy immediately and proceeded to drop a depth bomb where she thot the submersible lay. What happened to "our enemy the enemy" I don't know but the destroyer circled around a number of times and then joined the convoy again after which we proceeded on our way a little more interested in life in general and this trip in particular. Some "gob" says that the "depth bombs" are only used when the destroyer is sure of a hit, but I don't believe that. They also say that a torpedo passed across the bow of the ship just behind us but I take that also with a grain of salt. We were all disappointed not to have seen even the periscope. During the seance there was a natural and pardonable excitement which was no doubt enhanced by Captain Whitney who paced up and down between us and the rail cautioning us against rushing the boats which would be lowered past our deck in case we were hit. The army with a commendable effort at justness but with doubtful good judgement had arranged that those who were assigned to places in the lifeboats should stay in the cabin during the show while those of us who were to leap wildly into the sea and grab a raft were given a point of vantage. The men preserved very good order however and it was quite unnecessary, in my opinion, for the Captain to brandish his "Gat" even tho it was cased. As soon as we were dismissed the excitement caused a good deal of talking and a careful listener could compile quite a history of this attack in particular and "sub" attacks in general. Anyway it broke up a long dreary afternoon and we are quite ready to believe the ass't. engineer when he tells us that this is to be our most dangerous night so far in as much as there is danger both from submarines and floating mines.

Mon. Aug. 20. Nothing of moment occured during the night and I had a fair night's rest. Deac stayed up all night helping Smith in the condensing room and to see that if we were hit *our* section would get out via the condensing and engine rooms. This was our only hope of escape as we are too far from the hatchway and besides it would be too crowded to make good time. The morning was wonderfully warm and clear and we all settled down on the deck for quite sun bath and additional rest. Neal Lynch and I had found a space together and Neal had just observed that all danger was past when we saw the destroyer off our starboard bow fire and then give the "sub" signal of six blasts from her whistle. The other boats took up the whistle, another destroyer rushed to help the first and our convoy scattered in all directions for all the world like a flock of mud hens, screeching as they ploughed thru the water. Our vessel turned nearly at right angles, zig zagged for all she was worth and put on every ounce of steam there was in the boilers. By this time we were all at our various stations. Neal got into his life belt the wrong way and I changed it for him then we settled down to watch the show which was promising to be considerably bigger than the one Sunday. Captain Whitney seemed to feel the same way and as he paced before us he carried his "Gat" uncased & ready for action. I asked a doughboy for a match and was amused to have him answer "Match hell! there's too damn much going on." For an hour and a half every gun on every ship kept firing. There were at least two hundred shell fired in all and the two guns on the old "San Jac" fired 17 times. There seemed to be a perfect nest of subs and our shells were falling everywhere. I wondered at the time why it was our own ships weren't hit. The destroyers made a beautiful sight as they rushed from place to place. One destroyer sneaked up close behind our ship and let go a depth charge which as we didn't see the destroyer produced considerable excitement on our boat. Everyone thot of course that we'd been hit and I remarked to Lynch that I guessed here was where we stepped over and for him to stay close because one of us ought to have enough luck to be picked up. A torpedo missed our bow by 10 ft and only because the wheelman saw it coming in time, jumped on the wheel and managed to turn it in time. After missing us it barely missed the Henderson which was astern. After it was all over the surface was littered with dead fish and some wreckage tho that probably came from the shore which was only about 30 miles away. I can honestly say that I wasn't afraid. I was excited of course but was perfectly deliberate in everything I did. I hope I'm never more frightened than I was during that hour and a half. Everyone is keen to know how he'll act in a tight place what you fear is that when the test comes you'll show fear. All the fellows behaved admirably and seemed to consider it all a matter of course. What a queer world this is! I bet there were a couple hundred men on board who had read, in open mouthed awe and admiration, stories of sea battles in our previous wars. Here they were holding box seats at a modern sea fight which is even more nerve straining because your foe is hidden and they seemed to enjoy it

immensely and as soon as it was over they went about their
business as if nothing very unusual had happened. We're now
entering the channel safe and sound after fourteen days of a
rather disagreeable voyage. Our rolls are packed and in an hour
or so we will land thereby completing our second lap. Quite an
auspicious start for that final trek to the front. I forgot to mention the two French airplanes which came out to aid us and
added their quota of bombs. Just as we entered the straits one of
the airplanes flew close beside our boat at a low height. The pilot
waved his hand and laughed. A laugh of comradeship! a laugh of
welcome to his new blood brothers! Soon after one of our own
destroyers came close in while the crew cheered and waved to us.
We answered in a like manner tho I personally couldn't cheer
because there was a big lump in my throat and my eyes were a
bit misty. It was a funny feeling it gave one these were our
brothers in arms, men of our own kind and 14 German subs had
been driven off! I don't know if any subs were sunk they say the
official report is four I wish it were eight. A little French tug
comes out to guide us thru the mine fields. After considerable
wait while the French pilot was attempting to make himself understood in broken English we got under way again. Our first
sight of France was beautiful and seemed more so because we
were so heartily sick of this rolling, plunging craft. As we passed
up the Loire River (Belle Isle off the port) the country grew less
beautiful and became barren and rocky and blistered looking.
Surely this is not La Belle France. Anyway a bad beginning
makes a good ending. Sergt. Johnny is sick in the hospital so
Lynch and I went to see him. The most artistic marine scene I
have ever witnessed presents itself—the light green water of the
river, the deep blue sky filled with heavy banks of low hanging,
pure white clouds and a goodly number of peculiarly rigged little
fishing boats with their multi colored sails. Red, green, black,
blue, white, brown and various combinations of these colors. We
go thru the locks which are lined with a huge mixed crowd of
very excited people. French soldiers and sailors, French civilians
of both sexes and all ages and our own American soldiers. Orders
are issued saying that we will spend the night on board. This
brings down plentiful and picturesque curses upon the heads of
the army. Nearly everyone stays on deck pressing close to the
rails to see just what these French are like. The chocolate venders

gather on the docks and as the men are starved for sugar money passes chocolate cakes in the air till the venders' stocks are sold out. After mess Lyman and I climbed into the rigging determined to see as much of France as we could tonight. The name of this town is St. Nazaire and as far as we can see it's not a wonderful city by any means.

Tues. Aug. 21. Reveille at 4:30, disembark and march to Concentration Camp No 1. The town is very interesting and our march is rather ragged because we act more like tourists than soldiers. The streets are narrow and paved mostly with cobble stones. The houses are nearly all square and have tiled roofs usually red. The style of architecture is decidedly simple and plain and the houses are set close to the street from which they are separated by high stone walls and high ornate iron gates. We felt the effects of our ocean trip on the 2 mile up hill hike to the camp. It was hot before we'd gone half way and those packs seemed to weigh tons. One fellow called out to his sergeant, "Hey Serg., have you got my name on the roster?" The Sergt. replied, "Why Simpson of course." "That's all right then" said the first fellow "I thot you'd made a mistake and had it Sampson." The camp is a large one and shows very plainly how new it is and how quickly it was built. The barracks are long low tar papered affairs with oiled-paper windows and dirt floors. They remind one of the pictures of the long houses of the Virginia Indians, which one saw in the grammar school historys. We locate several farm houses and manage to buy some hay with which we "bed ourselves down" like a bunch of cattle. May our first night on French soil be filled with pleasant dreams.

Wed. Aug. 22. Reveille at 5:30, calesthentics at 5:45. It's still dark and decidedly chilly. The regular routine goes into effect and it's hard to realize that we are on foreign soil 3000 miles from home.

Thurs. Aug. 23 to Thurs. Sept. 6. Three trips to town for meals and sightseeing, mostly the former as the latter is soon exhausted. The prices are rather high due chiefly to the mistaken impression the tradesmen have that "tous les Americaines sont richs." We have no little trouble in getting what we want and our attempts at French cause much amusement on both sides. The Frenchman laughs very good naturedly because he is naturally polite and wouldn't hurt our feelings if he could help. We manage however and for any special event we enlist the aid of Borden who, being

a French prof, speaks the language almost fluently. The town is
dirty, ill paved and they say that it's one of the worst towns in
France due chiefly to the fact that it is a sea port. Our camp is
only about a half mile from the ocean and we often go down for
a swim. Always marching in formation with Myrtle (Wharton's
nick-name) at the head, who sits around on the beach while we
swim, warning us about this, cautioning us about that like an old
hen watching her foster children take to their native element. On
the way back to camp we are allowed to buy fruit, chocolate etc
at the various booths which line all the roads from the city to
camp. That "Myrtle" is a card. Absolutely lacking a sense of proportion;
blindly adhering to orders which he invariably misinterprets
and tremendously narrow minded in everything in general
and censorship in particular. The climax was reached one day
when we took one of our daily long hikes. There was a boiling
hot sun and he made us wear our blouses. As a result Bates
nearly had sunstroke and had to fall out. The daily routine consists
of cleaning-up details; guard duty; stretcher drill; foot drill;
lectures on first aid and long hikes. The hikes are fine, they put
one in splendid condition and at the same time we are able to see
some very beautiful country which lies back from the coast. The
first mail arrived about a week after we landed. I drew eight
letters. The mess is fair but hardly sufficient and there is much
crabbing. My health has been fine with the exception of about a
week. The French hold "un grand fête pour les soldats Americaines"
a[t] La Baule, a second class sea resort. Googins, Green
and I rented bicycles and rode over arriving before any other
Americans. We were surrounded immediately after our arrival by
large crowds of curious and enthousiastic French civilians. The
outstanding features of the party were, the rain; the trouble getting
a meal; the crowds in a holiday mood; a fine time and the
dinner which Kirby and I had with a French family. A puncture
and a request for a pump from a young French lad led up to our
invitation. The party consisted of the mother, two daughters,
two sons, Kirby and myself. One of the girls spoke English so we
"got by" o.k. with the conversation. Kirby admitted that he knew
very little French but said that he spoke German quite well
whereupon one of the boys started questioning in German and
Kirby's bluff failed miserably much to his embarrassment and my
amusement. The father who was manager of the Dion Bouton

motor car factory in Paris was absent. The cuisine was not very elaborate but it was well cooked and satisfying. After dinner the two girls rode a way with us on their bicycles. We also had a trip to Nantes to see the Cathedral and other points of interest. Practically the whole Section went. "Myrtle" and the other officers forgot to get off at Nantes and rode a station farther on while we stood on the platform and cheered. We had a fine meal at the hotel where I tasted my first "Benedictine" and caused gales of laughter by my facial contortions. The Cathedral was very beautiful and interesting.

An interesting thing happened one night while I was on guard. I was just relieving the man before me when the marine guard, whos beat ran at right angles to mine, came to my end of his beat. Just as I came into the light of an arc lamp he called out "say bud what's your name?" I told him and as he came across into the light I saw it was Hughes with whom I had played football at the East Side H.S. in Salt Lake. It was pure luck, our meeting as neither one knew the other had "joined up." We had a short talk of mutual friends and resumed our "beats." It helps to bring home a little nearer to run across someone you know. God knows you need something to bring home nearer when you're 3000 miles away, a stranger in a strange land and not knowing if you'll ever see your own again. Under these conditions when all home ties are cut, except a few long delayed letters, home and your former home life seems like a pleasant and hazy dream.

There are about 8000 German prisoners in St. Nazaire who are doing scavenger work around the camps and working at the docks. They look healthy enough and well fed and seem contented. At least they don't work any harder than the ordinary railroad "wop." We are forbidden to speak with them for what reason I know not except that we Yanks being an effusive lot might give them some dope.

Detail for assembling Fords which seems to speak of departure. The Fords are shipped to this country "knocked-down," two bodies in one box and the engines and chassis separate. The boxes (like huge piano cases) are brought up on trucks from the docks, dumped on the ground where we take them and in a day have two brand new ambulance bodies ready for the chassis which are assembled in another camp, run up here when completed fitted with the bodies and parked till the time of some section's departure.

A man from Section 92 was killed while bathing, making our first casualty. Weber is operated on for appendicitis and is recovering nicely under the watchful eye of Myrtle.

There has been a big fire on the wharves which destroyed a large quantity of hay together with the Y.M.C.A. supplies. The U.S.A.A.S. [United States Army Ambulance Service] assisted heroically in fighting the flames tho they did not volunteer. Those unfortunates who ran to see the fires were commandeered on the pumps and poor Derek who was among the number swears that no Roman galley slave was ever harder driven. A man from #92 was overcome by a combination of French liquor smoke and heat.

We have our "up-setting" exercises by moon light and during the day it is very cold and the rain is plentiful. Wheredyaget this "Sunny France" stuff?

We got up a baseball team and challenged Harvard. Yale in France however proves to be less potent than Yale in America and we lose 4–2. Legore of football fame, and now a 1st lieut. in the Marines pitched for us. I met him after the game repeating Kipling's line in "If" "and walk with kings nor lose the common touch" as I shook hands with him.

The Y.M.C.A. has a big hut in this camp which is crowded most of the time. They have concerts, lectures, and vaudeville shows but the best attraction is the women canteen workers. It is great to hear a girl "speak the language."

Some more mail arrives to cheer us on our way. Three letters for yours truly, one being a letter from "Doc Pud" at Mercersburg with a heavy "line" and insinuations of an honor roll on the chapel door. Big stuff, I'll say. My chief regret is that I signed up without going home first. What a lot I missed. Think of all the pretty little girls who might have cried on my manly bosom!

Thurs. Sept. 6. Semaphore practice and I am given a job as instructor. Johnny procures a big box of eatables from the commissary and we take a few wrinkles out of our poor tummies. A short, snappy hike in our blouses. It was extremely hot and plentious maledictions fall upon Myrtle. Some transports come in with freight and the men who have field glasses say they see "assembled" Fords on the deck. No such luck! We should soon be on our way from this hole tho the Lord knows where.

Friday Sept. 7. Rained all morning. No details. A small game of cards at which I clean up. We receive our pay 184 francs for a "buck." Settle up my boat debts and come out even.

Sat. Sept. 8. Big detail for work at the docks unloading four freighters. I am lucky or rather unlucky for I stay in barracks only to lose 190 frs at the cards and dice. $20 left for the month. Oh Boy! Get a pass out of camp for a couple hours in the evening with Deak. A fair meal and much chewing of the rag.

Sunday Sept. 9. Off for the docks at 6:30. Spend the morning wrestling bales of hay into these queer dumpy little French freight cars. We were working on the "Dakotan" and it is a revelation to me how much a ship like that can hold. Besides the Dakotan there are three others: El Occidente, Albert Luckenbach and ?? They have brought huge loads of supplies, Fords, hay, grain, meal, staff cars and trucks. The German prisoners are supposed to push up the freight cars as we need them and to make up the trains with the loaded ones. They're lazier than a Southern darky. This is some job tho it is better than drilling at that. In the afternoon we unloaded a whole herd of frozen "hoss."

Mon. Sept. 10. Very sick during the night and answered sick call this morning. Stay in bed till afternoon, am well by supper time and eat a big meal.

Tues. Sept. 11. Off duty again. "Myrtle" thinks I need a rest.

Wed. Sept. 12. No work. Deak receives news of his brother's serious injury while bathing. I hope the kid pulls thru. Deak is certainly wrapped up in the lad. Four letters for me. A dandy one from M. I have serious ideas of proposing by mail but decide to adopt Wilson's plan of "watchful waiting."

Thurs. Sept. 13. The thirteenth of the month and 13 men on the dock detail. That looked bad to me from the start. My forebodings of evil were realized tonight after supper when "Myrtle" discovered that Deak and I went thru the lines "sans" a pass. I got all the blame, lost my passes for the remainder of our stay here and also was accused of having led poor innocent Deak from the way that he should go. The old reprobate! Lest posterity should condemn me as unjustly as Myrtle did I'll give the facts which may shed some light on army life and the officers of the new army. Deak had been on guard the night before. Besides fixing it up, with the man who relieved him, to be allowed to pass him unchallenged, he also kept one of the passes which he had collected. I had already asked for and had been granted a pass for tonight. Just as Bob Larkin and Googins who were on the same pass were going to H.Q. for the signature Deak came up and asked me to go with him. We argued a bit and ended by my taking the pass he had held out on H.Q. We got in early enough but someway Myrtle found out that I'd been out so he came over called me out and asked me if I had been. I answered yes and when he asked me how I told him on a false pass. He then questioned me as to who had given me the pass but I refused to tell. Growing rather excited he threatened me with court martial. About the third time he did this Deak, who had been listening to the conversation, stepped up and told him that he had given it to me. Then it was that Myrtle gave me my dose of discipline and uttered the classical expression If you men had done this ten weeks later yewed have caught H-E-double L!

The dock detail was a cinch today in spite of the double 13 and we spent most of our time eating "des gateaux" [cakes] in a "patisserie" across from the docks. They are at last getting some work out of the prisoners who have been placed under an evil looking Q.M. Sergt who looks like the dwarf in Hugo's "Notre Dame" and curses fluently in German.

Friday Sept. 14. Two letters from Mother. Detailed to Q.M. but have nothing to do. I have the afternoon off as I am scheduled for guard duty tonight. There are rumors about that two sections are leaving as soon as possible to relieve two American Field Service Sections. This rumor at least appears authentic. The camp looks more like a real ambulance camp every day. There are now about a hundred completed cars in the park not counting the Packard trucks.

Sat. Sept. 15. On guard till 6 P.M. Myrtle receives orders to proceed to Paris much to our joy. Lieut. Abbot who was formerly 1st Sergt of the Harvard Section, takes charge. He should fit well as he has a reputation for being "white" and has had six months at Verdun with the American Field Service. Some of the men are cool toward him because they don't like the idea of having a Harvard lieut. Went to a very good band concert at the "Y."

Sun. Sept. 16. H.Q. announce that "there will be no details today" but Sunday in the Army is like Monday on the farm and I help unload Ford boxes from trucks. It's back breaking work to say the least. A pass to town in the afternoon from 3 till 6. We have a good dinner at the hotel, see the sights for the 10th time and finish up with much ice cream lemonade and cakes at the downtown "Y" hut. Coming home in a carriage it developed that our cabby had one time been a cow puncher near Fort Worth Texas. Googins, who lives in F.W., was with us and so had quite a lengthy talk with him. Four sections left early this A.M. while it was still dark. We poor unfortunates who were left behind gathered around to say Godspeed. We were nearly as excited as they were but not quite for they broke up three cars before they had left the camp. One assaulted Sergt. Johnstone and myself but failed to harm us. I was in charge of a detail this A.M. Working up? Ah, to what dizzy heights of fame cannot one reach who but applies himself. Deak is giving a very fair imitation of the departed Myrtle. Deak is a great mimic and when we get the "blues" he pulls off his justly famous imitation of President Hadley [of Yale].

Mon. Sept. 17. Detailed all day to assembling ambulance bodies. The work is quite simple and interesting. Am going to bed early as I am fat-i-gued.

Tues. Sept. 18. Nice luck. Am still on body detail. I finished my first body today and I may be kept on as Gil seemed pleased with my work. Our detail put up four cars today and we'll try to speed up as we can't leave here till all the Fords are ready to roll. That means ten more days at least.

Eight sections from Allentown are said to have arrived in Liverpool. Two of the four sections which left Sun. are in Paris doing evacuation work, the other two are at the Front.

Wed. Sept. 19. Nothing of interest.

Thurs. Sept. 20. Eight sections arrive from Allentown via New York, Halifax, Liverpool and Le Havre. After 36 hrs. on the trains they sure were a dirty, tired looking lot of "veterans." "Oaky" and Kelly arrive with #52 and say they had some trip. They were hit by a torpedo which failed to explode. Their voyage lasted 25 days as they were held in the harbor at Halifax for some time. They complain of the treatment on English transports and in the camp near Liverpool.

Friday Sept. 21. Six transports came in yesterday with over 10,000 troops. As a consequence we move our barracks and wishing to install myself well in my new house I built a bed. It's some fine piece of carpentry but may hold out a while. As a result of moving I helped carry "Cliff" to the hospital as he had a badly strained back from lifting.

Rumor has it that our section is to leave with the next bunch.

Sun. Sept. 23. Have all the day off and Deak and I get a pass (Myrtle relented)* from 7:30 to 11:30 A.M. Having read Cobb's story of a shave in an English barber shop I decided to try a French one and compare the two. I certainly can't recommend it to anyone excepting members of the Inquisition. Cold water; straight chairs; short snappy strokes with the razor; perfume via an atomizer. You have to wash your own face and to cap the climax Monsieur le Coiffeur pleasantly but firmly withall demands "un franc M'sieur s'il vous plait." Later we went to the docks to look around abit and see what manner of men they are that go down to the sea in ships on this side of the Atlantic. The French sailors are a hardy looking lot with their blue uniforms and red tasseled caps but the others, the civilian sailors were very ordinary. After looking over the formerly-German boats Fredrich der Grosse and Princess Irene we stopped in at a patisserie and were tempted to over indulgence by the pretentious display of "gateaux de toutes sortes." Walking home along the bay we espied two freighters coming in and said a prayer to our Penates that we wouldn't have to unload them. We feel rather cocky now as there was a write-up in the Paris Herald concerning our good work in unloading those other boats. But we fear we may have to pay the price for such notoriety and would rather be considered very very rotten as stevadors. Lieut. Abbot takes us for a short hike to Saint-Marc in the afternoon. My left leg went on the fritz so I didn't enjoy the scenery much. No supper and feel sick. Why oh why did I eat all those cakes.

Mon. Sept. 24. More body assembling and it's boresome as the devil. "Pete" returns from the hospital and I find my laundry which he had taken to some farm house before he was taken sick. Secure a pass till 10 P.M. and Durant and I have dinner at the Hotel Grand for seven francs fifty. Afterwards we eat much ice cream, lemonade and sandwiches at the Y.M.C.A. hut. Ran

*The parenthetical comment was added when Bowerman recopied the diary, apparently forgetting that "Myrtle" (Sgt. Wharton) had left the section on September 15.

across Gates who used to be "Doc Pud's" secretary at Mercersburg. I was very surprised to see him, He is in the "Y." See by the paper that "Ghost" Hendrick is in the Field Service. They issue us our overcoats which one surely needs at night but the days are warm enough.

Thurs. Sept. 25. Same old detail. As Lyman remarked "Army life is just one mere detail after the other." Section #86 have been assigned cars and are having practise runs. I wonder when our happy day will come. Hear that the Kaiser offers 300 marks, 14 days "permission" and an iron cross of the 1st order to the Boche who captures the first American. Personally I'd rather be killed than taken prisoner. Poor Bill Cunningham is sick. It's pitiful to see a big husky bird like him who's never had an illness in his life laid low. We are assigned cars but they say that we will not leave with the next 6 sections who are going in a very short time. The first YMCA hut in France is dedicated with fitting ceremony. I wanted to go but volunteered for a little after supper detail putting equipement in our cars. The sooner we're ready the sooner we'll leave. Word just received thru the "Y" that Austria has broken with Germany. This is too good to be true; it has however given rise to a history discussion which is assuming alarming proportions as most of the debaters are seated on my bed. Ten men and a corporal from Section 53 left this afternoon at 3:30. Supposedly for hospital work near the Swiss Border. They took no ambulances with them.

Wed. Sept. 26. Nearly whole of section is detailed to fix up our cars. Houlihan and I have to finish a body which we started several days ago. Orders come to leave Saturday morning at four. Put on a special patrol along the road to town. Our duty is to see that drunks keep the peace and when they're too far gone we're to help them in. "Pete" and I are stationed near the downtown Y.M.C.A. Houlihan and Sjostrom try to quite a Marine and two women who were riding in a carriage. "Hap" gets knocked out largely because he was as tight as the Marine was.

Thurs. Sept. 27. The men are assigned to cars. I draw no. 12 for the trip and will not have an orderly. In P.M. we oil them up a bit and take a short run. My boat runs like a bird.

Friday Sept. 28. My day is spoiled—first I send Deak's clothes to the laundry instead of my own and secondly I learn that Corp. Lu[n]dgren is to ride with me. The line will be 25 cars divided into sections of 8 with a noncom in charge of each section. We are to have 22 ambulances; a Ford truck; a Packard truck and a Ford touring car which the Lieut. uses. My car is to be the 9th out. Oh boy! early to bed as tomorrow we're off on the last lap.

Sat. Sept. 29. Leave St. Nazaire at 7:20. Everything goes off nicely and we make a much better showing than the first bunch. Leaving camp our road lay thru a very pretty stretch of rather hilly country dotted with picturesque little towns usually nestling at the foot of a more or less beautiful chateau. Considering that we tear like mad and that many of the fellows never drove a car before it's surprising that the day held but one accident. Holbrook smashed into another car but that was to be expected. Lunch of hard tack and a sandwich in a little village. Stop for the night at Angers at 4:45 and parked the cars in the square. After oiling up and eating we were given passes till 9:30. Quite a little town and we are the object of much interest. In fact the whole day has been a series of exhibitions and we have been pelted with flowers and apples all the way.

Sun. Sept. 30. Leave Angers at 7:10. First stop at La Fleche where I bought bread, jam and cheese and filled my canteen with milk. Noon stop at Le Main [Le Mans?], where we had two hours rest. Looked over the town and bought some goggles as the dust is terrible. A hundred cars doing 35 per all day long raise hob with the roads. The trams were operated by women and the conductor used a fish horn [?] for a signal as they do on the railways. Stop for the night at Nogent [-le-Retrou] and park cars in the square. The townspeople offered to have us billeted in their homes. We drew lots for guard duty before the billets were given out and I drew 3rd on the list 11:30–1:30. The owner of the cinéma extended an invitation to his theatre and most of us accepted tho it was very tiresome. The men all wore their hats and I imagine they thot us crazy when we removed ours. The billets didn't pan out very well, most of the people were either out of town or dead. Those who were home didn't seem pleased and nearly all the fellows slept in the cars. It developed that the mayor had taken upon himself to give us the liberty of the city and his idea wasn't agreed to by "les citoyennes." Managed to get about four hours sleep.

Mon. Oct. 1. Leave Nogent at 7:15 and arrive in Chartres about 11:30. They gave us three quarters of an hour to see the cathedral which is reputed to be the most beautiful in the world after Rheims. It certainly was beautiful but too huge to see rightly in such a short time. We ran across an old priest who showed us thru and even took us down into the vaults below. These were dimly lit with thousands of candles and contained numerous shrines and tombs which gave one a "mediaeval" feeling. The windows; the flying butresses and the freizes are beyond my poor power of description suffice it to say that one came away with an awed reverence for those old ages in which such masterpieces were conceived and executed. It would take at least 2 hours to see the thing and a day would be interestingly spent. Deak and I were four minutes late in reporting and were told to stay with the cars. The other fellows lunched at the hotels while we ate "canned wobly." Met a wounded soldier with three decorations in lieu of his leg. He had boxed with Kilbane, Carpentier and other well known boxers. In return for a Boche bullet (it proved to be English) I gave him a can of tobacco. As we near Paris we see more and more soldiers mostly wounded or old Territorials who work around hospitals in the rear. Our next stop is at Versailles where we had a short time in which to see the palace. I had some work on my car so could not go there. I hope to do so sometime while on leave if I don't get picked off. The place looks beautiful from the outside at least. I had a very interesting talk with a Canadian soldier who had been at Vimy Ridge and Ypres for nine months. He said they were preparing for a big Fall drive which should come soon. I imagine we shall be in it. A French regiment which was to leave for the Front in the morning was drilling in front of Louis XIV's garrison. I imagine the old boy would have liked their appearance, for they certainly looked snappy in their new uniforms, new steel helmets and new equipment. As I watched them I failed to notice that they were exceptionally young or old or that they were physically unfit. I also talked with a French soldier who had been a prisoner in Germany. He said the food was terrible but the work was not hard. When I asked him if he had been wounded he said nothing but very dramatically removed his left eye! Thirty five miles more before we reach our Base Camp. Fine roads and we hit it up in great style. The road ran up hill and down, thru an avenue of very beautiful trees. "Pete" smashes into Voorhees our second accident. We stop to light our tail lamps and to turn off our headlights. Another stop to turn on our headlights and a distinct feeling of tension is felt thru the line. A big search light is sweeping the heavens and the moon half hidden by fog and mist gives a peculiar ghostly light. Off again running close together so as not to lose sight of the little red tail light on the car ahead. The lamps on the cars at the head of the line look like fire flies as the cars wind in and out and up and down. My brakes aren't working and I have to use my reverse, which is far from satisfactory when we're running so close together in the night. "Pete" & Gil lose the way. Several accidents occur at turns but nothing very serious and we arrive at the "chateau" at 10:30. After parking the cars close to the walls we literally dropped in our tracks we were so completely fagged out. Personally I was never so done up in all my driving experience.

Teus. Oct. 2. Sleep till 7:30 but am only partially rested. In the morning we fixed up our cars and loafed around till noon. We find that Base Camp is a "chateau" in name only. It is really nothing more or less than a large farm house with a court formed by the various farm buildings. It is prettily situated however in a little valley while the surrounding hills are covered with woods. Sandricourt is the name of the farm and is about 35 miles southwest of Paris.* When the wind is right one can hear the guns but very faintly. The American Red Cross formerly had their Ambulance Base Headquarters here. There are a couple of old A.R.C. Fords here but they are larger and more cumbersome than ours. In the afternoon we inspected some trenchs which are about a quarter of a mile from here and which were built to hold the Germans should they cross the Marne. The trenchs were never used for fighting tho the [illeg; original version of diary has "the German cavalry"] did pass not far from here and reached within 7 kilometers of Paris. I was impressed with the amount of work it must take to build such trenchs. They are not continuous but the flanks are so well protected that it amounts to the same thing. There is the first line with its strip of barbed wire in front, 15 ft across. One can easily appreciate what a job it would be to pass this wire under fire. Connecting the front line with the kitchen and officers' dugouts in a little wood to the rear runs a zig-zag communication trench. The trenchs are about shoulder

---

* Sandricourt is actually about twenty miles *north*west of Paris.

high, generously timbered and having wicker work to support the sides between the uprights. In some places they are covered over except for a foot wide space or firing slit. In certain of these "rooms" are machine gun emplacements built of earth and wicker work. There are numerous stairs leading out to the rear and also at the ends.

We are on French rations and the breakfasts are largely psychological consisting of war bread and thick black coffee. There is an option of hot milk which most of us prefer and which doesn't go badly with bread and jam. The other meals are good and we are issued vin rouge with them. I think the stuff is rotten and I much prefer the water from a wonderful spring nearby. There is a fairly good library here in which we spend a good deal of our time and our stomachs are catered to by a little French woman who keeps a stand of cakes and candy. We learn that the two sections which left St. Nazaire before us left for the Front the morning of the day we arrived.

Wed. Oct. 3. Volunteers were called for but the reason was not stated. Two men were wanted from each Section. Hap, Ted and Van Doran sign up due to a little trouble with Abbot and left for Paris to join Section 64 which is an old Field Service section that is being recruited. We are very sorry to see them leave especially Hap & Ted but they may "ride some gravy." I spoke to "Pete" about volunteering when I heard of it but he advised me not to. I'm just as happy because I prefer staying with the old gang. Deak has a detail putting up a fence around the car park which I am on. The gas they have given us is very poor and I have to strain new gas thru a chamois after drawing off all the old gas in my tank. Went thru the trenchs tonight and after we sit around on the grassy slope talking of home and watching the full red harvest moon come up thru a gap in the beautiful wooded hills across the valley. The countryside is a good deal like that of Conneticut only more beautiful. One gets homesick watching the moon and pities the poor devils in the trenchs. How useless war is; what a waste of human energy not to mention life and yet I suppose some good will come of it in the matter of government; social conditions; inventions and a closer bond between all peoples. Here are men with three years absolutely lost from their lives and existing under such conditions that should the war end tomorrow it will take 2 yrs more for them to readjust themselves.

Surely God wouldn't permit all of this for extermination only. It's hard tho for a ordinary man to reconcile this war and a conception of a gentle God.

Change my quarters from my "bus" to the "chateau" that is to a cellar of the chateau.

Thurs. Oct. 4. We are to leave Saturday morning to join our division at Bar-le-Duc. This town is near Verdun and is at present the object of nightly bombing raids. We will be getting into the thick of it I suppose, well I'm ready the Bowermans have a good name and I must keep it up. With God's help I will!

The truck, Yens driving and Wasilic [Wasilik] and Hank as passengers, left for Paris at 7 this morning. Their mission is unknown. We are to be paid either today or tomorrow. Johnny gave us some dope on our trip Sat. We are to take 10 ambulances, a Pacard truck and a Ford delivery truck which we will exchange with the section we relieve for their 20 cars and they will drive ours back here. Johnny also said that of their 20 cars there were 19 different makes. The truck returns from Paris at 12 P.M. Hank brings a "vic" from the branch office of the Aeolian Co. of which Hank's father is president.

Friday Oct. 5. No detail and played the Victrola nearly all day. We have rigged up a stove out of an old kettle. The chief feature of the stove is its ability to send the smoke up the pipe. Still it's a blessing for even smoke will help warm up and dry out this cold damp cellar. The room has every appearance of a pirate's cave as we crowd around the smoking kettle, dirty, ragged and unshaven while the smoke from cigarettes and pipes blends with the low hanging cloud born of the stove. Parisians' musical tastes prohibit rag time which is our "fort." Perkins (the "little Minister") insists on playing "Lead Kindly Light" tho we object strongly because it isn't Sunday in the first place and in the second we couldn't see a light anyway in this smoke. "The Little Grey Home in the West" puts an end to the talking and brings a far away look into everyone's eye. Home's an awfully long ways off and God only knows when we'll see it again.

Sat. Oct. 6. Volunteer for a truck detail to Meru, thinking it will be a nice ride. As usual I get "stung" and spend the whole day unloading wooden barrack sections from a freight car into a truck, carting em 5 miles and unloading them. It wasn't exactly a "gravy" job and to make matters worse there was a holiday declared this afternoon which we soon found out, "didn't apply to the truck detail." Something must have gone wrong with the orders cause it's Saturday night and we're still here.

Sun. Oct. 7. New orders come saying we are to leave Monday morning going by train and taking only 35 of the 45 men. We are to relieve Section 62 but no one seems to know where they are. We have to get out of this camp as four sections from St. Nazaire are due shortly, so we go to Paris until further orders. There is much speculation as to who the men will be who are to be left. Larsen and I walk over to a little village nearby for a good dinner as we were hungry after a morning's work. The fellows who are to stay were announced at 2 o'clock roll call. They are Sergt. Hubbard (who is trying to transfer to aviation) Core, Durant, Flint, Stevens, Thorpe and Holbrook. They are of course bitterly disappointed and we are very sorry to see our "family" broken up.

Mon. Oct. 8. Hurrah! Everybody is going! *New* orders are responsible for this. Such uncertainty and changing about is exasperating. We are ready to leave by 8 and the truck takes our barracks bags to the station about a mile and a half away. We march down in the rain but are so happy to leave that the wetting we get doesn't dampen our spirits. I am writing on the train comfortably seated in a 1st class compartment. We are pulling into Paris, Capital of the World. "So this is Paris" everyone cries as we descend from the train at the Gare du Nord. Red Cross Ambulances take us across town to the American Hospital at Neuilly. Our journey was swift and our view restricted so we don't see much to brag about. The hospital is a very large building originally intended for a girls' school but, the war breaking out just as it was finished the Red Cross took it over. It has a fine reputation and is famous among the soldiers. This popularity may be due to the many good looking nurses who looked down from windows as we marched in the gates. Sections 93 and 17 are evacuating the wounded brought in from the rear hospitals. It's not very exciting work but they have fine quarters, good meals and can get into Paris often as the gate of the city is only a few blocks away. They give us a very good meal served by girl waiters. There is a regular table service and all the comforts of home. Walking about the corridors and in the paths one sees many wounded who are convalescing. They seem happy enough tho many of them flap along on crutches with a decoration pinned to their dressing gowns and only one leg. We are supposed to stay around the hospital all afternoon but Paris proves a stronger attraction than orders or a tea given by the nurses and Hank, Lynch and I take a little walk down thru the city gate. The walk resolves itself into a shopping tour and when we start back we are loaded with chocolate. At the hospital commissary we are able to buy American cigarettes. I only got two packages but some "hogs" got away with a hundred. I inquired at the Information Bureau if they knew where Loyd's hospital unit was but they were unable to tell me. Supper at 4:45 then to the station at 5:15 again making the trip in R.C. Ambulances. It is dark and rainy. Leave Paris at 8 P.M. for Bar Le Duc, riding 3rd class on hard wooden seats, 16 men to a car. Section #92 is on its way to the Vosges but leaves by the same station. They said it would be a long ride so we tried to pass away the time with cards but it didn't go. Johnny came around to tell us that in case Bar le Duc was being bombed when we arrived we were to look for a sign saying "Cave Vouté" and run for it. Believe me I will! Altho six of us are in one section of compartment with all our baggage we managed a few hrs sleep during which I caught the deuce of a cold. Deac, Hank, Wassom, Durant, Holbrook and I are together.

Teus. Oct. 9. "All out for Bar le Duc!" It is raining and darker than the ace of spades for which we are duly thankful for the partially destroyed station gives evidence of frequent bombing parties. We unload our baggage from the train and into a huge camion. The baggage detail finished we crawl into what little space is left in two other camions after the other fellows have found places. Off for the front at 3:30 with 60 kilometers to cover. I tried to get some sleep but finally gave it up as twenty men to a truck doesn't permit comfortable seating much less lounging. I believe we all expected some shells to come our way, but they didn't and [the] ride and sightseeing was uninterupted. The roads were well camouflaged by brush and willow screens. This camouflage is stretched between poles about 15 ft high but is not continuous being placed only when the stretch of road is exposed to the enemy. The road is also hidden from airplane view by occaisonal strips of camouflage which hang down much like the "low bridge" warnings on railroads. We pass all kinds of French troops. Some on foot, some on horses, some riding bicycles, some in camions like ourselves, some in caissons and some in queer looking, low two wheeled, mule carts which carry ammunition to the machine guns. There are numerous parcs for engineers' material, wire, trench beams, duck boards and the like. Ammo dumps with seemingly acres of shells of all calibers piled up like cord wood tho the piles are small in height and area and are separated so an enemy shell lighting one pile won't necessarily touch off the whole affair. There are hospitals placed far enough back to be reasonably safe from shell fire tho they are nearly all in range. These are the evacuation hospitals to which the car[e?]lessly dressed wounded are brought, sorted as to nature of wounds, operated on if absolutely necessary and all wounds redressed. These are usually manned by a group of medical men called G.B.D or Groupe Brancordiers Divisional. They are usually old men (territorials) and are used to replace losses at the front. The roofs are marked with huge red crosses and usually there is the same design worked in white washed stones in the yard. I noticed one hospital put awfully close to an ammunition dump and would not censure the Germans if they should hit it with their shells. We come to a cross road bearing a sign "Verdun 12 Kilometers." What a vision it calls up, Verdun the sacrificial altar of France. An operating table upon which the staunch hearted poilu submitted to a serious blood letting that the life of sa Patrie might continue. Glorious Verdun! Glorious Poilu; Glorious France! Soon we shall know you better and learn the reason why the army of the Crown Prince failed. Surely we will see some action with Verdun only 7 miles away and may we so perform our duties that we shall be worthy of the friendship of these men who have made the city of Verdun an inspiration. We reach our camp about 7 a.m. The town or rather village is called Genicourt [Génicourt-sur-Meuse] and lies about three or four miles behind the front lines. It develops that we are to relieve Section 63 not #62 as we had supposed. Some of the men in 63 are from New Haven and eagerly ask news from our men who live there. The Section's 6 months enlistment is up and most of them are returning to the States. Lucky devils! After a very good breakfast at which #63 was host we looked the town over. It is pretty well demolished and is a most desolate place with the mud and the rain. Our quarters aren't so bad tho well ventilated through floors and walls. There is a room with a fire place and the sleeping quarters are on the second floor. We cleaned up the place and it sure was some job as the house was in filthy condition as is the case, I understand, with all Field Service quarters as they have no discipline. Two days before we arrived, the Boches bombed the town. A huge bomb nearly 3 ft tall and capable of containing 200 lbs. of powder fell about a hundred yards from the billet. Luckily for 63 it lighted on its side and failed to explode. The same day some 25 shells dropped in about 200 yards away when the Germans were trying for a narrow gauge railway and a cross road. No one in 63 was killed or injured during their 6 months and I hope our luck proves as kind. Looking over the cars we found 19 Fiats which carry 10 "assis" and five "couchés." I believe we will like these cars much better than the Fords because they are larger and have a gear shift. We are attached to an attacking division which is due for "repos" in a few days. Seven of our men go out to the "postes" as orderlies to the Field Service men in order to learn the roads. I was keen to go but Gil said I looked too "done up." We explored the hill where the shells had fallen, collected a French hand grenade which I guess was used for practise, as my first war trophy. After dinner I slept an hour or so and then walked up on a hill nearby to watch the firing. One hears the guns constantly and from the hill, can see their flashes. The star-shells too were very pretty. When one can forget their purpose. They go shooting up into the night like a rocket, growing gradually brighter and brighter, then hang suspended a moment and fall to earth as the light is extinguished. One looked just like a searchlight on an airplane and we thot he was coming straight for us. As if an airplane would use a light flying over the trenchs. Oh you green horns! The sound of the guns is like violent thunder and as we stand in the "hollow" of wide semi circle the flashes of the guns about us are beautiful. Sometimes they start way at one end of our semi circle and run to the other so that one can almost imagine there are relays of runners who bear flaming torches which blaze up as they are tossed from one runner to the other. Isn't there something in Scott about the "fiery crosses"? I must look that up. Funny how one ducks like a gun shy dog at every violent report as if one knew a shell was coming his way. As we came up the hill tonight, thru the dark muddy streets of the town whose windows were all carefully screened lest enemy "avions" should see we passed a large group of soldiers, mere phantoms they were in the black night, voices rather

than men but sounds of rattling equipment gave proof of more
materiality. As we stumbled by them some man called out "And
your section, when do you go up?" "Immediately" came the answer in a voice which impressed me with its concealed bitterness,
saying in that one word how much the war was hated but how
futile it was to attempt to escape its horrors and duties. These
men were going into the trenches—poor devils—poor cogs in the
pitiless, devastating machine of war! Our division they tell us is a
crack bunch who have seen some fierce fighting and have lost
nearly 50% of their men.

Wed. Oct. 10. At 2:30 four of us, Flint, Larsen, Durant, and myself
piled into an ambulance which the Lieut and Johnny were driving and started for our first trip to the front to relieve our men. I
am to relieve Bradley. The road was in good condition and the
country side quite beautiful in its Fall regalia. Scattered over the
hills are hundreds of dugouts, camps of soldiers more or less
camouflaged and huge munitions dumps completely covered
with a roofing of camouflage. In the woods are the batteries and
the search lights carefully concealed. Great swaths are cut in the
trees by the German shells which has broken off the trees about
15 ft from the ground on the average. The woods seem filled with
men, horses and guns, ammunition convoys are met and passed,
soldiers afoot, soldiers on horseback and soldiers on bicycles are
coming and going along the road. As we passed one battery close
by the road side, it fired and the concussion struck us thru the
open window of the ambulance. We all thot it was an exploding
shell and consequently gave a start then looked cautiously around
to see if the other men had started or if they had seen you. Our
first stop was at a "poste" called La Cloche where we found
Kirby who excitedly told us all about the war and expressed himself as favorably impressed with the whole affair. This dressing
station to which the men are brought after being temporarily
dressed if hit in the "lines" is about an eight[th] of a mile from
the front line. Shells were whistling over head and on both sides,
not all German of course as we are in front of our own batteries
which were a couple of kilometers behind us. Under the tutelage
of Kirby & the Red Cross man we were instructed in distinguishing between our own shells called "départs" and German
shells called "arrivées." Also we were told that a shell which did
not explode (about 2 out of five, they said) were "l[o]upés." Just

before we arrived a shell hit about 200 yards from the "abri" or dug out and we learned later that just after we left one struck the road so we counted ourselves fortunate. The "abri" was an interesting sort of place. It was simply a little room some 30 or forty feet underground fitted with some rough board bunks, a table and small stove and lighted with candles. The "brancardiers" (stretcher-bearers) were seated about the stove reading or around the table playing cards. Our next stop was at Mouilly where I was to relieve Bradley. As we drove up on the little hill just in front of the house which served as a "poste de Secours" two brancardiers and a guard rushed up to the car and warned us with excited gestures that unless we backed down the hill "tout de suite" we'd hold a reception for few bullets from a Boche "mitrailleuse" placed in the trees at the end of the road. Naturally we were only too glad to take their advice and we thanked them for their consideration. The lay out was like this

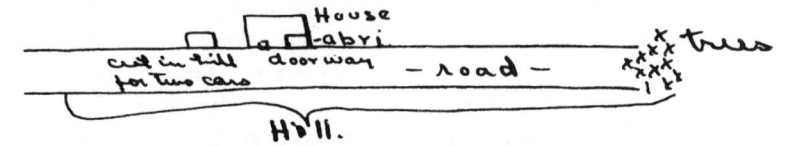

Bradley went off with the Lieut and I stayed with the R.C. man whose name was Lorenz and proved a very decent sort of chap. We soon got acquainted and he introduced me to the four brancardiers with whom we had a nice little chat before supper. One of the brancardiers is the wildest looking individual I ever laid eyes on, he's a cross between a Chinese pirate and a crazy sheep herder. Besides his ferocious looks he has a diabolic way of eating which is far from pleasant. The supper was well cooked and the cook fairly insisted that we do full justice to his meal. I tried to be decent and gorged myself tho I bought my favor dearly and was a victim to indigestion. After supper Lorenz and [I?] gather an armful of stones and went rat-hunting. The beasts fairly swarmed in the ditches along the road so the hunting was good tho our aim was poor and no trophies were secured. Lorenz told me that one of their fellows lighted a cigarette in the road before the house and was extensively shot at by the German machine gunners. He saved himself by ducking behind the wheels of his car which are solid. I stood in the doorway and threw lighted matches out into the road but nothing happened and I gave up.

Either that story was a "gag" or the machine gun & its crew had moved away. Our beds were in the abri under the house and were so placed next the door that if a shell lighted in the room next to the dug out we would be killed & not the Frenchmen. Oh well those old boys have had 3 years of this and it's only fair they should have the best.

Thurs. Oct. 11. Our breakfast (coffee and bread) was given us in bed at 8:30. Some life. As there was nothing to do we took a little exploring trip thru the town up the road about a hundred yards. The only building left standing as a whole in the town is the church and even that is holding on by the skin of its teeth. We pried open a box of ammunition which we found in an old cellar and took some of the stuff for souvenirs. Not knowing what they were we showed them to a Frenchman whom we ran across but he evidently didn't like the carelessness with which we treated our souvenirs and begged us to throw them away as they were unexploded hand grenades. We went back to the cellar and wasted a half hour throwing them at walls, perhaps that half hour wasn't wasted anyhow I'm just as glad none of them exploded. We were relieved about 10 o'clock that night by two men from Section 64# which has relieved our section. As Lorenz and I drove away from the "poste" the star shells from the lines were lighting up the road nearly as bright as day. I wrote a letter during the afternoon telling the folks everything that has happened since we left. Lorenz is going to try and mail it on the other side. I sure hope he gets it thru. I may be in a "brig" doing time if he doesn't.

Frid. Oct. 12. Left at one o'clock for our period of "repos." The division has already gone except for one or two small detachments. It was raining to beat the cars and was cold as the devil. I drove car 821 with Howie as an orderly. We arrived in the little village of Amanty about 5:30 after an 80 kilometer trip. We were absolutely saturated and half frozen. Our quarters are in the hay loft of a barn. They are fairly decent but over ventilated.

Sat. Oct. 13. Ballantyne, Bates, Borden, Lewis, Lynch, Googins, Peters and Tremaine are made 1st class privates—verily the lowly are exalted unto high places. I have no criticism except in the case of Peters he can't even drive a car.

Sun. Oct. 14. Move the kitchen to a less aromic and incidentley amoniac place and install the "bureau" in a house which will keep some rain off the records. Am on guard all day. Nothing much to guard except against the rain. This is quite futile and I give it up the 3rd watch.

Mon. Oct. 15. Larkin and I walked the 8 kilometers to Gondricourt [Gondrecourt] this morning to buy some cigarettes and see the encampment of the 1st Division of regulars who are in training there and will be the first American combat troops in the lines. After an engagement with a Q.M. Captain in which we sacrificed truth in order to gain our objective—2 cartons of Latinas we had lunch with three YMCA workers. One of them, a woman who lives in New York was very nice and we had a pleasant chat with her. Larkin, having used the expression "with the French Army" with considerable success on the Q.M. Captain evidently considered it an "open sesame" to all things. At least he employed it frequently during lunch. The 8 kilometers back from Gondricourt were a whole lot longer than the 8 kilometers from Amanty. As soon as we arrived home we both went to bed. Assembly blew at 9:30 and it was a sleepy grumbling crowd that piled out in the cold dark night. Ten cars were needed to evacuate a hospital train from Verdun. The train was due in Vaucouleur[s] at 2 A.M. so we left Amanty at 11 to be sure that everyone would be there on time. Howie Campbell was my orderly and was quite on edge during the ride because we carried no head lights then the side lamps on our bus gave out and finally the tail lamp on Bates' car which was ahead of me went blooey so that I could see nothing most of the time and merely trusted to luck. Despite Howie's admonitions we arrived safely only to find that the train was an hour late. The Frenchmen made a place for us by their fire in their barracks and gave us tea which kept us awake. I felt very fine despite the walk that afternoon and the lateness of the hour and caused a French major some merriment and more curiosity as to my civilian occupation by my singing and dancing act on the station platform. Finally after what seemed hours of waiting the silent dark train rolled in—silent yet strangely alive with I know not what. It reminded me of the time as a boy when I attended the removal of a body from the "Yellowstone Limited." Then the doors of the compartments opened and the "assis" descended and limped into the barracks. Men with frozen feet, slight wounds in the head, arms and legs. The assis cleared from the train and the platform the doors of the compartments containing the "couchées" were opened letting out the sickening smells of bad wounds and disinfectants. I had to sneak away for a little fresh air the stench was so remindful of my experience with chlorophorm which sickens me. Amid a good deal of shouting, joustling and swearing by the doctors and stretcher-bearers the couchées were slowly put into the waiting ambulances, five to a car and we were off to Rigny. I made two trips and was returning from the second just as day broke. What this day must mean to those poor devils who have waited so long in the cold and wet yearning for a comfortable warm bed, and someone to nurse them. I was impressed during the night with the total absence of any sign of impatience or word of complaint from the wounded. They were like well trained children, never questioning what was done to them. I can't imagine Americans behaving as well and—for opposite reasons—neither do I believe Germans would suffer so silently.

Teus. Oct. 16. There being no more wounded I drove home. It was so good to be able to go fast without causing suffering that I opened the "bus" up. Arrived home we ate a little cold breakfast and got ready to move at 10 o'clock to Bur[e]y en Vaux ten kilometers away. Certainly we're going from bad to worse in regards to towns and quarters. Everyone is disgusted with the town, the quarters, France, the French Army, the American Army and about everything else on earth, not to mention the filth in these little French villages which is always disgusting to an American no matter how good he feels. While the others were "crabbing" together I drifted over to inspect the barn which is to be our home and was rather awed by the date over the doorway. 1775. I wonder did the builders stop to listen when the "embattled farmers" fired on the British troops at Concord? did one of the hated "aristos" crouch in terror in one of these dark corners as the infuriated "citoyens" rushed past, their blazing torches lighting up the 10 yr old keystone with its date? To an American especially a Westerner old building[s] are rather impressive.

Wed. Oct. 17. I was detailed to help the mechanics fix up the cars. Thrilling work! They say 25 planes bombed Nancy today and dropped 80 bombs. I have been too long in the army to believe anything I don't see and then you're not sure—in the army.

Thurs. Oct. 18. Sergt. Peters and I made the "mail route" today which consists in visiting our four "postes" Gousancourt [Goussaincourt?], Maxey, Saint Germain and Domremy (birthplace of Joan D'Arc) and evacuating whatever malades there are to Toul 35 kilometers from Burey. The trip is about 60 kilometers in length and is much sought after. We left Burey at 11, took our malades to the H.O.E (Hôpital d'Evacuation) where they were sorted as to the nature of their wounds and were then taken by us to the various hospitals in the city. As we took so long in finding one hospital we didn't have much time to look around in tho we did visit the Cathedral. Toul is interesting to me for its huge wall which surrounds it. Trying to sight-see and drive in a convoy at the same time I ran into a wagon to the great anger of the Frenchman and some slight injury to my fender. These Frenchmen are very funny when properly excited and our collision was quite diverting. Home by five in time for a rather good supper prepared by l'Apache and Trefaux our maître de la Cuisine—Just after supper a American battalion came thru on their first trip to the Front. They have left the training camp at Gondricourt and are ready for a little of the real thing in a quite sector. They look trim and fit and are very enthusiastic. One young chap from the University of Oklahoma had supper with us tho l'Apache deemed it bad form on our part to invite guests after dinner had been served. Their helmets were mightly like the English one and are considerably heavier than those of the French. That reminds me—as Bob & I were returning from Gondricourt a string of Limousines passed with General Pershing, French generals and their staffs on the way to inspect this battallion. A German plane came over this evening and all uncovered lights were extinguished immediately indicating a wholesome respect for our enemy when he takes to wings. One old French woman hearing the noise came outside with a lighted candle to see what was up (a good pun). I answered her look of inquiry with a laconic "avion boche"—puff! the candle went out and she poured out a perfect torrent of words which I couldn't understand but knew from her flashing eyes that they were rather anathematizing to Germans in general and avions boches in particular. The aviator fortunately had bigger game in sight for we escaped and were duly thankful. It's the queerest sensation peering up into the sky trying to see an enemy plane and imagining all the time that a bomb is falling straight at you and will undoubtedly hit you full in the face.

Friday Oct. 19. "On call" all day but no call comes and I employ my time in washing and greasing my old tub. Lewis and Lyman, skippers of the good ship "Punt" run aground and their staunch craft is pounded to pieces on the rocks. The heroic Lewis attempts the rescue of Lyman but stumbles while carrying him to shore and they are both laid beneath the surging tide wet if not drowned.

Sat. Oct. 20. The Lieut. being continually harassed with the complaints caused by our quarters in the barn succeeds in getting an abandoned café for our use. The thing has four rooms and a fire place so I imagine our worries are at an end.

Sun. Oct. 21. Two months since we landed in this country. I wonder how much longer we're going to be shunted around in these dirty little villages only within hearing distance of the Front. We'll have to wait till our division is sent to an active sector or until we get a new one. Drew kitchen police duty which, however, permitted me to visit Vaucouleur in the afternoon with Sjostrom. We saw the gate thru which Joan D'Arc passed on her way to Nancy now barely 9 ft high. We also visited the old old chapel in which she prayed. It was at Vaucouleur that the Maid of Orleans got her first recruits. After a dinner at the Hotel Joan d'Arc we walked home arriving about 6:30.

Mon. Oct. 22. Lucky enough to draw the "mail route" again. Butler and Beecher go with me. "Long John" relieves Church at Gousancourt. We pick up four malades at Domremy and go to Toul dropping Church at Burey. Butler and I visited Wasilich who is ill with bronchitis in a hospital there. He seems much better and expects to be out soon. Returning from Toul we stopped at St. Germaine where we relieved Googins and Tremaine who, before leaving initiated us into the mysteries of Barsac, a sweet white wine. Have supper with 12 sous-officiers and find them a very jolly and interesting crowd. Sleep in the Poste de Secours with the Brancardiers. These Frenchmen have a positive dread of fresh air while they are sleeping and the minute you open a window they start yelling "current d'air" "current d'air" and don't cease till the window is closed. Besides the stuffiness of the room, one of the brancardiers who had been gassed at Verdun snored like a thresher so our sleep was troubled, to say the least.

Teus. Oct. 23. Up at seven and start the day abominally with a French breakfast. Write letters nearly all day attempting to catch up with my correspondance. In the afternoon we had a fine interesting talk with a young sergeant who styles himself L'Anarchiste. He is very pessimistic about nearly everything. He doesn't believe the Americans will make good fighters, believes the war will either be over in 3 months with a Boche victory or last as many years, thinks the English are "pas bon" and Wilson is not a fighter but merely a good lawyer and a moralist. Says he doesn't want Alsace Lorraine that none of the Frenchmen want it except the people who don't have to fight. He declares that the infantry are completely "fed-up" and are willing to quit any time regardless of who wins. He believes that the Germans have the best artillery and superior aviators. Says an enemy army will never enter Germany and the Germans would never have entered France if the French had had a good government. Finally he hates Poincaire, Lloyd George, the Russians and the French high staff which he declares hurried Joffre off to America because he opposed the wasting of men in useless attacks. Butler and I become very excited and seriously considered lamming the beggar. Never have I wished so much to be able to talk French. After supper while Madame cleared up the table and we sipped our wine L'Anarchiste proved himself a good story teller and held our attention for over an hr and a half. What stories! Two of them stand out in my mind. Guinemeyer fighting a Boche some 7000 ft up, the latter's fall in flames; the famous French Ace des Aces swooping down still firing; the landing; his salut to his dead opponent and his departure in a motor. Surely aviation is the 20th century chivalry and is the only department of war in which one still finds sportsmanship.—Four officers of a "75" battery killed by a shell, the funeral service in a sappers' trench dimly lighted by candles which go out each time as a shell explodes or one gun fires. The constant relighting of the candles. L'Anarchiste officiating as priest. The story ended with a bitter dramatic gesture and the words "Ils étaient des bonnes hommes" [They were good men] a sentence containing all this man's pent up hatred for war and its terrible cost. He is most satirical and can put more sarcasm into "Ah yes" "Ah yes" than most people could put in a book.

    The second "character" is the plump jovial little adjutant nicknamed the "Leetala Wooman." Champion of Paris, Parisian Women and the poilu. His imitation of Americans driving an ambulance under shell fire is rich as is also his imitation of Shep's stuttering. He shares the opinions of the young sergeant and having the floor did not hesitate to express them himself. Butler being able to speak French after a fashion argued hotly and I supplied enough emphatic gestures to keep Roosevelt going for a year. However no matter to what degree of warmth our conversation developed we always broke up the seance with the words "sans rancour [no hard feelings] eh?" and we agree "sans rancour" because these men have seen and done and tho they may not be exact in their statements surely they have earned the privilege of expressing their opinions before such neophytes as we Americans are.

Butler and I accepted an invitation from L'Anarchiste to visit his school of instruction tomorrow. He is teaching the young recruits the operation of the 75. To bed early so tired that our gassed friend who snores & coughs alternately the whole night thru, does not disturb me in the least.

Wed. Oct. 24. Visit the school in the morning. It would have been more interesting if I could have understood more of what the Sergeant said. He explained to us about barrages and the star shells used as artillery signals, the color, number and arrangement being changed whenever necessary. He admires the "75" but says the bigger guns are best as nothing can oppose them. He also explained that because the enemy has the exact range of their trenches it is almost impossible to hold them even tho they may be captured quite easily. His own gun has been fired 10253 times and in two hours during an attack at Verdun he fired 345 shots. Wrote some more letters in the afternoon and took a turn around the town seeing nothing of interest because one French village is exactly like the other. Brad and Borden relieve us bringing five assis and two officers whom we take to Toul. A captain sat in front with me but my attempts at conversation succeeded so poorly that we rode most of the way in silence. Having to wait some time for our officers [I] went around to see Wasilic again and found him doing very nicely under the care of two awfully good looking nurses—no wonder he recovers slowly. At four o'clock we met the officers and had a nice snappy ride home with my formerly silent captain yelling "doucement!" [slow down!] at every turn.

Thurs. Oct. 25. Spend entire morning wiring my lamps and straightening my fenders. Eat supper in a house near the barracks with Hank, Yens, Art and Kirby. Beaucoup frites [a lot of fried potatoes] for a franc. On guard for four hours 10–12; 4–6—a lonely job and permitting of much thinking of past, present and future mostly past which makes one very blue.

Frid. Oct. 26. Supper again at the home of M. Lewis. After the "family" had formed a ring around the fire place I was introduced as a Metropolitan star. Being obliging I acceded to the demands of M & Madame and sang while they listened with open mouths. Finally I couldn't help laughing and we all burst out to the evident astonishment of M & Mme.

Sat. Oct. 27 to Friday Nov. 2. This job of waiting for something to do is a wearisome one and we're dead of ennui. Besides the usual routine of K.P. and guard nothing has happened worth recording. Perhaps I should put down my impressions of France and the war but having seen such a rotten part of the former and so little of the latter I feel that it's better to wait. Cuss words don't appear well in a diary and I could use few others in recording my impressions. Thank Heaven the outfit is a small one and composed of men who are or at least have been gentlemen. I can't imagine how these days would pass in the company of men with whom you had nothing in common. I was on poste only once during this time going as orderly to Kirby to the poste at Gousancourt. We pooled our capital and spent most of our time in a little café which enabled us to look more cheerfully on life. Kirby was quite ill one evening and of course it was on that night that our only call came. We went to Toul, discharged our "malades" had supper and "homeward plod our weary way." Because we got on the wrong road we nearly had to swim our weary way at least the old Fiat must have considered herself a motorboat. The next day was All Saints and the weather was perfect. Kirby and I took a walk in the afternoon during which we got perfectly homesick. That malady was not dispelled either by a trip thru a nearby cemetery inspecting old tombstones. Later in the afternoon the division band gave a concert which we attended only to increase our homesickness. That evening as we sat around the fire place in the Poste de Secours we heard the church bells ringing and I asked a Frenchman if there was another Mass. "No" he replied "they're celebrating the Italian victory." This completed our cup of woe as it recalled to us that our allies the Italians were rapidly being driven back.* Not withstanding the seriousness of the situation to which the Frenchman alluded I considered this remark quite clever and about the best bit of humor I've heard in France.

The division pulled out that night and when we awakened in the morning the little town was quite deserted. The French Lieut's orderly brought us orders to return to barracks at once so we left immediately after breakfast. We signed the pay roll when we returned but are not hopeful about receiving our money.

Friday Nov. 2. Today was some sort of a French Memorial Day and the Section took part in the ceremonies. Leaving the village we marched slowly up the hill behind it to the cemetery where we first made a tour of the graves in single file each man removing his hat as he entered the cemetery. This tour finished we drew up near a large vault to listen to a French captain whose words were for the most part not understood. The Captain's speech however eloquent was not necessary—the hundred or more wooden crosses bearing the name rank and the division of the soldier, the date he was killed, the words Mort Pour La France [Died for France] and a tri colored disk with streamers were eloquent enough to impress us with the seriousness of our business and the devotion which these men had had for their beloved country. The speech ended we marched down behind the brancardiers who left us when we reached the edge of the village to attend the decorating of five of their number. As soon as we were given "fall out" we hurried to the field where the ceremony was to take place. The company formed in a three sided square with those to be awarded the Croix de Guerre placed half way and facing the open side. The company formed an officer proceeded to read off the citations. At the end of each citation a captain handed a Croix to a major who made a short speech pinned the medal on the faded blue overcoat and shook hands with the honored man. I had supposed those decorated were always kissed on both cheeks but I suppose that is only done by a general and a major is forbidden the osculatory rite. Of the five one was a young priest who was rather flustered during the proceeding and certainly was the most pleased of them all.

---

*On October 24, 1917, the Austrians nearly encircled Italian units near the Isonzo River. The rout at Caporetto, which resulted in 300,000 Italians being taken prisoner and even more deserting, was depicted in Hemingway's *A Farewell to Arms*.

Sat. Nov. 3. Left Burey en Vaux for Cuistine [Custines] which is near the front beyond Nancy. The trip was quite interesting as we passed thru that famous city Nancy. Despite the repeated reports of bombing I saw no evidences of the raids in the section thru which our road lay. I was surprised to see a statue of Abraham Lincoln standing in one of the squares. I never appreciated before that Abe was an international figure. Just before reaching Cuistines we drove thru the town of Pompeii [Pompey] which is subjected to numerous air attacks because it is the site of one of the largest munition factories in France. A kilometer away we passed a young forest of lamp poles which were used to delude Friend Boche at night. When these lights are going and the ones at Pompeii are out he is expected to unload his bombs on the harmless lamp posts. Whether he does or not I haven't found out. Custines needs no description or comment as it is exactly like the hundreds of other small French villages. It is 30 kilometers from the German border and from certain nearby hills one can see the spire of Metz, that supposedly impregnable stronghold which controls Alsace-Lorraine.

Our barracks are fair at least no water came thru the roof. Outside of this blessing they are very ordinary, being drafty, dark and cold as there is no place for a stove. We went to bed directly after supper as that was the easiest way to keep warm. I, being on guard, slept in my car. I was supposed to wake Larsen at 10 but my watch was wrong and I awakened him at 9 much to his disgust. To make matters even, I waited till 10:30 before calling him again. Shep who was third guard believed I was sleeping in the barracks and woke everyone trying to find me. There were threats of a double lynching, poor Shep being exhibit A and myself being exhibit B as an accomplish to Shep's crime.

Sun. Nov. 4. UNEVENTFUL——

Mon. Nov. 5. Having been on guard last night I exercised my right to sleep late. There was much excitement in camp this noon when a Boche plane came over on a reconnoiter and was the target for some 60 shells fired by the A.A. guns on the hill nearby. We all dashed wildly into the middle of the road to watch the airman's luck and to pray for the worst. He obligingly flew directly overhead, his plane surrounded by puffs of white and black smoke. The white being from flame shells the black from shrapnel. No Frenchmen were in evidence when he flew overhead and we were cautioned to follow their example and get under protection but being inexperienced we remained where we were until the "éclat" began to fall and one missed Vorhees only by a foot. After supper Yens, Shep, Weber, "Papa Joffre" and I went up on the hill to see the anti air craft guns. The battery consists of two 75's so mounted that they can be elevated to 87° and swing completely around. Near the dug outs for the officers & men are the instruments for gauging the height of the planes and the direction they are going. A telescope, a wind velocity guage, a search light, a series of stretched wires to catch vibrations and a number of huge horns which enable the crew to hear the motor a long ways off. Near the guns is a dugout for the telephones over which notice of an airplane's approach is given to another station toward which he is going. We had a great time learning the workings of the various instruments & the guns and our friendship being pledged by a liberal gift of American cigarettes we were permitted to have our picture taken as we manned the guns. Shortly afterwards notice came from another battery over the phone that a German was coming. The crew jumped to their places at the guns & instruments, cotton was given us for our ears and we prepared to witness some lively "Hun strafing" but the blame fool went off on a tangent and we were forced to content ourselves with a sight of him thru the telescope. It seems that one can usually distinguish between French and enemy planes by the sound of the motors and in case that means fails friendly planes signal with colored lights or wireless. We waited for the appearance of another Boche till hunger drove us home to Harper's slum gullion.

Tues. Nov. 6. Draw K.P. detail along with Wassom. There is plenty of work to be done but we are spurred on by special grub so we don't mind. Six sacks of packages arrived about noon and the camp resembled an Indian village during a war dance. I only drew one containing tobacco, chocolate, chewing gum and shaving stuff but I was very pleased. Some of the fellows received 6 or seven packages. I guess I'll get some more later on.

Wed. Nov. 7. Hubbard returned from Paris today having driven a staff car for the Lieut up from Sandricourt. He had left us to take an exam for aviation and we plied with him questions concerning aviation, Parisian life, news of the war and news of home. The only interesting information he could give us was that he'd heard at Headquarters in Paris & at Sandricourt that 11 men from Section 25 had been directed over the wrong road and were all either captured or killed. At any rate they are missing and 11 men have been sent from Sandricourt to fill up the Section. This story is very probably "hoi" but it is very possible. And if we stay in this sector long we'll probably do the same thing as there is a perfect net work of roads.

Thurs. November 8. Cunningham and I were detailed to reconstruct the garage. The idea was to close up the cracks, so lacking lumber we used tar paper, rags, blankets and bits of wood. The result was so decidedly futuristic that we had to do the thing all over again to the great indignation of "Wild Bill" who filled the spaces between hammer blows with fluent cuss words. To complete the day Thorpe and I were detailed to wash my car. About six Sergt Johnny told me to get my car ready as I was to go out to Jean-[de]laincourt where Shep and Church had broken down. Everything seemed to go wrong. First only one of my headlights would work so Gil, Sergt J and the Lieut got sore and told me to stop my motor. While they were looking for another car Larkin gave me a burner from his car so they decided to let me go. Crane, Gil & Johnny piled in and we were off. When we'd gone about a quarter of a mile down the road Gil suddenly remembered that he had forgotten his rope so he got out and ran back. I started to back up when Johnny noticed that my tail lamp wasn't lighted and his anger rekindled. I lighted the lamp but the glass was gone and the light kept threatening to go out. I backed very slowly stopping each time I saw the light flicker. Finally Gil returned and we got under way again. About half way up a long steep hill the old tub started to boil like a steamer. I finally decided to stop & hunt for water as the radiator had evidently run dry tho I had filled it a couple of days before. There seemed small hope of finding any water in the dark and at that time of year but Johnny went searching for some only to return in a short time empty handed (he'd have been out of luck if he had found it because he didn't have a bucket). Neither Gil nor Johnny said a word but one could feel the atmosphere becoming charged till at last it settled like a blanket on my soul. I decided to try my luck and after a frantic search for my bucket finally found it tucked away in the last tool box after I'd decided that I'd left the thing at home. After looking around awhile I ran across some stairs leading down into a ravine. There was a sign which forbade anyone to descend the stairs because of danger but that was no time to believe in signs nor obey them so I stumbled down wondering what in the world could be at the bottom. All I saw when I got down was a narrow guage track, a dump car and what looked like a mine all covered by a heavy overhead screen of camouflage. But there was no evidence of water and I was about to give up when I saw something glisten in the dump cart. Upon investigation I discovered the car a quarter filled with rain water enough at least for my needs and I was overcome with joy. That's about the best bit of luck I've had for years. Filling the radiator we started on our way a third time praying fervently that nothing more would happen. The roads on that hill side were the worst I've ever seen, the mud was hub deep and very slippery so that we had to crawl along bumping and sloughing around in the darkness until we nearly bumped into Church's car. Gil tried to repair the car but could not so we tried to tow it but found this impossible also due to the deep & slippery mud so we ended up transferring the malade to my car. Arriving in Nancy we had the car disinfected (the malade had the measles) and got home about 10. I hope I didn't catch the measles. Had a bite to eat & turned in.

Frid. Nov. 9. Missed roll call as I couldn't locate my socks in the deep gloom of our quarters and as a penalty had to work on my car all day.

Sat. Nov. 10. "RIEN À FAIRE."

Sun. Nov. 11. Overslept for the first time in my army experience due to the fact that I read late last night and because only two men in my room got up so there was not the usual noise. Because of my thus far perfect score Johnny thot I was sick. There are 6 men on the sick list now and this may have caused his belief anyway I like a darn fool in emulation of the Father of his Country told the Sergt the true state of affairs and was rewarded for my truthfulness by a gift of guard at the noon assembly. After this I shall alow all officers to remain undisillusioned. I volunteered to chop wood for the kitchen in the morning so I must have been completely saturated with virtue. In the afternoon "Hub," Jimmy and I walked to Pompeii stopping en route to inspect a large rolling mill. The sign on the gate forbade any one to enter but we walked brasenly in confident that our uniforms and professed ignorance of French would get us by. It was all very interesting and we followed the raw product thru its various processes from the blast furnace till it was a finished product ready to be made into a thousand & one things. They showed us the dynamo room where a bomb had struck wrecking a steam turbine and bellying out two huge iron doors like sails. As seven bombs have struck the place they now protect all the machinery with thick "abris" of sand bags. We also saw girl factory hands for the first time. They were dressed in bloomers and jumpers and sure were a hard looking lot. We crossed the bridge at Pompeii without being stopped but on our return a guard asked us for our passes. We couldn't produce any but they let us go after cautioning us against repeating the offense. Am now on guard. I shouldn't be writing but am taking a chance as everyone else does. It's so black outside you can't see a car five feet away & a lantern is supposed to attract "avions" so what is there to do. A call came in for a call just as I relieved Cliff. "Bal" & Church answered it but had a hard time getting away. Our quarters are very poor. There is no heat at all and only one small window for ventilation and light. To add to our discomfiture the weather is beastly and the pay master refuses to come. I made a 25 to 50 franc bet with Deak today that hostilities would cease by October 1st 1918. Things look very dark just now and I believe the end will come as a surprise and Germany will have more of a "say" in dictating peace than we wish her to have. I count upon this winter to reduce Germany's reserve food supply as we have at last placed an embargo on supplies going to continental neutrals. Everything is extremely quite on this front as was to be expected but we are bored to distraction.

Mon. Nov. 12.——NOTHING DOING.——

Tues. Nov. 13. Big battle with two Boche avions by three A.A. batteries about 6:45 this evening. It was a wonderful sight to our unaccustomed eyes. Yens and I had decided to go up on the hill near the battery as it was a beautiful night and they were sure to be over. We had just left the house when we heard a motor in the air near by. A moment later two huge searchlights swept the sky and the guns opened up. Bedlam seemed to have broken lose, the 75's were barking away like watch dogs, the mitrailleuses sounded like a platoon of police beating their night sticks on the pavement and now and then we caught the sound of the Germans' motor—the thief in the night who had come to take lives and property. The bursting shells were beautiful to see—big red blotches of flame way up in the heavens, like a tremendous Fourth of July spectacle. We stood in a doorway to escape the shrapnel and well we did for it rattled down on the titled roofs of the houses all around us. Amid all this noise we heard three loud booms which came distincly to our ears and we learned later, tho we guessed it at the time, that they were bombs falling upon Pompeii, tho no great damage was done. The firing ceased as suddenly as it began and Yens, Hub, Crane and I went up on the hill to be near the seat of action. Nothing more happened that night and we returned home disgusted.

Wed. Nov. 14. Six of us, Hank, Kirby, Hub Weber Lewis and myself having secured permission from the Lieut move into new quarters. We have rented a fair sized room which is warm well lighted and so clean that we feel almost civilized again. It sure will be great to get back to a decent house again when this bloomin war is over, tho we'll not be allowed indoors perhaps for the odor of our many barns may hang to us still. A little more anti avion work tonight but it was on a very small scale and Hubbard alone evidenced enough curiosity to go outside.

Thurs. Nov. 15. Another visit by friend Boche but he passes quickly and the few A.A. shots did not even interest Hubbard.

Friday Nov. 16. Altho rather late we gave a house warming last night that was a hummer. Poker and drinking was indulged in by all and a pleasant evening was spent among scenes which recalled the days at New Haven. We didn't turn in till 11 and are really ashamed of ourselves such late hours are positively indecent. Noticed a novel thing when I arose this morning. Six capitive[?] balloons, arranged in three's were in the air with nets stretched between them. They are used only at night and should be quite effective in bagging boches. Some boob gave notice that a general was coming so we all fell to and cleaned up. The general didn't materialize and if it happens again I shall be convinced that inspections by generals are merely hoaxes to cause us to do a real good job of cleaning.

Sat. Nov. 17 to Wed. Nov. 22. Nothing seems to happen and we are getting sick and tired of all this hanging around. There should be enough work at the Front and I don't see why we don't go there at once. We're tired of "repos" and quite sectors.

I was on sick call with a bad cold when Kirby burst into the room with his usual superlatives and informed us that we are to leave at once for Nancy where we are to store the Fiats and return to Sandricourt. Much consternation and conjecture. This seems the final straw we shall probably remain at Sandricourt now till the war is over. Someone suggested that they might be going to make stretcher bearers out of us. I wouldn't care if they did it would be better than laying around here or at Sandricourt. Everyone is pretty downhearted and I'd hate to have Pershing hear the remarks about his army.

Thurs. Nov. 23. We pack up and leave Custines. Arriving in Nancy about 9 o'clock, we drove to the motor park where we turned over the Fiats. I really hated to leave old "821" she was a darned good bus. But the Fiats are too heavy & burn too much gas so we had to get rid of them. Coming into Nancy Holbrook tried to make a jumper out of his car and "take" a canal bridge. Deak became excited and jumped doing better than the car from all reports for it didn't go over the rail. Holbrook seemed disappointed. In the evening we attended a cinèma tho I believe we're all sorry we did because the music and more especially the American picture made us all homesick. Hank and I are on guard so that along with my cold I get hardly any sleep.

Sat. Nov. 24. Leave Nancy by train at 5:30. The night is dark and cloudy for which we are duly thankful. The station shows the signs of numerous air attacks and to leave Nancy by train on a clear night is considered to be more dangerous than a week in the front lines. We travelled 3rd class in 16 man compartements— two of them into which the whole section crowded with their packs and other impedimentia so there wasn't much room to sleep in. I finally got settled in a luggage rack but it was too much like the Spanish Inquisition and I slept but little. Thank Heaven the pay master managed to find us finally so we were paid before leaving.

Sun. Nov. 25. We arrived in Paris about 11 this morning tired and dirty. The Lieut gave us all 45 minutes in which to eat and we all dashed out in search of a restaurant. Deak and I decided to visit a barber shop first and we had everything in the place excepting a manicure. Deak finished first and when I joined him outside he had met some priest who took us in tow for a sightseeing trip of the town. We left our guide shortly because it was time to return to the station. As it was we had mistaken the hour for return and came about 15 minutes late. Johnny was raving and after we'd changed stations he put us as guards over the baggage and gave the others 3 hours off. The others may have had a better time but I doubt if they saw more people for we were constantly surrounded by a traffic-stopping crowd which regarded us with friendly curiosity. At 6 they gave us 15 min. in which to eat and tho I hadn't eaten a meal since Thursday and was hungry we barely had time to snatch a few bites. Arrived in Sandricourt at 9:30 and were taken to the camp in trucks. "Oaky" Connors is still here having been left when 52 cut down its number. A bite to eat and then to bed. I understand we are to leave 8 men here when we go. I hope I'm not among the 8.

Mon. Nov. 26. We are given our motive equipment consisting of twenty ambulances (Fords); a Ford light delivery; an Indian motor cycle with side car; a Packard truck and a kitchen trailer. The Fords are in rotten shape as is, in fact, the whole camp. I guess too many officers spoil a camp especially when they have few men to command.

Teus. Nov. 27. The eight men left are Balmer; Durant; Core; Sheppard; Sjostrom; Thorpe; Holbrook and Lynch who is trying to transfer to naval aviation with his brother. Poor "Shep" is broken-hearted and everyone feels particularly sorry for him. Poor chap his diary is ruined if he stays here all the time and he will never be content with any other outfit. Before leaving for Nancy at 2 I laid in a supply of camels and chocolate at the YMCA which is the one bright spot in Sandricourt. I heard at the "Y" that Phil Allison of Salt Lake is in camp but I didn't have time to see him. The cars are running abomnially and will never reach Nancy at this rate. Our first night's stop is at Ecouten [Ecouen] where the new kitchen trailer is put thru its paces and makes good.

Wed. Nov. 28. After spending half of last night and half of this morning fixing the cars they are running much better and we make good time all day. Stop for the night at Sezanne where we are quartered in a darn cold barn with a bunch of louzy Frenchmen. Tomorrow is Thanksgiving and our prospects of eating a dinner of hard tack & corned willy out of the back end of the Ford truck are good. Well, c'est la guerre.

Thurs. Nov. 29. Thanks giving! Before leaving Sezanne we filled up with gas and enjoyed a fine run to Vitry le Francois. I had to drop out of line once with commutator trouble but soon fixed it and made things burn afterwards. This traveling in convois is like an auto race, not so fast of course but nearly as exciting. We had three quarters of an hour in which to eat at Vitry and spent most of the time locating a restaurant. When we finally found one we only had time to eat bread & "confiture" and drink some chocolate. I drank mine so fast I burnt my tongue. Well as I said last night "c'est la guerre." We reached Void by night and before going to bed were able to get a very good meal for 8 frances. Thus passed our first Thanksgiving à l'armée.

Friday Nov. 30. Arrive in Nancy at 11 A.M. Went first to the Parc where we received our mail and ate lunch. Then to our new quarters—large barracks well built and fairly warm.

Sat. Dec. 1. There are only 25 days till Xmas so I wrote a Xmas letter to the family. I hope it will reach them in time. Spend the rest of the day cleaning quarters and installing ourselves therein we shall be fairly comfortable in time.

Sun. Dec. 2. Go into town on a three hour pass and indulge in a luxurious hot tub bath, trully the best thing I've struck in France. One can rent a tub and two towels for 1 fr 50 and I'm a liar if I don't have one every Sunday. We had our delayed Thanksgiving dinner tonight and it was some dinner. I'm uncomfortable still. The menu—veal, mashed potatoes; gravy; macaroni au gratin, jam, figs, dates & nuts. I took out $10000 worth of life insurance at a cost of $6.50 a month. I wrote Dad about it and hope he approves as it looked too good to me to pass up. If I am to be killed it's a lot better the folks should get $10000 & some trinkets than just the trinkets.

Mon. Dec. 3, 1917 to Mon. Jan. 14, 1918. Our stay at Nancy was quite uneventful. The clear nights were occaisons for air raids but excepting shrapnel from the A.A. guns nothing fell close to us. One evening as we we[re] watching the progress of a raid, a Frenchman who was in the yard yelled something to us which I understood was that an airplane was falling. I rushed outside but saw no airplane. The fellows in the doorway started yelling to me to come in because the shrapnel was falling all around me. My attention being distracted from the airplane I did notice the shrapnel sure enough so I hurried to cover. That is no stuff to fool with unless you have on a helmet. The next day on a trip to town we saw a Boche plane in the public square. It had been brought down near Custines and was badly damaged. The upper wings were gone but the bottom ones and the engine were practically intact. The plane was beautifully camouflaged in mosaics differing from the French one which is wavy lines. For recreation during our stay we played football during the noon hour and in the afternoons either roller skated at a nearby rink; took walks into the country or trips into town for meals and shopping. Just as we were at the point of dying of ennui orders came to move tho like all the rest they didn't say where to so altho we were keen to leave Nancy we were exceedingly pessimistic as to where the orders would take us. I was sick in bed at the time but the joy of leaving worked wonders and I fell to the job of packing with great vim. As soon as everything was packed and while we were waiting to go new orders came to wait till the next day. We chafed exceedingly at the delay but having been so long in the army we took the disappointment philosophically and unpacked such things as we needed for our night's stay. The morning of the 23rd we did leave turning the flivers towards the South East. Reaching Luneville about noon we parked in the square near a huge caserne [barracks] and proceeded to eat. While there a Boche plane came over at a surprisingly low height and was promptly fired upon by some French soldiers with rifles. Needless to say the shots missed and the aviator flew rapidly away determined no doubt that he had made a mistake in his bearings for unless he knew that there was no A.A. Battery nearby (which seems unlikely) he must have taken the nearby French aviation camp for his own. We arrived at Baccarat about 3:30 and stopped outside the town for about 8 hours shivering in the cold and roundly cursing the French Lieut who was taking so long in locating some quarters for us. That night we relieved Section #92 and slept in their barracks at the Crystallerie, or glass factory. Crane and I being sick secured permission to sleep in a hotel. We dosed up with quinine, aspirin and hot todies and I perspired like a horse but failed to get rid of my cold. The next morning the Section moved to temporary quarters in the Caserne. Crane & I slept in the hotel again.

Dec. 25. Teus. XMAS! Santa Claus brought me one package which I appreciated more than all the gifts I ever received on a previous Xmas. The Lieut took Crane & I to the hospital to be examined. The doctor said there was nothing serious so returned to the barracks and went to bed. That evening we had a fair sized Xmas dinner which tasted very good and was a credit to the cooks.

Wed. Dec. 26–Sat. Dec. 29. Another trip to the Hôpital H.O.E. and we are sent to an infirmary ambulance 12/16 where we stayed till the afternoon of the 29th. Even in a hospital the French won't open a window and the air was so rotten that we both sneaked out every afternoon. I'd rather die in the open. Lieut. Abbot came over the morning of the 29th and told us the Section was to have a banquet at the Hotel du Pont as the Xmas turkey issue had finally arrived. We begged him to get us out of there in time to be present which he very kindly did. The banquet was a great success in every respect.

Sun. Dec. 30. As Section 92 has left we moved into their old quarters at the Crystallerie. They are spacious, well lighted & ventilated and can be heated.

Mon. Dec. 31, 1917. NEW YEARS EVE! Kirby and I are on duty at H.O.E. Went to bed at 8 listening to a regimental band playing in the square and the joyous outbursts of numerous parties preparing to welcome 1918. May this year be the Year of Peace and our Victory.

Teus. Jan. 1, 1918. "Happy New Year to you!" "Thanks, the same to you, and *many* of them." New Year's in the army is like Monday on a farm so we work all day. Little convivial gathering at the Hotel du Pont in the evening.

Wed. Jan. 2. Lewis and I go on poste at Montigny where we spend five unexciting days, getting a call about once a day from the several advance postes. One night call. While Lewis ate his dinner I went up with a Frenchman after the blessé. Coming back thru Montigny I picked Lewis up and we went in to Baccarat. It was very dark but near the Front the star shells helped a lot. A few shells came over during our stay but fell some distance away so our only troubles were with a stove which refused to burn when a south west wind blows as it does four days out of the five. The meals were good and we had an opportunity to improve our French as we ate with the brancardiers. The last day of our stay a brancardier brought in a German tract which had been dropped in the lines and behind them by an airplane. It was written in French and quite cleverly urged the poilu to revolt. It was signed by "une committé des Poilus Boches." Art asked the brancardier if he believed in it but he said no as it was undoubtedly written by German officers. Relieved Mon. Jan. 7 by Lyman and Voorhees.

Thurs. Jan. 10. Received my Xmas packages six in all and gorge my self on the good things they brought.

Sun. Jan. 13. "Bal" and "Hub" while bringing in a blessé at night collide with a dispatch rider on a motorcycle. The Ford's axel was badly bent and Gil went out to straighten it but no one was hurt.

Mon. Jan. 14. Kitchen Police.

Thurs. Jan. 15. Ten cars called out in the morning to assist in a "coup de main" (raid) the others being held ready in reserve. Flint and I leave Baccarat at 12 with a Medecin Chef and a Pharmacist whom we take to Pexonne. From there we went to Badonvillers where I replaced Hubbard as orderly on Ballantyne's car while Bill returns to Pexonne four kilometers back. There are four cars at B. "Bal" "Hank" "Brad" and Gougins also Gil with the Packard fitted up to carry "assis." B. is 600 yrds behind the lines and when the batteries open up at 1:05 in preparation for the attack at 4:00 we can hear the guns boom, the shells screech overhead and hear them land zoom! among the barbed wire in front of the lines. The 75's, 105's and machine guns tore away at the entanglements and German trenches almost continually till 9:30 with a short respite at four when the men went over. At 5:30 the wounded and prisoners started coming in and Brad & Art went up to a farther advanced poste Rendez-vous des Chasseurs. Gil leaves about 6 with 15 "petits blessés" men who are wounded but can either walk or sit up. It soon got black as ink and the rain fell which together with the passing soldiers, prisoners and wounded made a weird scene when the gun flashes and the star shells lighted up the battered little village. Bal & I left with three couchés. At Pexonne I transferred to Russel's car in order to guide him to B. The night was so black that we were forced to go on low most of the way excepting when a star shell or a gun flash lighted up the road for a brief while. By the time I returned the abri was filled up with French & German wounded so I went down to see the doctors dress the wounds. As I stood in the narrow winding gallery they brought in three wounded, one with his shoulder torn off, another minus half his arm and the third with raw meat and blood where his eye should have been. Being my first close-up of wounded I got rather sick at the stomach and decided I needed some fresh air. My curiosity soon got the better of me and I returned. This time some wounded Germans were brought in looking rather sunken cheeked and old. They are the Landstrummers, men from 35 yrs up who like the French Territorials are used to hold quite sectors or work on the roads. Two of them impressed me, one a grey-haired man of about 43, bitterly tired out, wet, covered with mud and the strangest mixed expression of fear and dejection. The other was a lad of about 21 with his fore arm shot away. As the French wounded are cared for first he had to lie on a dirty little bunk built into the side of the abri till his turn came. He bled profusely, his clothes and the mattress upon which he lay were soaked with blood which dripped off the boards to form a reddish pool on the earthen floor and reflected the light of the wavering candles. Tho he must have suffered intense pain he remained absolutely quite possibly thru fear for they have been told the same stories about French atrocities to German prisoners that we are told are perpetrated by the Boches. I had more pity for the young fellow because every time I looked at the old one I saw Belgian women raped, French peasants shot down and the memory of the little Belgian boy who had showed me his arm with the hand gone at the wrist the night we stopped in Sezanne. Russel got a trip and I went to Pexonne with him returning with Bradley. Brad got a trip and I returned from Pexonne with Cunningham. By this time the show was nearly over, three more cars get a load and Bill and I are left to clean up. We finally secured our load—two Germans, a brancardier, the pharmacist and the Medecin Chef. As the Lieut and Howie had gone up to Rendezvous des Chasseurs we waited for them since we did not know the road from Pexonne home. The Lieut didn't show up so we shoved off with orders to send up a car from Pexonne which should go to R. des C. in search of them. Picked up Tony [?] in Pexonne who knew the road so we buzzed along home in the darkness and the mud feeling a good deal as if we were returning from a late but very exciting party. Despite the fact that we all expected return fire from the Germans and that I had figured my chances of being picked off were about 80% better than the others the only thing that happened to me was when Bill missed a bridge in the darkness and a pole knocked me off the running board. Luckily I was wearing my helmet or I would have been knocked cold. I picked myself out of the mud and examined the car which was unhurt except for a slightly bent axel. For then on I lay on the fender with a search light. We passed Gil about half way home. The truck has skidded off the road and nothing could be done till morning. Later we met Brad who returned with us to Baccarat. We took our Boches to H.O.E then to Mixte and got home at 12:30 the last car in at the hospital. Bill tried to get a German helmet but was too kind hearted. I got a gas mask. There was a box of preserves awaiting me in the barracks so we dug up some bread and had a bite to eat before returning. It seems that Steve and Bill Flint had quite an experience when they took the wrong road and ran past the sentry.

Wed. Jan. 16. Sleep till 10:30 then out to Migneville with Van Doran. Before leaving Baccarat we inspected some 28 Boche prisoners assembled in the court yard of the État-Major and awaiting to be questioned. They all had no uniforms and fatigue caps which the German govt. sends for issue by the French I guess. Stop at Montigny to tell Weber and Larkin that there are some blessés at Habla[i]nville. From M. we went to Rary [Reherry?] but there were no malades so we continued to Migneville. We are stationed at the Poste de Secours in a rather decent looking house. Our rooms are on the second floor but give directly upon the roof of a concrete "abri" so we can exit hastily and soon be safe in case of shelling. The food is rotten consisting mostly of beans and cabbage. We relieved Wassom and Perkins. Kirby & Ted remaining with us. Write a letter home. Quite tired so go to bed early.

Thurs. Jan. 17. A young wireless operator came in to try out his English. He succeed[ed] poorly and his visit was concluded in French. We're not "sharks" but we speak it better than he did English.

Friday Jan. 18. Kirby & Ted get a trip at noon and shortly after Van and I had four assis to take in. Houlihan and Clifford relieve Kirby & Ted.

Sat. Jan. 19. This is a quite sector and we have little to do. The firing is nearly all in the back areas tho now and then we get wounded from the trenches. Having little to do we play "hearts" nearly all day and night. Van Doran who is learning the game "gives the party." A French telephone operator came in this evening for a chat. He has lived in Montana since he was two yrs old so he speaks English very well. His American accent and his fluent cuss words are unusual in a Frenchman as they nearly all have learned English in England.

Sun. Jan. 20. More "hearts" Van Doran being again "elected." Later in the evening there was a gas alarm. We all assembled in one room and closed the door and windows so there was hardly no gas where we were. It was our first experience with gas and we were all rather nervous. A couple of the poilus put on their masks and I followed suit. Hap thot it was unnecessary and said so; to which I replied that that old frog had seen four years of gas and was wearing his so I felt that I'd follow his action, my experience being so limited.

Mon. Jan. 21. Van Doran and I leave making a round of the postes near Migneville to pick up whatever malades or blessés there may be. Hap and Clif also get a trip with some blessés. We have been using a road which runs over a hill past some 75 batteries and is not supposed to be used in the daytime. It is much shorter than the other way so we usually take it. Today we had passed the battery when Van discovered that he had forgotten his gloves so we went back. Four times over that road in so short a time is going too far, those Germans will think it's full of traffic and send over a present or two.

Teus. Jan. 22. Baccarat. Rien à faire.

Thurs. Jan. 23 [actually Jan. 24]. Gas test at the Caserne to find out if our masks will resist gas. A room had been made air tight and we went in with our masks on. Inside someone fired a pistol which contained a gas cartridge and the room was soon filled with a thick grayish vapor. After leaving the masks on for some minutes we were ordered to take them off in order that we might know gas when we smelled it. Some of the men took deep breaths and nearly passed out but the only affect on the others was the smarting of the eyes. The French masks which we use are different from those of the English. They are flat bags lined with felt and soaked in some kind of chemical which resists or changes the gas. They are lighter and more easily put on that most masks but are more uncomfortable. One feels at first as if he were being smothered. I imagine my mask will resist gas at least I didn't smell any of the stuff while I had it on. Come to think of it—perhaps the reason they had us remove our masks while in the room was to prove to us that there really *was* gas and that the masks really worked. One hears of the Germans being issued new masks & put thru the same kind of test only without the gas. I don't believe that the Germans would be fools enough to lose men by issuing bum masks.

Fri. Jan. 24 [actually Jan. 25] to Wed. Jan. 30. Kirby, Hank and Gil are away on their permissions. The new parts for the Vocalion [record player] arrive and we enjoy ourselves by getting homesick. Music may have charms to sooth the savage beast but it certainly hath the power of bringing visions of home to men who are far away. Go again to Migneville, this time with Cunningham. We relieved Wassom & "Tony." The place has been fixed up and is not half bad. We now have a stove and a table in the room and are eating at a peasant's house. One man goes to the kitchen every morning before 9 and draws our rations for the day which Madame prepares. We signed the payroll before leaving B. so we should be getting some more pay in a month or so.

Thurs. Jan. 31. Bill goes to the kitchen for the rations while I chop wood for our vest pocket stove. A pick is my axe and a house my wood pile so it's slow & tedious work. There is a battery of old 90's near by which fires on and off all during the day and night. Whenever they shell the town or batteries around it we can hear the "chef" give the firing order, bang go the guns and no more Boche shells come over. I guess the battery must have a pretty good line on friend Boche. They try vainly to get the battery sending over about a hundred and fifty shells in 24 hrs but our battery never gets touched & we have never carried a wounded man from it yet. A few shells came into the edge of town today which is unusual as they mostly go over it or around it searching out batteries. The Lieut. came out today bringing the pay roll which Lewis and Van Doran signed. We had cleaned up the place anticipating his visit but he never came up to the room much to our disgust.

Frid. Feb. 1. Russel and Voorhies relieve Van and Lewis.

Sat. Feb. 2. Bill and I had an "urgent" call at 8 for Gare Écuereille [Ecureil?] for a blessé who had half his face shot away. We to[ok] him to H.O.E. at B and then to Mixte. It is very cold driving now. The trees are covered with ice and shine like diamonds in the sun. Coming back to M. the ice was falling from the trees like hail and stung our faces like the deuce.

Sun. Feb. 3. A call to Ancervilliers [Ancerviller]. It was Voorhees & Russel's turn but they were promenading in search of a battery so Bill and I took their place. Found 14 letters for me in Baccarat. Just as we returned, 16 "avions francais" flew over the town headed for the lines. They were bombing planes and were evidently bent on evening up for the Paris raid of the other night in which Kirby Hank & Gil were spectators.

Mon. Feb. 4. Sergt. Johnny returns from officer's school at Meaux and will stay with us till his commission arrives. I bought a kodak from Voorhees today for fifty francs, he's going on a leave and needs some money. Four of us were playing cards about 9:30 this evening when Hub came in and told Flint and me to get our packs and go to Badonvillers. To send out a car with blankets at 9:30 is so unusual we wondered what was going to happen or had happened. A Boche attack? a car on poste smashed by a shell? The Lieut, Jamon and Howie went in the staff car with Bill and I following closely in order not to get lost. We had to stop a while at Vacqueville and the Lieut told us there was a French gas attack coming off at Nervillier [probably Neuviller or Merviller] and that we were to relieve Yens & Bates who alone knew the road to Nervilliers. Nothing happened at Badon during the night.

Friday Feb. 8. Hank and I were relieved and brought in a "couchée" and three "assis." Passing thru Mervilliers we saw some 500 Italians who have come into this sector to do road work. I expected to hear one of them call out "Hey youse guys, do ya wanta da shine?"

Wed. Feb. 13. Thank Heaven it isn't Friday today. Russel and I relieve Beech and Deak at Badon. The time on poste was quite exciting according to them. Deak was partly gassed and every shell the Germans fired seems to have been fired at them. This is a very good poste as we live in the house of Madame Thomas who cooks splendidly and besides has a very attractive daughter—Alice. Cunningham and Perkins are here with us and "Wild Bill" courts Alice continually not without success.

Thurs. Feb. 14. "Perk" brings in a French priest named Moussus who speaks a little English and is desirous of learning more. He seems an exceptionally fine man, well educated, traveled and with some culture. I accepted the position as tutor and our first lesson went off nicely.

Friday Feb. 15. Kirby and Ted relieve Bill and Perk, bringing me a package from home. M. Moussus came in after lunch and has offered to take Kirby and me thru the trenches tomorrow at 8. I like him better each time I see him. It is a relief to find a man, not an officer, who is refined.

Sat. Feb. 16. Moussus tapped on the window at 8 and we soon joined him. It is a fine, bright day and we start gayly on our "grand tour" as Moussus calls it. Before we started he cautioned us to wear our helmets and we obeyed tho we thot it unnecessary in such a quite sector. Going down the main street of the town which runs parallel to the trenchs we turned to our right thru an alley and into the communication trench which led to the first lines. It is what my French friend calls a "luxurious trench," the sides are well braced, even floored, quite high for Frenchmen tho I had to stoop and concealed from airplanes as it runs nearly straight a thing very unusual. The side braces are made firm by cross bars overhead which I continually struck with my head and told me why we were told to wear our helmets. The floor of the trench was as I said, even, and walking was further aided by sections of latticed walk called duck board. We stopped from time to time to look at the surrounding country tho we saw little of interest until, after diverging into a side trench much bending and many remarks about taking care less the Boches see us we arrived at a machine gun emplacement guarding a road which led from the front lines and ran near the communication trench. Our curiosity aroused by a bulging musette carried by Moussus, was satisfied when he took from it numerous packages of cigarettes and little pamphlets which he distributed among the men. So that was the reason he made this "grand tour" of his so often! Surely it was a fine thing to do and my respect for the man increased. There was little to be seen in or from the emplacement so we said our au revoirs and "bon chances" and returning to the main trench continued our way to the lines. There were numerous firing steps, exit trenches and trenches for drawing here and there all being strategically placed to perform the work assigned to them. Arrived at last in the front lines we paused a moment to take in our surroundings and then rushed up to the sentinel standing armed with an open gas mask rifle and grenades all ready for instant use. He seemed to be looking so intently across no man's land that we felt sure he must have located some Germans so we asked him how far off they were at this point. Over the hill? how disappointing! We had hoped to see a few of them in their native haunts. Disappointed at this point our next question was if we could get closer. Here Moussus stepped up from a nearby dugout and told us to follow him and he'd show us "une petite poste" (listening post). We walked down the main line a short distance, turned to our right and towards the Boches, traveled a short trench (not luxurious merely a deep ditch) and found ourselves in a little open hollow filled with machine guns, rifle grenades. This was a petit poste, the Germans were only 200 yards away and a Frenchman who came up from a deep dugout where the men sleep in the day time gave us permission to take a picture. I got up on the firing step and snapped a picture of barbed wire, blackened broken trees and utter desolation but no Boche. Another Frenchman who had come from the bowels of the earth to receive his visitors saw me standing there and remarked that that was a very good way to get killed. I didn't want to get killed of course but I did want that picture. Before returning to the main trench I took a picture of two enormous rats which were drying in the sun suspended from telephone wires. I was interested having heard so much about rats in the trenchs and also felt that I could talk more convincingly about them if I had their picture. The whole front line system was not at all what I had expected, the trenchs were crudely built, mere ditches, they offered poor protection from shells, no continuous firing step, no trench ladders, there were no bristling arms, few men could be seen (they were asleep in the dug outs) and above all they were dry! This last was a blow. I had expected to wallow in mud and water up to my knees and I didn't even get the soles of my shoes wet. I felt much like the youngster who suddenly realizes that there is no Santa Claus. There were numerous transverses behind which one could command the trench sections if the Boches should get in the lines. There were drain trenches running off to the rear, machine gun emplacements and many little dugouts in which the grenades and torpedoes were stored. As we turned into another short trench leading to a second petite poste we passed an officer making an inspection but he was the only officer we saw. This time we were even closer than in the first poste and I couldn't resist taking another picture tho I saw no more than I had in the first one. Having come, having seen and having taken pictures we decided to return home and were confirmed in our decision by several loud reports in the direction we had just come. Moussus remarked carelessly that they were shelling our lines and resumed his walk. I was keen to leave because they might just as well shell our part of the trench as the other. As I say, I was keen to "partir" but naturally didn't let my companions see it and waited with affected sang froid while the priest stopped several times to distribute the contents of his bag. Each successive shell sounded closer and I gave a inarticulate mutter of relief when at last we turned off into another communication trench which would take us back to the village. This trench was not as well built as the first communication trench was nor was it straight but wound in and out like a huge snake crawling into the woods a short distance away. Wonderful thing—woods! For some unknown and nearly groundless reason one feels secure from shell fire. In case of shelling or bombing the first instinct is to hide, any sort of covering lends confidence and a feeling of safety to a man. It is laughable to see a man dive into a bush or under a thick covering of wood or tin yet if the shell comes your way you will do the same unless you are an old hand at the game. Some 1000 yrds behind the front line we came across a signal station from which battery fire is regulated by phone, runners or star shells. It was situated on a hill and commanded a fair view of the trenchs as the trees were thin here and one looked over the top of the denser growth. The place looked like it was preparing for a Fourth of July display being packed with star shells of all sizes, shapes and colors. The large rockets are shot from troughs the smallest ones from short fat barrelled pistols. Leaving this station we continued our winding way till we came to the "second line" or reserve trenchs. At the junction was a round steel observatory carefully camouflaged but nevertheless conspicuous. As it was empty I entered and peered thru a narrow slit in the direction of the lines. As the elevation was high a very good view of both our front line and the Germans' was given tho I still saw no enemy soldier or evidence of life. I can't imagine why an enemy shell hasn't ruined that observatory long ago because at close view it appears as evident as a plateau on a plain and gazing out thru the narrow apperture one feels that the whole German artillery must know it's there and that you are inside. Just as we left this point we met the men bringing up the dinner in pans and pails. Meat, soup, bread, wine and mustard comprised the meal and I must say it looked uninviting. The ration party was accompanied by a paymaster sergeant, the sight of whom caused M. Moussus to chuckle and tell us in English that it was a very unusual sight to see a paymaster in the trenchs. At places the trench was so narrow that one man alone could pass. This Moussus explained was caused by shells landing nearby and causing the sides to cave in and often bur[y]ing men alive. That was a nice pleasant thot—buried alive!—and we walked more briskly. Finally we reached the end of the trench passed another telephone poste and machine gun emplacements and walked into the village. As we approached Madame Thomas three Boches flew directly overhead surrounded by a generous collection of shell-puffs. Our anti air craft batteries were doing exceptionally good work and one plane suddenly swooped down, seemingly hit but doing his best to regain control and his own lines. Our fervent prayers went up that he should fail in both his attempts but either he was not hit or the German Gott was with him for he soon passed beyond our sight. Tho we had seen plenty of airplanes fired upon we had never seen one brought down. The A.A. guns' work is extremely haphazardous and for every plane brought down 80000 shells are fired. They first bracket with three shells in order to find their target but by the time they find him he swoops or rises and the rest of the shots are placed where they think he is going. So far we'd never seen a gun crew out guess a Boche airman and we entered the house cursing the latter's good fortune.

Mon. Feb. 18. We are relieved by Bradley and Borden. Bill C. meets us at Pexonne and took some of the eleven malades who were waiting us at the "poste de secours." Bill went on to another tour and we went home. The road from Vacqueville to Pexonne has been made a one-way road and the other roads and the towns are crowded as our Division is moving out to give the 42nd American Division (Rainbow) which is now at Baccarat a chance in the lines.

Wed. Feb. 20. Pete, "Papa Joffre" "Pop" Clifford and "Wild Bill" start off on their "permission" all smiles and rosey hued hopes. They are going to Nice as Paris is forbidden except by special permission.

Thurs. Feb. 21. As the Rainbow Division has only been across two months we look down upon them from the lofty heights which veterans of 6 months attain. As we are under the French some of the American officers find fault with our costumes and can't seem to understand why we should wear French helmets, rain coats, etc.

Friday Feb. 22. Voorhees and I relieve Hank and Gil at Migneville.

Sat. Feb. 23. One trip today, an Italian with frozen feet.

Mon. Feb. 25. Kirby and Wasilik relieve "Art" and Larkin. About 7 Ed & I got a call to Herblevilliers [Herbéviller?] which is beyond Gare Ecureil and very near the lines. An ammunition convoy was blocking the road in the woods and as it was very dark we had a hard time getting past. When I used a pocket flash light to guide our way the French captain in charge of the convoy nearly went crazy. Don't blame him. The blessé had been shot in the face and his features were rather spilled about so that he was far from a pleasing sight. Face wounds are the worst appearing if they're bad and I dread that worse than anything next to being blinded which could be the same thing.

Tues. Feb. 26. After five days of rain the sun appeared this morning bringing with it many French & Boche planes. One fight developed about 2000 ft up and tho the Frenchman chased the Boche back to his lines he could not bring him down. It was a very pretty sight to see them climbing and diving while attempting to get in a vantage point. When they swoop the engines make a perfect roar and it is this sound usually which announces a fight and causes one to look up. One very seldom watches planes any more unless they are fighting or being fired upon. During the fight we stood in a field and rooted loudly for our ally. Kirby in fact nearly went crazy with his enthusiasm. Just as the two planes passed beyond sight some shells came over into our field and we dug for an "abri." The Americans evidently took those shells for a challenge for their artillery is booming away directed by a French observation plane which circles over me as I write.

Wed. Feb. 27. Flint and Ted relieve us. A brancardier told me today that the Germans were bombarding Nancy with big guns and the division which had been stationed there has been moved to Baccarat. Can this be the start of the much heralded German super-offensive.

Thurs. March [actually Feb.] 28. We now are very busy taking care of three divisions, two French and the Rainbow. The Americans have their own ambulance service tho it is modeled along different lines and is an integral part of the medical department, that is the medical men rotate as ambulance drivers, hospital attendants and stretcher bearers, also they have big G.M.C. ambulances. These men will take care of their own division as soon as they can adjust themselves to the work but their officers don't seem to know much about it. I was sent out tonight to guide one of their cars to Hablanville. It was snowing and that G.M.C. didn't get along nearly as well as the little old Ford. We can't carry so many but we can make more trips and when it is a question of speed between life & death we'll beat them a long ways besides we can get places where they can't and pass convoys that stall them.

Friday March 1. The Lieut sent me out again as a guide for an American ambulance and again it was snowing but much colder and a whole lot darker. These birds haven't become accustomed to driving without lights yet and we took so long I nearly froze to death and had to change completely when I returned. Johnny has left for Paris, having received his commission. Everyone wished him the best of luck and he received a Sam Browne[?] belt as a reminder of old 585.

Sat. March 2. Reported to Captain Baskerville at 1:15 to guide him on an inspection trip of the "postes." When I reported at his headquarters and asked for the captain the bucks in the room all rose to their feet and took off their caps and answered my question with a "sir." I had received several salutes while on the street but this was too much and I explained that while my make up might look like an officer's I was only a buck private. As it turned out the Capt. went with the Médécin Divisionaire, Lieut. Abbot and Lieut. Jamon in a colonel's car and I was left to guide a lieut to a rendezvous at Montigny this being accomplished I was merely a passenger for the rest of the trip. As the lieut rode in the front seat with the driver and both had helmets, one couldn't tell that he was the officer and not I who sat in the back seat neatly clad in one of those swagger French issue rain coats, leather boots, and a campaign hat whose turned up brim hid the hat cord. The trip was a succession of salutes, a triumphal procession and I enjoyed it immensely being thus received as an officer but having none of an officer's worries. We made a round trip including every poste except Migneville. At Ancervilliers [Ancerviller] there was rather heavy artillery action, the Boche shells bursting in a wood about a kilometer away. Some 8 shells had fallen in the town that morning and the Americans were quite enthusiastic about it. The Americans are everywhere in the sector now and things have picked up in an amazing fashion. We who knew this sector for what it was—a real trully quite sector used for resting troops—the change is great but we do not welcome [it] because there is no advantage to be gained by firing all day long or by pulling off attacks. The guns have not been changed for three years. Boche aviators know every gun emplacement, every rock, every village on our side as well as they know their own and the retaliation fire means not a gain but merely work, death and suffering. The doughboys deride the poilu as a fighter and ask sneeringly if this is war. They tell us they are going to put some pep into the game and bring it to an end. But war nowadays is not a matter of heart it's a matter of head. Why? the poilu says, should we make this an active front and suffer when we can gain no object by which we can better our position or help end the war. The country here is unfitted for a big drive and only a big drive can prove anything. These poilus have just come down from Verdun, and they've seen three years still the Americans laugh and proceed to fire everything from a star shell to a 220. The Germans retaliate we carry off the wounded, see the dead buried, the homes destroyed and incidentaly dodge a few shells because it is generally upon the back areas that the most firing is done. It may be good training for Americans but it's damned Grant like in its cost. At Pexonne we took aboard a captain who told me with great show of secrecy that an officer in the intelligence department told him that there was need for quick and thorough preparation of the defenses here. I guessed that he intimated a German offensive, but why the German should attempt to come thru here is beyond me. There were some big new shell holes in the Badonvilliers road which I carefully noted and tucked away in a memory pigeon hole for use some dark night as it is very hard to avoid them unless you know where they are. Larsen & Hank had an exciting half hour at Village Negre the other day due to the fact that the Germans can locate the roads so easily. Jimmy Weber swears that on the same road two shells hit simultaneously on either side of him and he drove under the two bursts. Anyway the road is lined perfectly with shell holes mostly 77's. I returned to the barracks too late for mess so I ate at a café. Talking with three poilus they told me that there is to be a coup de main in three or four days near Migneville and probably in the Bois le Compte. This will be a bad place for us as it was here that Larkin had the machine gun turned on him.

Sun. March 3. A Letter from Johnny to Lieut Abbot says that Holbrook has died at base camp as a result of a pie eating contest. I am very sorry to hear this but can't help thinking what an appropriate death it is for Holbrook. Wild Bill greeted the news—"Well I'm damned he owed me ten francs." Johnny says also that Church Durant is at Dr. Blake's Hospital in Paris with very serious heart trouble and if he does pull thru he will be returned to the U.S.

Mon. March 4. Houlihan and I relieve Hank at Badonvilliers.

Teus. March 5. At 4:30 this morning we were awakened by a terrific bombardment. I thot at first that it was a French barrage but soon realized that it was Boche instead and I called out to Gil evidently with the idea of awakening him. Gil lighted a candle and we put on our shoes to be ready for any call that might come. That candle made all the difference in the world, it seems to be true that one is less afraid in the day time or at least when he can see things than at night, a survival I suppose of our earlier ancestors who kow towed to things they couldn't understand. The big shells were coming over in great style tho most of them were falling on the lines and just in front of the town while the shrapnel was being used on the town and the batteries behind it. Madame Thomas and Alice had gotten up and were rather frightened at first but soon calmed down, the mother busying herself making coffee (we would probably not eat for some time) and the daughter began shining her shoes. This puzzled us because we could see no need of polished shoes when you're dead but Alice said that the Germans had captured the town twice before and might again and she was going to be ready. Hap and I went outside to get his car warmed up and as I was cranking the car an éclat hit about 2 ft from my head making a metallic sound when it struck that caused Hap to think it had struck me on the helmet so he called to see if I was wounded. We finally got the car going tho the shells made so much noise one could hardly hear the motor and we went into the kitchen again which was fairly safe and was the best we had because the Americans had filled the abri under the house to overflowing. I started up the "Money Blues" on the Vic and we sat around waiting either for a shell to hit the house or a call to come. Our counter barrage had begun about

4:45 and to hear those 75s' barking away like a whole kennel which had been aroused was the sweetest music in the world. It's nice to know that your enemy is getting just as badly scared as you are. The racket stopped about 6 after lasting an hour and a half during which time 500 shells must have dropped in the town and among this number were many big 105's which make a huge racket and tear their way thru almost anything. A call came from Village Negre so Hap & I went outside. We found that the éclat which had nearly hit me had struck a water pipe also that a little area way 12 × 4 contained 8 pieces of shell which is going some. As the communication trenchs had been smashed up so badly the American wounded did not start to come in till 8 o'clock so we took in a French blessé and returned. Coming up the road from Pexonne which runs perpendicular to the lines we found that the Boches had put up a saucisse which looked straight down the road so we hung close to the camouflage which lined the road and gave old Lizzie the gun. The Americans lost 19 killed and 28 wounded tho the Boche raid had failed. The Germans had worked their barrage fire skillfully by shifting it to the back area and bringing it back on the lines again when the doughboys rushed out of their dugouts to repel the attacks. They say that the Americans stood up on the parapet and cursed & cried for the Boches to come over and when they finally did they gave them such a hot reception that they were forced to retreat to their own lines. All honor to the Americans, they showed themselves worthy descendants of the men of 61. How I wish l'Anarchiste could be here to see what raw untrained Americans can do. There were numerous incidents of courage and good spirit and the wounded were heroic Spartans to the core. They have been weighed and not found wanting. They are veterans now and have astonished the Boche and the French and also myself in that they were not only not afraid but seem to like it. To those with whom I talked of course it is their first affair and they were still keyed up which accounts for their enthusiasm. After they have seen more they will realize what a dirty rotten seemingly endless game it is. Hap and I made only two trips before noon as 6 other cars had been sent out.

What a difference it makes when you carry American wounded, it brings the war home with a bang. These are the men you knew at home, the clerk in the little store, the bank teller, the grocery boy, these are the men who cry out in your own tongue and their cries tho they are no more intelligible than those of the French seem to strike your ear in a different manner or at least the sound is relayed clear to your heart, which is not so with men who do not belong to your race.

The fellow with the éclat in his leg.

The three Boches who got in the trench.

Our first couché.

The Alabama boys' patrol party.

After supper we heard cries of "gas" and a man walking thru the street beating a piece of shell to give the alarm. A gendarme poked his head in the door and told us that the gas was coming so we hurriedly put on our masks. By way of diversion we started up the "vic" and I began some interpretative dancing to amuse the boys. Dropping my handkerchief I stooped to pick it up and became as dizzy as the deuce. Then my imagination got to working and I thot I could smell gas and told Gil that my mask must be leaking and I must be a goner. I was sure scared for a while but Gil saw what was wrong and advised me to sit down awhile & take it easy. I followed his advice and soon felt better realizing that it was the exertion and not gas which made me feel so funny. Gil was a pitiful sight in his mask. I shall never forget the dejected whipped-puppy manner in which he slumped near the wall and cursed the man who invented poison gas and forced a human being to well nigh suffocate in a mask. Alice was the limit she absolutely refused to wear her mask, saying that she simply couldn't stand it and prefered to be gassed. Soon the call came to unmask and we learned that it had been a false alarm much to the amusement of Alice. Hap and I decided to walk down the street to the dressing station to find out what was going on. When we were about 30 ft from the "poste" I heard a shell coming and crouched close to the wall of a house. The shell burst just over the street a short ways from me and as I heard another coming I turned to tell Hap to stay close to the wall and try and find a cellar. But Hap was gone and all the answer I got was his footfalls as he raced back to the house. As soon as the second shell burst I too tore for the house and despite Hap's head start nearly tied him. Gil had been going to accompany us but had evidently heard the shell before we did and had decided to stay where he was. That night everyone expected a Boche attack as the wire was all down and the communications were still pretty badly mussed up. The abri under our house was filled with reserve troops and the fellows at the dressing station were sleeping in a dug out so we decided that we should have at least a guard who could awaken us in case of gas. Our room in the house faced the lines and tho there were low houses across the street, shells aren't fired on a flat trajectory and our window seems fairly yawning to swallow a shell or two. We would have preferred an abri but the thing was full so we dropped off to sleep with Gil and Art on the first and second watch. Art woke me at 2:30 but I went to sleep and fortunately awoke at 4:30. I roused Hap and cautioned him against lying down as I had done on my watch and soon was pounding my ear with my gas mask open by my head ready for instant use.

Wed. March 6. Nothing happened during the night so our precautions were in vain. In the afternoon Hap and I got a call. On our return just as we were about 500 meters from the town we saw two Americans hurriedly putting on their masks. They told us that some gas shells had just fallen in the road ahead so we put our masks on and gave Lizzie the gun, thinking that if any shells had fallen they must be landing in the same place on the bad corner at the bottom of the hill. We went down the Hill and around the corner in next to nothing nor drew an easy breath till we entered the town and learned that this was a second false alarm. These false alarms get on one's nerves about as much as the real thing.

Thurs. March 7. Three lieuts and an interpreter visited our room last night and we had a concert with the "vic." They are medicoes and a mighty fine crowd. It is unusual where an American officer treats a buck private like an equal. Thank Heaven we are with the French. Shortly after dinner today we took in an American captain who had been hit in the head. The batteries around Pexonne were being shelled and some of the shrapnel was being used on the road but we got in o.k. I don't mind shrapnel nearly as much as H.E. I guess it's because they make less noise and when they burst fountains of earth don't shoot up which show one what would happen if you were where the earth was. Fixed a puncture at the barracks and started back. Leaving Vacqueville we were accompanied by shrapnel all the way tho it was dark and the shells were bursting close to the ground evidently for we could not tell just where they were landing. They sounded mighty near however and occaisionally we would hear an éclat whistle. Hap argued that the sounds we heard were "départs" and as I claimed they were "arrivées" we had quite a discussion which lasted till we entered Pexonne where a French guard stopped us and told us we could not take the regular road to Badon' because of the shelling but must go thru the woods. Another guard came up and told us we *could* go the regular way tho we weren't encouraged any for these Frenchmen don't care whether an empty ambulance gets hit or not. We decided to go the regular way as it is shorter and we knew we could go faster than thru the woods. To drive fast relieves the strain of waiting for that shell to smash you into kingdom come. As we went thru Pexonne there was an enormous flash to our right but we couldn't tell what it was. It was too big for a shell and yet not like an ammo dump. Perhaps it was a small pile of shells which exploded. We got to Badon all right but we sighed our relief when we got back to Madame Thomas' house.

Frid. March 8. Madame wanted some wood so Voorhees and I took a saw and went up into an orchard nearly in the second line. The shells were whistling over trying to get some road or battery behind us. There were too many fresh looking shell holes in the orchard for comfort and furthermore no one wants to be up a tree when a shell lands so we hurriedly cut off a large limb and "partied" [left] tout de suite. Larabee and Shiv. brought out a load of brancardiers in the truck. They say there's to be an attack tonight. Wasilik came out without an orderly and relieved us so Hap and I went up to Village Negre' for three malades. The road is lined on both sides with shell holes and is going to be an unhealthy thoroughfare during the attack. Hap & I were sure glad to be relieved as these four days have been darned exciting. We must have been "cookooed" coming down for we forgot to stop in Neufmaison[s] and Vacqueville for the "malades."

Sat. March 9. The attack is to be pulled off tonight. All the cars are out excepting four. Hap is "on call" and I am doing nothing. I guess they're giving us a "petite repos" after our strenuous four days. I hope I can go out tonight tho I guess I will if there's much doing. *later*—I went out with Brad to Pexonne. Three Americans stopped us this side of the town and asked us to take in the bodies of three Americans who had been killed by falling with a bag of hand grenades as they came out of the communication trench and were now lying in the road. We told them we were sorry but that we had had strict orders not to carry dead as long as there were any wounded. A captain in charge of an artillery convoy then butted in and ordered us to take them but we told him the same thing and suggested that he put them on stretchers and carry them in on his caissons, but we couldn't carry them as we had to hurry to Pexonne and then go up to Badon after wounded. Arrived at Pexonne we had to wait awhile for a car to come down from the front and while we waited the artillery convoy came in. I went over to help unload the dead men from the caissons. They were shot all to pieces and as we were lifting our stretcher the man's leg rolled off and swung to & fro by a single tendon. We finally placed the stretcher on the ground and were walking away when the captain came up with a flash light, turned it on the stretch & yelled "for C—sake come back here and pick up those guts." We walked back and there in the circle of light we saw the man's entrails lying on the ground. The man with me reached down, rolled them up and slapped them down on the stretcher cursing the captain who made him do such a rotten job. Shortly afterwards a car came and we went up to Village Negre where we loaded in a lieut. and a private, both of whom had been shot in the leg. They said the Boches evidently knew of the attack and had pulled out of the first three lines and the four companies had only found four prisoners. The Boche had been shelling the road and the lower end of Badonvilliers but fortunately no shells fell when we passed. The car began to run on two cylinders and we had a devil of a time getting up the hill to Bertrachamps [Bertrichamps]. These Americans are certainly game.

Sun. March 10. A day of rest thank the Lord.

Mon. March 11. At 10 the Lieut told Ted, Sergt Peters, Bill Flint and myself to get ready to go to the saw mill. I went out with Flint we were going ahead to buy some food at the canteen in Montigny as we did not know how long we'd be out. Flint & I took out a doctor and the truck brought out a load of brancardiers, splints and other medical supplies. We arrived at the saw mill safely enough tho the road from St. Pole to the "Scierie" [sawmill] is "défendu" [forbidden] in day time as it is in full sight of the German lines and that truck of ours being uncamouflaged must have loomed up like a mountain. It looks about as much like an ambulance as a baby carriage does and the Boches have every right to fire on it tho they do on an ambulance any way.

Yens came out on the motorcycle bringing us food, blankets and orders to stay all night. We didn't know just what was going to be pulled off but supposed another coup de main, this time by the French alone. After eating we looked around for a place to sleep. Bill and I chose a room off the kitchen with some Frenchmen while Pete and Ted decided on a second story room in a house across the court yard. We went to bed early and I slept fine till we were awakened by a barrage which we thot was French. One of the Poilus lighted the electric lights in the room and prepared to make some coffee while Bill and I and two other Frenchmen stayed in bed it being then only about 10 min. to six. Suddenly the lights went out and there was a terrific explosion and a blinding flash just outside our window. The Frenchmen sprang from their beds crying "à la cave!" "à la cave!" [to the cellar] and we followed closely. Half way to the cave I stepped in a pool of water and realized that I had left my gas mask and shoes by my stretcher and said I to myself, you may have to stand in a wet cave all day not to mention gas, which I fear more than shells. I yelled to Bill to return for his mask also and we ran back together. Returning to the cave we could not locate the opening but a Frenchman gave me a shove and I catapaulted thru a mere window into a little cellar about 6 × 12 ×6. Besides Bill and myself there were five Frenchmen two of them having forgotten like Bill to put on their shoes. The conversation had a wide range as to subjects but the whole theme was discouraging especially to one so newly initiated into these mysteries of war. One little Frog whom I shall hate eternally kept poking his dirtiest digit at the low vaulted roof and exclaiming "pas solide," "pas solide." We all knew very well that it wasn't solid but didn't care to be reminded of it. Another sniffed like a Lewellan setter, interrupting his snifs by questions as to whether the smell he smelt was gas or powder. Bill & I couldn't tell the difference so we believed the worst. A third went into a detailed account of the German method of following up their barrage with troops and as such "strafing" was unusual our morbid friend could but believe that this was the "grand attaque" of which the Boches had boasted and that soon we would all be prisoners. The other two thank Heaven were silent except for strenuous cursing of the Germans. The noise was terrific. Every time a shell exploded we heard the plaster, glass, timbers and tile tumbling down. The waiting after each shell for the next one was the worst. It was then that I was grateful to the falling house which drowned out the chatter of my teeth. I blamed that chattering on the cold damp cellar but think it only just to admit that the cold was not entirely to blame. Those tense moments when one waited for a shell to hit directly on the cave were terrible and I discovered that I was not the only one who was nervous when I lighted a cigarette from a candle held by an old poilu—the candle shook! and I secretly rejoiced. It would be terrible to be the only one afraid. I worried considerably about Ted and Pete wondering if they had found a cave. Once in a lull I heard voices and called out but a Frenchman said that there was a cave adjoining ours and the voices came from there. At the end of 45 minutes the shelling ceased and we started to leave but could not till one of the Frenchmen called "qui va là" [who goes there] and, receiving a French reply, was assured that we were spared a German prison camp. We found Ted & Pete in the courtyard examining the truck which had caught the devil from a shell which had exploded some 15 feet away. There were 70 holes in the radiator and easily 30 or 40 in the tarpaulin. Bill's car had received but two slight wounds much to his disgust. As the truck was out for the count we telephoned the barracks & demanded a tow. Over a hundred shells had fallen and of this no. the only dud had lodged itself in the wall of Ted & Pete's house too feet from the window beneath which they were sleeping. Ted who had hitherto been rather unreligious looked at the shell and remarked in an awed voice that there must be a God. One shell had struck a thin roof directly over our cave but luckily had exploded before reaching the cave itself. We learned later that had a shell struck the embankment of the lake just behind our house we would have been drowned like rats. One Frenchman had been killed by a shell which burst five feet from him. I saw him as he "lay in state" waiting till a ditch could be dug and a rude cross fashioned. He had received the full burst and was not good to look upon. We walked up the railroad track some 150 yrds to see if there were any new shell holes near the bridge. There were none and we came back hurriedly fearing lest

M. Boche should start another racket and catch us away from our base. We were about 75 yards from the cave when we heard them coming over again. I did those 75 yrds in nothing. This time they left us alone and shelled the station at St. Maurice a half kilometer away. Jamon who evidently doesn't believe a private can tell when a truck is out of commission came out in the motorcycle and attempted to start the Packard. All he started was a razzing party which was highly unmilitary but effective as he dashed away in a rage after a tow. Abbot came out also bringing the Médecin Divisionaire with him. The M.D. is considering making this place a "poste"—if he does I sleep in a cave. While waiting for the tow we hung around an abri and talked over the night's work. It was then that Bill Flint made [the] famous remark that if he were a prisoner he'd juggle hand grenades if they asked him to. As soon as an American truck came we left and with few regrets. At Montigny the guard stopped us as they were shelling the town. Having no blessés we descended and lay down behind a low stone wall watching them burst. As they were all shrapnel they sounded like pop guns after hearing those H.E's. As soon as they stopped shelling the town I suggested we depart before they had time to change the range as it was evidently "at home" day for this part of the front. We ended a doubtful trip with Bill driving successfully and all voted it the most exciting 24 hours any of us had ever spent.

Thurs. March 14. Things are picking up on this front. Nearly all the roads are being shelled as well as the towns where our postes are located. Bates and Perkins had an exciting trip from Badon. The road was being shelled so heavily that the American officers refused to let them drive over it. They finally secured permission from a French major and left with the Americans censuring them for their foolishness and declaring they were under no orders from them. That's what an ambulance man must do most of he time, proceed under his own initiative and he has always the opportunity for not going ahead or disabling his car. Bates & Perk should get a "Croix" for no man can do more than risk his life to save another's.

Tues. March 19. Three cars sent to Gare Ecureil tonight about 8 o'clock to wait for a gas attack which the French pulled off. I went with Kirby, the others being Pete, Lewis, Dereck and Bradley. Just as we entered the woods a 75 barked twice and we heard a team coming down the road at a dead run. Someone yelled to watch out as they were hitched to a caisson full of "ammo." We drew aside and watched them tear past waiting to here an explosion when they hit a tree but nothing happened so we drove up on the road again and continued. We stopped a little way beyond the poste near a rail road culvert which was to serve as an abri. As far as we could see there were four possible objectives for German fire, the battery just behind us in the wood, the railroad and the open stretch of road where we had stopped. Several times we sought shelter as they tried for the battery. Crouching in a low narrow culvert with 6 inches of water running thru it was not a physical comfort and being perpendicular to the lines and "pas solide" it gave us little mental comfort. About four thirty or five the "brancardiers" returned without any gasseés or wounded and we left joyfully as we could hear machine gun bullets whistling around tho they were falling short. Also we had no desire to be on that road in daytime. Four hours sleep.

Wed. March 20. Brad and I go to Migneville for five days and every single night we were there they shelled the place with gas which made sleep impossible. All night long they fired at intervals of 15 to 30 min. All day they shelled the roads and one night dropped a few in the town. One huge shell fell just in front of the house where we eat and the people left next day as did nearly all the other civilians in the town. We only had one night call, a Frenchman horribly gassed who came sobbing into the dugout about four o'clock. Just as we were starting the shells began coming over again falling either on the batteries or roads we could not tell which. I wasn't keen about going but it had to be done so off we went, fortunately taking a road that was not being shelled. Returning to Migneville by another road we counted scores of fresh shell holes on & around the road. When our five days were up I was worn out practically no sleep for 6 nights.

Hank came in from Badon today with the tail end of his car smashed by a shell. It was struck while standing in front of Madame Thomas' house which Hank says is now practically ruined. Badon has become a mean poste, the town is shelled every night and the roads have been forbidden to all except ambulances, supplies being taken up on pack mules thru the fields. God's kindness is alone responsible for some of the miraculous escapes. The Americans have ordered the civilians to leave but they cling on desperately and must be moved by force. Poor beings they are so ignorant they fear to leave their homes more than the German shells. The French are crazy because the American has stirred up the sector so they call it "Le Petit Verdun." The Yanks on the other hand are crazy because the poilu who knows the value of a rest sector and knows nothing can be gained by attacking does not fire continually. The other day the captain of a battery near Pexonne kept firing with a Boche plane in the air. That noon when they were having mess some shells dropped in and five were killed. The captain like the fool that rocked the boat lived and is up before a court martial.

Sun. March 31. Easter Sunday. We are going to a sector just on our left and then to the Somme perhaps. Section 92 is at St. Clement. Six of our cars are going up this A.M. to take over the postes and the others to follow Monday morning at seven. How his Easter differs from the others I have spent, today the biggest battle in the history of the world's history is being fought.* The heroic French and English are valiantly fighting against overwhelming odds. Petain has issued an inspiring message to the armies. "The enemy has thrown himself upon us. He wishes to seperate us from the English and force a route to Paris. Hold on to the land. Stand firm! Your comrades are coming. United we still stop him. Shoulder to shoulder we'll hurl him back. This is *the* battle. The fortune of France depends upon it." Petain. A stirring appeal to which his troops are hotly responding.

Mon. April 1. One trip this noon. I hope it stays quite as I would like to rest up a bit.

Teus. April 2. Nothing doing in the night. A trip to Benamenil at noon then to St. Clemens [St. Clément). Some town and our barracks are rotten which occaisons much grumbling against the Lieut. The former section rented rooms but such luxury is not for the men under "Conscientious John."

Wed. April 3. Saw an observer jump from a "saucisse" to escape a Boche aviator. The parachute opened nicely and he landed safely. On days when there are low hanging clouds the "saucisses" have a rough time as the enemy planes can sneak up easily.

Thurs. April 4. A German visited us early this A.M. and dropped a few bombs on the railroad station tho he did no damage. Later

---

*The "Great March Offensive," which began on March 21, 1918, forced the English to retreat some forty miles. The German advance lasted nearly two weeks.

two shells whistled over the house, one exploded in a field the other was a dud. Whether they were Boche or fired by our own A.A. guns I do not know, but probably the latter as no more came after them. All permissions in the French armies have been cancelled and every available man is being rushed to the Somme. At a formation today the Lieut told us that few people realized the dire peril that France was in the first day of the big attack and that two complete divisions of cavalry had been sacrificed. These two units one French the other English alone saved the day and allowed the Allies to retreat successfully. How insignificant the charge of the 600 is alongside of this. Two whole divisions 18000 men. The Boche has paid a terrible price for his victory it being claimed that their cost has been 500,000 men. If they can only be held an Allied victory is sure because Germany cannot afford to lose so many men. Grant lost more men than Lee at Cold Harbor and didn't take his objective but it was practically a victory for the Union because Lee's losses could not be replaced. We expect to go to the Somme directly but today there are rumors of a Boche attack in this sector which seem to mean that we will stay here. Why they should attack here is a question but it was on this very front that the bloodiest battles of the war took place in '15. There seems to be some ground for believing the rumors for the front line towns are being evacuated. Yesterday on a trip to Moyen and Luneville with Cunningham I saw the most completely destroyed town I have ever seen. The whole place was literally razed to the ground and presented a most vivid picture of war's desolation. In the midst of the ruined houses a little wooden structure fittingly named the "Café des Ruines" sat like a Phoenix (if a Phoenix ever sits). It was a testimony to the fineness of the French.

Richard, Jamon's orderly, returned from his "permission" at Paris today filled with contempt for the shells of the new German gun which has been firing on the Capital for the past two weeks. According to Richard the shells are nothing and no one cares a whit about them.

As to events on the Somme one can only guess and pray for the best. The newspapers say that they are holding a little, but one can place little confidence in newspaper reports. But surely Germany cannot succeed. Why if all else fails God would be with us and [stop] these ravages. Just now it is hard to believe Pope's philosophy that "whatever is, is right" and surely "God works in mysterious ways his wonders to perform." When I stop to think of our going to the Somme or of a big offensive here I wish to write here my opinions on duty and death so that if I should be killed the family will not mourn me, death is not a thing to cause unhappiness—(two pages written in the original diary and then cut out and burned due to some natural aversions which a man has to making a will or to talking about death in this war. Death is something one sees constanly and while one hides his fear of it, it is disappointing when you're young and is never mentioned except jokingly. A serious consideration of death is kept secret, I know not why either thru superstition or the effect talking about it has on one's morale.[ )]

Today Jimmy & I made a trip to Luneville and bought two Belgian police puppies for 50 francs each. We have named them Pinard and Grenade. Pinard being "le mien" [mine] and much the better dog tho James thinks otherwise. They still drink milk and we have paid a woman to take care of them while we remain here. Two months is an early age at which to go to the wars but I guess they'll survive and I hope we can take them home with us.

Mon. April 22. We are relieved by Section #34 just down from the Somme and we leave for a 10 day "repose" near Baccarat.

Teus. April 23. Stayed last night in Baccarat and were "sitting pretty" being billeted in good houses. We thot we would stay there and were very sore when the order came to pull out for Bazien, a wretched little village without a church and only one café. (It's a rotten French town which has only one café.) Our "esprit de corps" having sunk to such a low level we criticised Abbot & Jamon freely, openly and above all strenously. Overhearing our remarks he (Abbot) called an assembly that we might arrive at an understanding. Maybe he understands us but we certainly don't him. He's a poor "nut" with no push at all. Blind adherence to idiotic orders, overconscientiousness and a meek disposition never gets one anything or anywhere in the Army.

Still April. Rain! Rain!! Rain!!! I never believed it could rain so much.

May 3. Friday. We're off for the Somme! Left Bazien today with orders to proceed Westward. This is pretty indefinite, but surely we're going to the "Big one." Rumor has it that we are going to

Meaux where we will stay some time. The "Permissionaires" are to assemble at Ramblevilliers [Rambervillers?] and join us later. They are going to miss out on a fine trip. Dereck and Pinard are riding with us. Madame cried exceedingly when she said adieux to Pinard and Grenade and they themselves whimpered a good deal. Poor little tikes this army life is going to be hard on them. I only hope we don't run out of condensed milk before they are weaned. A dog is a wonderful thing yet a man doesn't notice their loyalty and companionship as much in war time as in civil life because he is so closely bound to other men and their [illeg.] is so striking. End the day's journey in Charme[s], a rather pretty town with a better class of people than we have encountered before.

Sat. May 4. Emery and I go for "ravitaillement" (supplies) to Bayon. We have to wait a long while for the train but it is better than waiting around Charmes. On the way back to camp we saw some Americans with a battery of machine [?] guns mounted on rail way tracks, huge things which will fire a shell 25 or 30 miles. Four of our cars are going by train to some unknown place. The Lieut chose Green, Googins, Wassem, Wasilick and Hubbard who is in charge. The division is also going to entrain here while we are to drive overland.

Sun. May 5. Leave Charmes at 3 o'clock in the morning. The dust is terrible and we all look like millers. Stop for lunch at Chaumont and park the cars in front of General Pershing's headquarters. M. Moussus lives here but I didn't know his address so I could not call on his family. We saw some real honest to goodness American girls and they looked like a million dollars. They are mostly telephone operators, tho they are riding around in staff limousines. We also ran across our friends the Field Clerks who look like officers and are called "Spooks" by the privates. Left soon after lunch Emery replacing Dereck as my orderly. Driving from 3:30 is no fun and I was getting pretty tired long before we stopped for the night at Troyes famous in history for some battle or other. As we drove into town Hank had the misfortune to hit a little boy. The youngster ran blindly across the street and tho Hank did his best to avoid him, [the boy] stumbled and fell headlong striking his head on the braces of the tool box. He bled profusely. He was rushed off to a hospital where they say he is not fatally hurt. It makes a lot of difference to see a child lying unconscious in a pool of blood and I can't see how the Germans could have shot them. Hank feels terribly but I was directly behind him and know that he was not to blame. During mess some blasted Frog stole the sound box for the Vocalion. We have covered 350 kilos today and are dead tired.

May 6. Mon. Stop at noon in Nogent des Belles Tours [presumably Nogent-sur-Seine]. By night we reached a small village near Meaux [Chaucorin]. Hap, Bob and Mathe [?] take French leave and walk to Meaux. Hap & Bob craved excitement and Mathe [?] has a family there. They wanted me to go too but I felt too tired. The meals are rotten, d—n those cooks of ours.

May 7. Teus. Our rumored stay at Meaux proves erroneous and we leave at 8 arriving at Beauvais at noon after having skirted Paris. Just north of Paris one first sees the signs of a big offensive. The roads are all guarded to keep the traffic moving, convoys must be split up into small sections which must run 100 ft apart and there is a constant stream of traffic both ways. That [which is] going towards the front is composed of staff cars, dispatch riders & camions loaded with fresh troops who have a superficial gayety which attempts to conceal but does not, the grim determination in their hearts and the perfectly rational fear of the horrible experiences of a big battle. Coming back are also staff cars empty camions and trucks trailing broken artillery pieces which will be patched up & returned as soon as possible. The men coming down are dead tired and dirty, those who can are sleeping in positions which seem impossible and on the faces of those who must keep awake are the most peculiar expressions in the world. The eyes seem to burn under the nearly closed eyelids and they are made more prominent by the thick white dirt which covers the rest of the face. In the set faces and burning eyes one sees the utter fatigue of these men and feels rather than sees the awful hours they have seen. The men impress one as having been struck dumb by some great shock, dazed by the magnitude of the noise and death. Now and then some dust colored poilu shakes off his lethargy to yell savagely and a little wildly "on les aura" [we will beat them] to the Americans. "On les aura," the expression made famous forever at Verdun. When men like these can yell "on les aura" the Germans can't win. We were held up by a traffic jam for nearly an hour in Beauvaise. I never saw so many camions in my life. Beauvaise is simply filled with troops some of whom are disembarking from trains, others from camions. Some are marched off for a brief rest while others are piled into camions and tear off for the front. Motorcycles tear past bearing important messages, staff cars whiz by piled full of officers who are returning to their commands, being lately returned from leave. For a while we move along nicely enough then a jam occurs as some little bewildered [illeg.] turns to the left instead of to the right, stalls his motor, and thoroughly frightened by the ravings of a frantic gendarme, has to be helped by some poilu. Finally the line moves on while everyone prays that no other tie up will occur till we are out of the city. Outside of Beauvaise hundreds of men are working on the roads trying to keep them in shape for the tremendous traffic. Along the road one sees abandoned trucks, wagons and motors which have broken down and have been pushed aside to remain till the crisis is passed and time can be taken to repair them. About five in the afternoon we arrived in Aumale where the men who went by train are awaiting us. Aumale is quite a decent little town and we are given billets in an orphan asylum. The roar of the guns near Amiens can be heard plainly. What a noise and we will soon be there ourselves.

Wed. May 8. With Emery for RVF 8 kilometers away where we had a long wait before the train pulled in. The whole division gets its supplies here and the wagons were lined up for a half mile. When the train did arrive and they began to unload a carload of bread we saw why it is the poilu always cuts off the crust. The men climb into the car and walk all over the stuff and shoes get awfully dirty in this country. After a bite to eat at a farm house we returned to Aumale.

Thurs. May 9. Revellie at 2:15, mess and we leave at 4, destination unknown. It must be somewhere near Amiens and I guess we're going to have a pretty warm time. End our trip about noon at Picquinny [Picquigny], a little town 12 miles behind Amiens. Tho Amiens was formerly a city of 140,000 people the Boches have shelled and bombed it so much that hardly 200 are left. The refugées stream thru Picquinny in a seemingly endless line being carried mostly by British trucks, tho a few are walking. We are given a garden to pitch our pup tents in and Deack and I bunk together not mentioning Pinard and Grenade who are supposed to sleep in a box but prefer our blankets. There is a huge rail road

gun near us which, I hope, does not attract the attention of the German air men. If it does I hope they don't miss *to the left*.
No mail.

Friday. May 10. Nothing of note. As yet we do not know whether we are to work from here or move on. No mail and I doubt if we get any till we move back on repos.

Sat. May 11. There is a splendid old castle here which was built in 800. It is a huge affair and tho rather badly ruined one is still able to get an idea of its former size and strength. Troops have been quartered in it, but there are none now and we can roam thru it to our hearts' content, climbing up on the high battlements from which we gain a fair view of Amiens (the Cathedral does not appear badly damaged) and prying into old damp dungeons where one's imagination runs riot.

This is the first time we have been with the English and one is struck by the excellence of their equipment. A comparison of their horses and their tractors for hauling the big guns with those of the French makes one wonder how the Frenchmen ever get any where. The Australiens are a splendid lot and being less reserved than the English they impress us Americans much more favorably. They are more like Americans than any other soldier not excepting the Canadiens and we hit it off in great style, "Diggers" and "Yanks." The English don't seem to be liked by anyone the French, the Australiens and the Canadiens hate them if one is to judge by what is said. The Australiens call them "Woodbines" which is the name of a cheap English cigarette and the main remark of the "Diggers" is that "these xx—*! Woodbines let us down again." True this is usually said by those who are drunk but the Latins have a saying "In vino veritas." The English have such a supperior air and while they must be commended for not boasting still they so overdue this virtue that their very modesty is more boasting than American brag. However the Tommy doesn't seem the least downhearted as one would expect and they have every confidence that "Jerry" will be held and believe he has lost more men than the ground gained is worth.

The guns roar more plainly and the air is full of avions tho one rarely sees a German this far back. That's one thing I'll hand it to the English on—their aviation which is the best of the lot tho the Canadiens will tell you the service is largely composed of colonials. A Frenchman who had been shot down came into camp today and later two Englishmen whose observation plane had been struck nearly 2000 ft up by the A.A. éclat which took away their propeller. They landed safely and were waiting for a R.F.C. [Royal Flying Corps] car to get their plane. Deak and I took the observer to a café for a drink. He chose a table far in the rear and kept watching the door. Finally he explained that he would be bawled out if he were caught drinking with a private. To complete the list of visitors today a French Colonel came into our garden ostentatiously to inspect the quarters but really attracted by the pups I believe, in which he seemed more interested than in us. Madame in whose garden we are encamped also came down from her house attracted perhaps by the colonel tho ostentatiously to see the pups. The colonel whose knowledge of English consists of "Will you kiss me?" put the question to her and she having undoubtedly learned in the same school and not to be out dared by the officer answered "oui," so the old duffer kissed her on both cheeks while we all smiled discreetly at his daring and her gameness. Funny that two kisses one on each cheek are considered a mere token of esteem while one alone means other things. Later Madame who must have seen that we were a little shocked by this oculatory display explained to us saying "We Parisians you know are very frank and open." I could but agree with her. These French are splendid.

The several regimental bands of the division are being worked to death. A concert and a parade is given daily to cheer the men up for the coming battle. The poor cusses sure need it they've had four years of this sort of thing but they still have an awful punch when they meet the Hun.

May 12. Sunday. An air raid last night and tho they only dropped two bombs near the castle they succeeded in killing three civilians and injuring two others. Our cars answered the call and did their work so well and quickly that the men were complimented by an English Capt. of M.P.'s. The baby killers lived up to their rep for one of those hit was a little girl who died on the way to the hospital. The other two killed were an old man and a middle aged woman. Three generations wiped out! Surely this is every one's war and we Americans can thank God that the war is being fought on this side. Night before last they came over and I heard them as I lay awake in my pup tent cutting off their motors and expected to hear each time the express train noise of a bomb but nothing happened. Three cut-outs had me worried considerably as a pup tent is no protection whatever.

May 13. Monday. We have left our lovely garden and are now installed in factory sheds situated nearer the railroad and close by a bridge. We should surely collect a few bombs in this place. Deak & I had a fine ride to Poix on an evacuation. We were fortunate enough to miss a bomb which fell in the road thru a small village by three to five min. Despite the fact that I had never seen such a huge bomb hole there were no casualties unless you consider a dead horse one. The opinion is that we will move tomorrow. I guess we'll get in it pretty soon at any rate as the German's second drive is expected daily. Each night that we are awakened by a particularly heavy barrage some one says (and everyone thinks) "Well boys she's started." I don't know what the others think on such an occaison but for myself I'm decidedly thoughtful. These attacks are such terrifficly huge unnatural affairs and so many thousands of men are being killed that one can't help wondering whether he will come thru ok or not. Today an Australian told us of the work of the English Ambulance Service and how it is considered in the English army. Among other things he said that if our work in the "Forward Area" was the same as theirs he could only offer us his sympathy in the next offensive. He also said that you couldn't get men to ride with you unless of course they were wounded. One Australian Ambulance driver, according to the Daily Mail, received the Victoria Cross in the last attack and that's going some.

Mon. May 20. A week ago we left our garden and today we left Picqui[g]ny. We are now in Esquinoy [Esquennoy] just behind Mont[d]idier towards which the Boches' second attack is being directed. We are now in a French sector and besides feeling more at home we also, strangely enough, feel greater confidence in the French than in the English. We had a most interesting drive today. Skirting Amiens we got a closer view of the Cathedral which stands out like a moutain peak. A few shells were falling in the city but we could not determine their effect. Just beyond Amiens we saw a whole "tank" corps "en repos." They were carefully camouflaged and I was disappointed as I had never seen a tank before. As we got up closer to the front the traffic because more dense; piles of ammunition lines the roads and every now and then one would hear the ta-ta-ta of the machine guns on airplanes [but the] machines were generally so high up one could not see them. As I was driving some officers in Jamoux's [Jamon's] car I took them into Bretieul [Breteuil] and returned about a kilometer to a factory which is our quarters. Near by there is a very large park where we have pitched our tents. The park is badly run down and I hope it is [not] further ruined by the Boche thinking that it contains a munitions dump.

Teus. May 21. Well "they" certainly did give us a "park warming" last night. The bombs all dropped on Breteiul and an aviation field a quarter of a mile away but the éclat from the A.A. gun barrage fell like rain in the woods. I have never hear[d] such a barrage against avions before. This p.m. we sat on the stone wall of our park watching the shells drop into Bretieul. One can hear the report of the German gun, the sharp whistle and then the explosion as the shell falls. Later we visited the aviation field near by. The machines are mostly two seaters used for observation. We tried to get them to take us up but the attack is on and they're not doing any passenger work.

Wed. May 22. Hank and I got a trip to Beauvais. It certainly is some town and we had a peach of a dinner in a very decent sort of a restaurant. After dinner we went around to see Miss Lewis. She was out but we saw Pinard & Grenade. They have changed a lot but both knew me and I could hardly resist taking Pinard home with me. Damn this matriculation des chiens de la guerre [registration of war dogs] rule anyhow. Returning we brought an American lieut. He is with the first division and says there are eight others in these parts.

May 26. Sunday. There was a terrific barrage last night and we all expected that we would be called today but no orders have come. This waiting around while so much is going on is rotten work. I'm sure we'd all prefer getting in to it even knowing as we do how terrible it all is. "Pete" is going to leave soon for the officers' school at Meaux. I am very glad for his sake but we all hate to see him go. Van Doran reached the end of his tether today and has been returned to headquarters. He has been arrested twice as a spy and tho acquited each time he has caused no end of trouble. I never liked him but now that he is gone I feel sorry for him. He may be playing in luck tho for this isn't going to be any pick-nic. Nearly every section has lost three or four men and one lost 14 cars.

Mon. May 27. Monday—one forgets days, dates and even months over here. 8 cars called out to evacuate 32 men who have La Grippe to Crevecours [Crèvecoeur]. Wiley [Wylie], our new man replacing Van arrives and seems a likeable chap. Rumor has it that we are not going up till the counter attack.

Teus. May 28. Ten cars called out to evacuate 60 men of our division who have the grippe. They're getting rid of all the sick so I imagine something will be doing pretty soon. I don't know why it is but since we have known that we are to leave soon and go into the lines we have carried half the division sick with the grippe. Deak went with me and we led the convoi both ways. Leaving the place where we got the malades I turned on the lights but an avion opened his machine gun on us. We turned the lights out in a hurry and it being the first experience of this sort I tried to out run him but fortunately I used my head after a little while and drew up under the trees at the side of the road. It doesn't do any good to try and out run those boys and it's surprising with what accuracy they hit the road. Later—going down into a little valley we could see the bombs landing just ahead of us. They make a beautiful sight, huge fountains of sparks and flames. Arriving at the bottom we could not see the car immediately behind us because of the smoke. Driving some five kilometers further and entering a little village we were again subjected to the aerial bombardment. This time the bombs fell all around us and we were saved by the fact that at this point the road had been cut thru a hill and the bombs were all falling some five feet above our heads. Thinking that I had missed a turn to the right I had stopped the convoy just at this point but the howls & curses which came from the night behind us soon awakened me to the precariousness of our position and we drove rapidly into the country. Stopping to learn if all had survived the bombardment Lewis took the occaison to drive alongside and enquire in tones of mingled anger and pity if I had been the one so devoid of brains as to stop all the crowd in the little town. Having replied meekly that I had been the one I was next forced to listen to a rather long and profane discourse dealing with the matter of stopping in a bombarded town just because one thought he had run past a turn. Returning from the hospital which we reached in several parts the avions were over Bretieul, but they held their loads till after we had passed thru. As there were no shells falling in Breteiul (as is usual) we arrived home safely about 2 o'clock where we were informed that the early morning would see us on our way to Champagne where the Boche has reopened his offensive and is pushing back the French Army, due they say again to that damned English 5th army.

Wed. May 29. Up at five of the clock after two hours of delightful sleep. I am driving Jamon's car (he is away "en permi") and am accompanied by two officers whom I picked up in Breteiul. Tho we are moving South I am unaware of our ultimate destination and there seems small chance of finding out as my officers are unusually reticent. We entered Compiegn [Compiègne] about 11 and being given 3 hours freedom I busied myself with a hot bath, a shave and a good luncheon in the Hotel Palais. After lunch I prowled about the city which must have been a considerable town in its time but now shows the effect of bombs and shells. Down near the river I ran into some men from Bob Nourse's section and had a very pleasant chat with them. The Section tired, dirty and a bit on the qui vive because their destination is unknown arrived about 2:30 and my officers and I left for Le Meux arriving there about 3 A.M.

Thurs. May 30.* Up at five tho we really hadn't slept at all as the airplanes were greatly in evidence and we had to sleep under our cars to avoid the falling "éclats" from the A.A. guns. Assembly was called and Lieut Abbott gave us a little talk something as follows "Our division has orders to hold on the left bank of the Oise River where they will remain till the last man. We are going to get some very stiff work and I know you will do your best" and then the customary order "Start your engines." In the early morning with airplanes overhead, with the barking of anti air craft guns and machine guns and especially because of the tenseness of everyone's nerves due to lack of sleep and an appreciation of the seriousness of coming events his words sounded quite

---

* General Ludendorff, hoping to draw French reserves from Flanders preparatory to the main German offensive there, ordered an attack between Soissons and Reims on May 27. Known as the Third Battle of the Aisne, this diversionary action gained its own momentum. The Germans took Soissons on May 29 and reached the Marne the following day.

thrilling and all of us I'm sure felt that queer ticklish sensation along the spine that is caused by a thrill of any sort. It was not till 10 o'clock after four hours of low gear work past convoys, infantry and refugées fleeing terrified before the German that we arrived in Retrounes [Rethondes] 30 kilometers behind Soissons. Leaving my officers at the hastily established headquarters I returned to Compiegne with the Medecin Divisionaire. The shells were falling in several places and at about fifteen minute intervals. Tho we drove all about the town we fortunately missed connecting with any and the closest we came was when [one] lighted close to a troop camion about five minutes before we caught up with it. Of the twenty men in the camion five were wounded and three killed. Two of the dead bore no visible shell marks on their bodies and seemed merely to be resting, their heads resting on their extended arms. After picking up one blessé we chased the convoy, some five trucks loaded with brancardiers. One fellow had lost two fingers from his right hand and was exultingly displaying his marred hand to his companions who shook their heads in uncomprehension of some men's luck and muttered under their breath that they too would be happy to lose two fingers now before the "grand attaque." After returning to Retonnes [Rethondes] the Lieut sent me out with Yens in the motorcycle to deliver orders to leave to the various medecin chefs. Things must be going pretty badly with us and I guess we must be retreating, not having arrived soon enough to take up our position on the "left bank of the Oise." As I handed the orders to one medecin chef he bowed his head on his breast and murmured "Ah! La pauvre France, la pauvre France." Everyone is downcast and some of the old bearded veterans wipe tears from their eyes without shame as they curse the Boche. Others react differently and seem to be glad that the end is near even tho it means the defeat of France. "Let them take Alsace-Lorraine and Paris too if they wish" some say. "We are tired of fighting and will not fire another shot." We left Retonnes at four and nearly met disaster on a small bridge at the edge of the town. A Boche avion had evidently noticed that the roads were full of retreating troops, guns and supplies and determined to stop them all by bombing the bridge over which they all must pass. As our section was on the bridge when he decided to make his "coup" for the Vaterland we were greatly interested in his success. Luckily a

Frenchman saw him before he got low enough and managed to bring him down. His plane fell in an adjacent field at the edge of some woods into which our German friend (evidently unharmed) plunged to escape the mob of outraged Poilus who had grabbed whatever lay at hand and rushed toward the plane. Going thru Le Meux I took aboard my two officers after I had dined at an officers' mess with colonels, majors, captains, and lesser fry. Leaving Le Meux early in the evening about five we drove to Villers-Cotterets over the roughest cobblestone roads in France and then one of the darkest nights this neck of the woods has seen in some time. About five kilometers from V.C. I was nearly frightened out of my senses by one of those new German airplane flares. The thing must have been dropped four miles away but even at that distance it lighted up the road we were on and made half the Heavens appear as light as day. At first we believed that a munitions dump had been exploded but it burned with such a continued & steady brilliance that this did not seem likely. None of us had ever seen such a thing before and personally I believed that the world was coming to an end. One officer believed it was a French flare to dazzle an enemy plane while the other thot (and correctly, we learned later) it a Boche contrivance for locating objects to bomb. As the Section had passed thru Le Meux before we left they were ahead of us and about 3 kilometers in front of V.C. Dereck stopped me to show where the Section was parked for the night and where I was to return after letting down my officers at V.C. Arrived in V.C. we drew up in a square just off the main thoroughfare over which all the supplies were passing to the men who were battling desperately a few kilometers beyond in the seemingly futile attempt to stay the advance of the Germans in their most recent and most elaborate offensive. Tho the officers told me they would return directly I was forced to wait three seemingly interminable hours. During this time the traffic passed in two unbroken lines. Besides the huge Paris busses which had brought up one regiment of our division (the 167) and were being vacated at this point, big guns, little guns, cavalry, ammunition trains, supply trains and ambulances in flocks streamed by in such an endless line that one imagined the whole French army must be concentrated at this point. It is on such a night as this and during such a time of uncertainty and suspense that this war seems the least bit romantic and as one conceives of it. In the darkness men guns and trucks appear phanthom like, indistinct beings of another world, even the voices of the men and the creak of wagons & gun [illeg.] take a different unreal character. But in the broad light of day these things appear the realities that they are and war realities have no romance. Crouched up close to a sheltering wall (some shells were falling in a nearby section of the town) I had ample time to collect my thoughts and consider calmly what the events of the past two days really meant. Would I be content to see the war end in a German victory tomorrow? It would mean the end of all this misery & suffering, an end of sleepless nights, an end of crawling slowly thru pitch blackness alone and badly frightened, an end of being 3000 miles from home and in a strange land. But we have been long enough in France to have caught the Frenchman's infectious love of his country and his hatred for the Boches and I decided then that if only France could be saved, if only the Germans' wrongs could be avenged, I would gladly endure the discomfort, fears and hardships of war for five more years. When we enlisted it was from no love of France and not from any poignant hatred of the Germans. It was a duty, a duty to be accepted gladly because thru its performance we should see new sights and experience thrills and strange sensations. Tonight all this is changed the cause of France has become our own real cause and her hatred has become our own real hatred. We are no longer supernumeraries in a show we are part of the cast itself. When I returned at three to Vez, Rouget met me and demanded excitedly what had delayed me and did I know what had become of Voorhees & Russel. Telling him that I had not seen them he said he had been greatly worried that V.C. had been captured & that we all were prisoners as no one seemed [to] know just how far the Germans had advanced.

Sat. June 1. Got away from Vez at 8 o'clock tho we were up at five. By nine we were unloaded in our billet at V.C., a huge old chateau of Francis I, now used as an evacuation hospital. As yet the town has not been greatly harmed by shell fire tho practically every civilian has left and in such haste and so recently that in some houses the dinner table is still prepared and in some others food is still cooking on the stove. Immediately after unloading my baggage I gathered up my officer friends of the night before and we chased about the country looking for a lost ravitaillement convoy. Home at 7 where I had a bite to eat and then out from 8 till 9:30. To bed at 10 so completely fagged out that tho shells fell in our wing of the chateau and one a short ways from our room I was not worried the least and after waking with the noise went back to sleep immediately not caring a whit whether a shell crawled into bed with me or not. This attack, the paper says, is outdoing all previous efforts and V.C. is the object of the offensive. We are in the center of the German line.

Sunday June 2. Out to Dampleux about noon. Tho the village is four kilos from the lines, because of the preparations for a hasty retreat it is the foremost dressing station and Abbot said that he never expected to see the 10 cars again which he sent here early this morning. While waiting for blessés we had great fun rummaging thru the evacuated stores & houses, which present the appearance of having been ransacked by robbers due to the haste of the inhabitants' departure. This is the sad part of war and behind here the roads are filled with refugées trudging along carrying in wagons, hand carts or in their hands what few necessities they were able to snatch up.

It is not very fine to loot these places but it's better that we should have them than the Boche who is expected here daily. Finding a house near the dressing station, we crawled into those queer French beds and went to sleep with the sweet music of seventy-fives behind us barking out a terrific barrage.

Mon. June 3. Awakened at five or thereabouts by two huge "arivées" (shells coming in) which landed close to our house. In this "guerre de mouvement" [moving war] there are no regularly constructed abriis and not knowing that there was a fine cellar in the dressing station we hurriedly jumped out of bed and ran behind a little brick house adjacent to the dressing station. By this time things were going in great style; the H.E. was landing all around us and the air was spotted with shrapnel bursts. The seven of us lay down on our bellies and tried not to show each other how badly frightened we were. A Frenchman lay about 50 ft from us and Larabee seeking information as to a dugout yelled out "ou est une cave?" (where's a cellar?). Receiving no response he crawled over and shook the Frenchman by the shoulder thereby discovering that the least of the poilu's worries was a dugout as half his head had been blown off. After 20 min five of the fellows discovered a small window leading into a small half cellar into which they crawled leaving Wassom & myself still lying behind the building. For the next 10 min Was and I spent the time in crawling from one end of our building to the other and indulging in the following dialogue: *Was* (as we looked cautiously around the corner next to the fields) "Do you suppose Bowie we can make it out there into the fields? We'd be safer in a ditch." *Me* "I guess we might if we had damned good luck but what good would it do look at the shrapnel." *Was* (at the other corner peeping with one eye at the dead poilu & with the other on the exploding shells just in front) "There's a damn fine 'abri' under the church up there on the hill and if we stay here much longer we'll be in the same fix as our friend there." Me "I'm willing to try it." Was "But it's a long way off. Let's have another look at the fields." Wassom finally dove thru the little two by twice cellaret window and I, not wishing to die alone soon followed. Because I had misjudged the depth of the cellar my arrival inside was like Satan's except that I lay prone on a very dusty dirt floor and not on a fiery lake. I shall never forget the vehemence with which Was censured me for raising a cloud of dust in the cellar when outside the shells were raising six times as much. After huddling in the cellar about 10 minutes the consensus of opinion was that as a protection from shells it was of little use and that we would prefer dying in the open. Outside once more a Frenchman crouching in a little hole in the foundation of a house across the street whistled and we dashed to his cubby hole but found it too small for more than three so we left there against the advice of the poilu and arrived at last in a "belle cave" directly under the room in which we had spent the night. The shelling continued with its full force for about 20 minutes when a lull came and with it a call for an ambulance. Bill left the cave to take it after expressing the common belief that there wasn't a car fit to drive. No one I'm sure was the least bit envious of Bill and were only hoping that when "their" call came there would be no shells at all. Contrary to belief and seemingly to the laws of chance the cars were still intact and I followed Bill shortly after he left mine being the second car on call. I sure hated to leave that cave and especially the companionship of the other men. My load was three couchées, one a Boche who clamoured so unceasingly and so piteously for "eine drink vasser" that I dashed around the house to the pump much to the disgust of the brancardiers who said it was a shame to get a Boche anything. My trip in was decidedly uneventful as not a shell fell near me. The road however showed evidence of the intensity and extent of the bombardment. A number of trees had fallen and three dead horses lay in the ditch. Kirby had the next trip after mine and a very lucky escape as he was loading his car at the door of the dugout. Immediately after my departure the shelling had recommenced and one shell coming directly over the car struck the stretcher & "blessé" whom the four stretcher bearers had placed on the ground just behind the ambulance. The four brancardiers were killed, two doctors who stood in the dug out door and the blessé was blown to atoms a search later revealing only a piece of his overcoat and a foot of the stretcher arm. Kirby who had been sitting in the seat of the ambulance was absolutely untouched another proof that there is a Providence which watches over ambulance men. Kirby I hear is to receive a "Croix." Return with Googins to Maison Forrestiere where we find quite a number of blessés and about 50 Boche prisoners, some of whom are badly wounded. I had the opportunity to get any number of souvenirs but it rather went against my grain to take things from prisoners I haven't captured myself. I would have bought some if I had had money but rather reckon that that would be "bad form" in the eyes of the poilus. Drove to Betz with two Boche, a gassed poilu and two "assises." Returning to Maison we dined al fresco and "à la refugée" with a group of "genis" or engineers. When a French cook has the pick of a farm yard and its garden one is pretty sure of a delicious meal.

June 4. Tues. Fairly good night's sleep. A couple of shells struck pretty near and I awoke to find the Frenchman next [to] me raised on his elbow. "Pas loin," [not far] says I. "Non, juste en face" [no, right across from us] says he and we both lay down and slept too beastly fagged out to have a couple of shells rob us of our much needed sleep. This morning I saw my first man die. Poor devil he was badly wounded and tho the doctors did their best he was too far gone. We gathered round him as he lay on his stretcher in the court yard and watched the peculiar slate colour come into his face. He was unconscious and therefore died peacefully enough. As he grew nearer death he blew small bubbles from his lips evidently a sign of the end for a priest leaned over him saying the last rites. Hoping that an operation might still save his life they loaded him into Googins' car and he drove as speedily as possible to V.C. but in turning around at Maison the wounded man had fallen from the top stretcher rack and had bled to death. When Gooch returned his running gear was covered with blood. More prisoners came in and I got hold of some Boche war bread. Terrible black stuff that burns one's tongue and would soon give a delicate stomach a bad jolt. From the insignia on the Boche uniform we learned that the Imperial Guard had attacked this morning. The Imperial Guard! Germany's finest, her shock troops de luxe and the old division held! They have not only held but have rewon some three kilometers and richly deserved the praise of a general who said today that they were the best division which had occupied this sector and the only one to hold. The 128th is expecting a citation and I believe the Section will have a like honor in a lesser degree. "Old Whiskers" it is reported tapped the panel of an ambulance the other day muttering "Croix de Guerre" "Croix de Guerre" thru his facial screen. Besides Kirby, three others it is said, have had their names handed in for work done at Dampleux. They are Googins, Larkin and Wiley. Wiley's car was completely wrecked by a shell which exploded just under the tail end. He had just left the car but would not have been wounded even had he been in the front seat as there was not a single hole in the front panel.

Wed. June 5. Back in the chateau at V.C. There is nothing much to do tho the town is shelled a bit. Today they planted one squarely in the town pump and clock which stands at one end of the principal square.

Thurs. June 6. Three shells dropped squarely in the hospital (chateau) today and they have shelled the town quite promiscuously. After the first shell hit our barracks we all made for a splendid old wine cellar of Francis' well buried and "bien solide." For some reason or other I stayed outside under an archway. Deak was with me and while we were talking I saw Lieut Abbot cranking up an ambulance. Not liking the idea of our Lieut doing our work I ran out into the courtyard to help him and offer myself as driver. Instead of letting me take the call he told me to jump in with him as orderly. Just then they yelled out that two cars would be needed so I ran back to the lineup and got another. Meanwhile Wasilik had come up for air and learning the trouble jumped on my car as I drove out. Rouget speechless with excitement came out of some place & joined us and we followed Abbot to a street running into the square where most of the shelling was. The street was badly ruined and being one that they shell almost continuously we didn't care to remain long. The brancardiers evidently were in haste also for they put a blesse (half his head blown off and a terrible sight) into my car so poorly that the tail gate would not close. Rouget who was off his nut told me to put him in and then take him out. I then asked Abbot what to do as "that damned frog was nutty" and he told me to rush him to the hospital. Seeing that the Frenchmen in their haste and excitement had neglected to put up the legs on the stretcher I told Wasilik to get in and hold up the tailgate but he fumbled around so that I told him to drive and I got in. On the way to the hospital he ran past the right turn which we always make and stopped right in the worst part of the town and I don't like to sit in the back end of an ambulance waiting for a shell.

Friday June 7. Lieut Abbot, Beech, and Butler left for Paris today to get a new car. I have asked them to send a cablegram for me and cash a check but they will be so busy I'm sure they won't have time to do much running around for the men. Section 36 is camped just behind our chateau and while visiting them today I ran into Wallace who used to be in a Sunday School class with me in Salt Lake. Also Jude Burton who is a Sergt and has a Croix with Divisional citation. We had a great time talking over prewar days and acquaintances.

I was just getting ready for a good snooze when Hub tells me I am to go to Oigny as Bates had to bring in his car which was missing badly. As it is a very hard place to find at night when you haven't been there before Bates returned with me as orderly. We had just arrived at the grotto or quarry when orders came to pick up five assises in the town, which is about a kilometer away. That town is no place for a rest cure and as I was fixing up my car while Bates went in to get the blessés the shrapnel was clanking all around the car. Left Bates at V.C. and continued on to Betz. I hated like the devil to take the road along the railroad tracks for it is shelled promiscuously for a kilometer or more but it is a shorter and better road (the other is cobbles) so I went that way. These forests around here make night driving particularly rotten because the trees in some places arch over the road and any ways it's darker than all get out. One doesn't attempt to watch the road but looks rather at the thin winding strip of sky overhead. This sort of steering is all very well on a wide empty road but no fun with convoys disputing the right of way and shell holes to jar one up. Returned to V.C. by 2 o'clock. Hub was up anxiously waiting for Ted who was an hour overdue from Dampleux. Hub showed me the way out of town and I started again for Oigny, wondering where the devil I would end up. It's darned easy to run into "Germany" nowadays.

Sat. June 8. A trip with 3 couchées and two assis this morning.

Sun. June 9. Bradley relieves Art. "All quite on the Potomac." This afternoon 21 planes mixed it up over Faverole [Faverolles]. It was a marvelous and unusual sight to see so many avions fighting at once and tho the fight lasted five minutes only one plane went down. Following the fall of the one plane whose nationality we could not distinguish, the whole show suddenly disappeared in the low hanging clouds. Pick up a blessé in the town of Oigny and go into V.C.

Mon. June 10. The barracks were shelled again a little today and 585 suffers its first casualty. Poor Bates who was preparing to go to Dampleux was severely wounded when a "130" fell in the courtyard 18 ft from where he was bending over a tire. Tho he lost half his foot, had both arms broken in two places, and suffered numerous body wounds it is a veritable miracle that he was not killed. His life was saved by a pocket kodak which he carried in his left breast pocket. A piece of éclat damaged the camera beyond repair but protected his heart. Three Frenchmen who were 25 feet from the shell and in a door way were killed outright and four more died during the day of their wounds. Borden also received a slight wound in his wrist which entitles him to a stripe but no convalescence. Bates owes his life to being wounded where he could get immediate attention. He suffered greatly from shell shock and small hope was held for his recovery during the night.

Three cars were pretty badly damaged but Bates' is a total and complete wreck. Following this misfortune we all decided to move our blankets to the big cave where we slept peacefully in the same place in which Francis I kept his choice wines.

Teus. June 11. About 2 am Jamoux came down into the cave telling us to be ready to leave whenever we should be called. Everyone immediately got in readiness to clear out but we were all wondering whether the Boche had broken thru, whether we were merely going to evacuate the hospital or [whether] there was another Boche attack to be staged. Lieut Abbot said our last guess was correct but he must have had a "bum-steer" for 12 o'clock noon found us still in V.C. It finally developed that we were to evacuate the chateau and take up quarters in the Village of Boursonne some 10 kilometers away. The Boches are not really to be blamed for shelling the hospital since the French had installed a battery of big guns directly behind us. I am of the opinion that that is generally the case and certainly I have seen enough hospitals surrounded by ammo dumps and parks for materiel. Just before we left V.C. a Boche brought down a "saucisse" near the edge of town. Tho we don't ordinarily cheer greatly when a saucisse is attacked successfully we could not help but admire the aviator's courage as he dove three times thru all the machine gun & A.A. fire the French could bring to bear upon him. I heard several Frenchmen express their admiration for his nerve with suppressed "Bon Dieus" tho they cursed him bitterly as soon as the balloon was down. This is an unhealthy place for the saucisse the score today being three down. On the fourth down I trust the German will get the ball (or several of them) and that it will prove fatal. Today we witnessed a scene which might have been taken from "Diamond Dick." The observer, seeing that he was not being pulled down quickly enough, jumped with his parachute but in some way became entangled and hung for some minutes head downwards. We all thot his death certain in as much as the German began shooting at him with his mitrailleuse and were most agreeably surprised when a bullet cut the entangling cord & down came the observer right side up and handled with care. Later, Hank took a call and brought in two French aviators whose engine had been completely carried away by a passing shell. This sort of thing is extremely unusual but why it shouldn't happen every day is beyond my ken. Our quarters at Boursonne are agreeable enough. We are now installed in a farm of the better sort. The hospital is installed in the house the stables & garage in the side buildings and ourselves in a loft over the gate. Directly below us is the morgue whose location some declare may be detected by the smells which arise thru the cracks in our floor.

Section #77 is here also and will take care of the evacuation work leaving us free for the front line work. Perkins was evacuated to Betz today and at last accounts was en route for Orleans where we hope he will speedily recover.

Wed. June 12 Out to Maison Forestier where we have established a reserve depot which will supply the poste at Dampleux, the two at Fleury, the artillery postes behind us in the woods, and also take care of the wounded which come in here. The idea is to have four cars always at Maison and an orderly is stationed here to regulate the traffic. Today I have drawn this job and I can now sympathise with a traffic cop tho I believe he has a soft job in comparison. As the Boche was quite active with gas this morning we were decidedly busy. Some of the men neglected to report to me as they came in from the front line postes and Lewis lost his way so that in a short time I found myself without a car. "Shrive" finally arrived on the scene with a crippled car and I eagerly seized him and loaded seven "asphixiés" (gassed) who had been standing around for a half hour or more. Shrive protested that he would never reach B. with that load but I begged him to at least get out of sight as the medécin was "getting on his ear" and I dreaded the consequences of such acrobatics. No sooner had I collected my required four cars when three more appeared and I sent them back. I do hope Abbot will approve and not be horrified at the waste of essence [gasoline] caused by their futile journey. I didn't send for seven cars and whoever is in charge at B must have got worried. I should [have] thot either Rouget, Jamou or "Hub" were in charge.

Thurs. June 13. On poste at Fleury. Old "Mary Jane" couldn't make the hill to M.F. with four assis. Fortunately Brad came along and we managed to get the old girl to the top where Brad & I changed cars & I returned to Fleury. Fleury is a G.B.D. poste located in the woods near the town of Fleury. Tho there are plenty of wounded here it is also a relay poste for Gare Ramée and there are generally two cars here. There is a rather large dug out used as a dressing room while the stretcher bearers have divided up into small groups of four or less & dug themselves fairly decent "foxholes" in the side of the hill. The only drawback to these small "abris" is the fact that they are pervious alike to rain & shell so that one is sure to get wet and has a fair chance of being killed. Anyway we can be happy that this isn't Friday.

*Friday June 14.** About 4:30 this A.M. the Boches developed a violent dislike for our woods and from the quantity & quality of their shells I do believe they had some evil intention against our persons. Whatever their intention they seemed to have let loose with everything they had and the shells were landing "partout" [everywhere] as a poilu very aptly expressed it. I had been the house guest of three Frenchmen who had not, it seemed to me, taken sufficient pains to make their abode shell or éclat proof. Being awakened at the first shell we spent several years (so it seemed) mostly in discussing the marksmanship of our friend the enemy. "Ils approchent" "Pas loin ça" "Juste en derrier" and "Ah les vaches, c'était tout en face"** are phrases which will give a general idea of what the Germans were aiming at. During the breathless pauses which continued from the first whistle of a shell till it exploded we crouched low and hoped fervently that *that* shell also would not pay us a visit nor send an éclat as a representative. Bill Flint was up at the advance poste Gare Ramé and I prayed that he would stay there till it was all over. Alas the gods were against me for I heard his motor chugging up the hill and saying a sorrowful goodbye to my hosts I crawled out into daylight about the most unhappy cuss in the world. Bill's face was an open book in which I read how badly he had been frightened. "Bowie," he said "as soon as you pass under the bridge go like the devil. It's hell on that road they're shelling hell out of it." Comforting words these and my spirits rose accordingly. Borrowing Bill's helmet (I had left my own at M.F.) I hurriedly cranked my car saying a little prayer that I would have the guts to go thru with it. The car started. I yelled for a guide who would show me the way as I had never been over it and didn't care to loiter along looking for the place. As we left the poste we could seem them breaking on both sides of the bridge, sending up big

---

*Astounded by the success of his attacks upon the French center, Ludendorff postponed plans for a major offensive in Flanders and decided to concentrate on an advance to Compiègne and Paris. The Battle of the Matz, June 9–14 (also called the Montdidier-Noyon offensive), eventually ground to a halt as French reserves were brought to bear upon the German salient.

**"They're approaching," "Not far, that one," "Right behind us," and "Swine! (literally, "Oh the cows"), that was right in front of us."

clouds of dust & smoke. I saw them but somehow they didn't seem to register on my brain. I saw them & that was all. The road surely had been & was being shelled. Shell holes, branches & wires littered the road. Despite this I had had from the time I said my prayer the most peculiar feeling almost of abstraction, the shells didn't worry me in the least because something inside me kept saying "you're safe"; "they won't hit you"; "don't be afraid." As we dashed along the road I recall how it seemed that I was merely driving along a country road at home. A most peculiar feeling and I believe I have failed to express just exactly what it was. Turning at last from the main road we ran some 50 yards toward a little stone house which stood beside a lake. Reaching the house we lost no time in reaching the cave tho we were somewhat delayed by a rather huge tree which had been shading the house but now lay across our path. Bill had said that the blessés were coming in fast but I had to wait nearly an hour before the wounded came in. Meanwhile the thundering went on about us and by stepping to the door of the cellar one could here the small 88's (we were 200 yrds from the front) go swish, swish, swish past till you would have sworn that by stepping outside you would be cut in several pieces as by a giant scythe. The shells which fell in the lake exploded with a peculiar dull boom and so well was its force transmitted that our house shook from bow to stern each time. At the end of the hour a couchée and an assis were brought in both having been wounded on the main road. While I fixed up my car some brancardiers went down the road a ways to remove a tree which had fallen since we passed there. As soon as they returned we left the poste losing no time on the way. About a kilo and a half from the poste and about 200 yrds from the first bridge another tree had fallen which completely blocked our road. As it was too huge to move it was necessary that I return to Gare Ramée for men & saws. My guide seeing that I had no further use of him, said that he would get out & walk up to the bridge while I was gone. Returned to the poste I yelled to the cellar that I wanted some men & saws. I shall never forget the look of disgust and anger on the faces of those men who were detailed to go with me. The assis had followed me into the cellar but the poor couché had to stay in the car. I felt sorry for him but the time was too short to permit of taking him inside too. Returned to the three I left the car in the road while we piled out to cut the tree in two. The assis being useless there decided that he'd beat it up to the bridge which being of heavy stone offered fair protection. Just as we were fairly started with our work a Boche avion flew overhead & spotted us. He opened up his machine for a moment & then flew away. If he shot at us he was a poor marksman, but I decided to run the car off to one side where it would not be so apt to cause another visit by enemy aircraft. Shortly after the avion left a couple of shells landed about 100 yards down the road. Evidently the aviator had reported our being there and the artillery was trying to precipitate a strike. Whatever the purposes of the Boche, he would have been delighted with the result of his firing. Four of us hastily threw ourselves in a ditch behind convenient trees while three jumped into the capacious & rather deep hole left by the trunk of the fallen tree. Recalling the advice to besieged ambulanciers I tried to get a brancardier who lay near me to assist in taking the couchée from the ambulance and placing him in the ditch with us. The idea didn't seem to appeal strongly to my French friend who added, as he refused to move, that the couché was well enough where he was and that for all of him he would remain where he was. Shortly after I called to the men and we started after the tree again. I have sawed some wood in my life but it was play compared to this. Despite the speed (almost frenzy) with which we worked it was a full half hour before the trunk was severed and moved aside sufficiently to allow us to pass. While stopping under the bridge for my assis and guide I thot I heard a shell coming and ducked my head. A Frenchman who saw my movement laughed and said "You're not dead yet" to which truism I answered "No not yet" and off we went. As I passed Fleury it was evident that the shelling had covered even more ground than I had at first believed for the trees were down almost to M.F. and Bill had a story of a wild ride. Returned to Boursonne I was sent out to Dampleux about 10 P.M. Entering the town I met Wassem wearing his mask. Seeing that I had none on he removed his and told me that there was a good deal of gas near the poste and some shelling. It being my first trip to Dampleux* I had the very devil of a time finding the poste. After standing in

---

* Actually he had been to Dampleux on June 2 according to both the earlier and the recopied versions of the diary. The statement about this being the first trip appears only in the recopied version.

the little square and calling I decided that my eyes must locate the poste if my mouth couldn't so I removed my mask and renewed my search. Finally a mere sliver of light in a window led me to the right house which I entered with considerable relief as there seemed to be a good deal of mustard gas about and I wasn't sure how much was necessary to breathe in order to be successfully gassed. A call came almost simultaneously with my entrance and I left taking with me a Frenchman who said he knew where he was going. That Frenchman was a darned liar for we covered most of the Foret de V.C. before we discovered our blessé and it was then so late that they decided to keep him till morning. I returned to Maison F. greatly disgusted and rather alarmed by the amount of gas I believed I had inhaled in Dampleux.

Sat. *June 15*. Returned to Boursonne in the morning and was able to indulge in a good rest till noon. Out to M.F. again with two evacuations to Betz to fill in the afternoon. Spent the night at M.F. my sleep being disturbed only by the big "155" just behind us which deluged us with a shower of hay leaves at each report. Besides the hay which tickles there remains constantly in one's mind the unanswerable question "Why don't the Germans try for that gun and why won't they blow us to bits when they do?"

Sun. *June 16*. Out to Fleury early in the morning. Rien à faire [nothing to do] and the food is très scarce. Fairly quite but they keep shelling both sides of us all the time and occaisonly treat us to shrapnel which makes one a bit cautious about exposing oneself.

Mon. *June 17*. Still at Fleury but no sign of a blessé and I industriously build a place under the trees where we may park our cars and keep them from the prying eyes of evening aviators.

Teus. *June 18*. Just as I had given up all hope of ever leaving Fleury one lone solitary blessé came in and I could have welcomed him with embraces & kisses. The impulse was even harder to resist when I listened to his boastful account of having killed three Boches single handed. Night at Boursonne.

Wed. *June 19*. To Maison then to Dampleux where I found Bal.

Thurs. *June 20*. Spend most of the day fixing up an abri which we discovered just behind the Poste. After cleaning out about 10 years' dirt we built the door up about 3 feet with big stones to keep the éclat from getting in bed with us. The home being built

it was now necessary to furnish it so we rummaged around town and succeeded in finding the following:
1. two lamps (one with shade), very artistic and somewhat useful.
2. A fur rug rather badly moth eaten and looking more like a much used battle flag than a rug. However it is highly decorative in spots.
3. Two tables—in good condition and the most likely looking furniture we have.
4. Two chairs—one kitchen, one morris. Sitting in the morris chair is like riding a camel (if you're too broad to sit between the humps).

The furniture in, two blankets were procured and a "gas curtain" erected at the door. The abri was finished and I sunk exhausted but proud into the "Inquisition" chair only to be called for an evacuation nor did I ever after have an occaison to enjoy the fruits of my labors. Such is life, we accumulate, others enjoy Kismet. Returned from barracks to M.F. Being the first "on call" I expected to spend the night either at Fleury or Dampleux but Bill Flint got stuck in the mud coming from Fleury and I was saved much to Hank's disgust who was second in order. I have never seen such a dark night in my life and it was most difficult to find my car in the woods. After taking Bill's load it was impossible to go faster than low speed and it seemed that I met every convoy in the French army. Now and then a battery near the road would fire and the flash would come just in time to save my neck. Several times I ran off the road and it was necessary to descend and search for the cobble stones with my feet. I am quite sure that I would never have returned to my car if I had not left the motor running. After some eternities I finally arrived at a place where I believed another road should turn off to the left & to Boursonne. If this *was* the turn then there should be a white milestone close beside the road & near the corner but my eyes could detect no white so I began a systematic search with my feet, walking up & down hoping to stumble against it. Even this proved hopless & I had about decided that this wasn't the turn when I began feeling the trees nearby and at last discovered a signboard. My bricquet would not light but I managed to get enough sparks from the flint to read the word Boursonne and I went merrily on my way. To Betz & return to Maison F. but it is now light.

Friday. June 21. Today, a shell from the 155 just behind us exploded just after it had left the gun. No one was hurt but Borden who was passing received a considerable scare. A trip about 5 so I spend the night in the barracks.

Sat. June 22. I have a lot of work to do on my car and would like also to write some letters so I hope I am not called out for a little while. Richard came up with his "felicitations" today. My "pourquoi?" [why] elicited the answer "Croix de Guerre" and in proof he showed me a list of 14 men who are to be decorated. The section is likewise to be cited. I'm awfully glad for the folks' sake; How proud old Dad will be and Mother too. I don't know as I deserve one certainly not when I think of what the Frenchmen in the trenchs go thru.

Sun. June 23. First clear night we've had in some time and the almost forgotten airplanes come over but do no dirty work. The papers all speak of large strikes in Vienna and of an ultimatum by the people, "Bread or Peace." According to "les journaux" there can be no bread so perhaps they'll get peace. Here's hoping. The Italiens are doing remarkably well and the Austrians have been driven back across the Piave. Evidently "Roman Punch" is too strong a potion for them. The betting element in the Section favor peace in 4 months tho no odds are given. I place 175 frs (Cunningham 25, Flint 100, Cliffor[d] 50) that next June won't see a peace signed. I hope I lose. The attack at Rheims by 3 of the Crown Prince's best divisions was a miserable failure. Surely peace can't be a *long* way off. Rumor has it that Germany has sued for Peace but under such unfavorable terms that the Allies refused to accept.

Out to M.F. but the Dampleux poste has been moved back and there were six cars there already so I returned to B.

Mon. June 24. Greene who is perhaps the most persistent rumor starter in the Section, has announced that the French are going to open up with the artillery at 10 because (here Greene was a bit hazy) either there is to be a Boche attack or they wish to shell the reserves which general report says they are massing in front of us. Green is always so confident that *he* has the right dope that we invariably believe him tho we know by experience that we are bound to be fooled. Ten o'clock arrived and strangely enough & contrary to custom there was practically no firing in our sector. Green stood up well under our gibes and immediately started rooting up another rumor like a hog hunting truffles. We are now supposed to ask the officers of the 150 battery near M.F. to cease firing while we pass. The reason for this is that Bal happened to be just in front of a gun when it was fired and as a result the whole side of his car was blown in and the car nearly left the road. There is to be a "Coup de Main" (raid) at Corcy tomorrow morning and I'm the first call out. May the Gods smile and allow me to see the light of a new day *from my bed at Maison*.

Teus. June 25. My usual luck! Steve came down from Fleury about 12 and I had to pile out. Thank Heaven it wasn't a dark night for all other roads being impassable we are now routed via Dampleux and I did not know the road. Arrived at Fleury I was assigned to a chambre à terre and prepared for a good snooze but the two cups of coffee at supper had played their usual low trick and I was still awake when "Pop" Campbell came down from the advance poste some two hours after my arrival at Fleury. Even at Gare Ramé I was not able to sleep till 7 and was awakened shortly after by the brancardier making his rounds with the canteen of coffee and calling "au jus, messieurs." In all probability I will be here two or three days and possibly longer a stay which no one particularly relishes as this is no health resort by a whole lot tho they have reinforced the cellar considerably. Having drunk my coffee I fell to sleep again but was awakened shortly by a second poilu who told me that it would perhaps be a bit wiser if I should camouflage "Little Eva" (as my car is now christened). When I had done collecting branches (already cut by éclats) and draping them over & about the old girl she was hardly recognizable. Further sleep being out of the question I wandered some 50 yards to the edge of the lake where I squatted on the shore & watched two Frenchmen who had rowed out in the middle & were fishing with hand grenades. The sport is very profitable and has its thrills also when they hear the shell coming near. It is a very funny sight to see them row to shore during a spell of shelling. Surely those men would break the world's record for row boat speed if they were timed. How those backs and oars do bend and how they cut the water!

Wed. June 26. All hands participated in building a dug out today.

Even the two officers helped and the hardy old poilus had considerable fun at our expenses as we were so soft. The cellar which we now inhabit has been unanimously declared "pas assez solide" [not strong enough] and the new dug out will have the house for protection so we should be fairly safe there. Because we are so close to the lines (200 yrds) it is necessary to be constantly on the lookout for airplanes & our work was interrupted many times. When the look out yelled "Avion Boche, Messieurs" we hastily camouflaged the hole & the fresh dirt with branches and beat a hasty retreat to the cover of the house or the adjacent trees.

Thurs. June 27. It has been so signally quite lately that everyone is wondering just what the Germans are up to. Some say that they have sent their reserves to Italy where, by newspaper accounts, the Austrians sure need help.* Vive "L'Italie," "Bully for the Wops."

Upon my own solicitation I was initiated into the mysteries of a French gambling game called La Banque. The seance was very interesting but the tuition came to 25 Francs. I hope I'm relieved before I forget how to speak "the language" as English is fondly called by the American doughboy.

Friday. June 28. Just one year from today since I held up the old "lunch book[?]" and said "I do." What a change there has been in me and in my life. Wonderful experiences; sad experiences, dangers with all their thrills and uncertain consequences, all these shared with the finest fellows God ever made and commencing true honest to God friendships which shall, I hope endure as long as we all live. "He who has never faced death can never know the joy of living" I don't remember who said that but he spoke trully. Life which is uncertain is doubly sweet things which formerly were necessities have become luxuries and give more satisfaction and joy than any luxury formerly did. Say what you will and admitting that war is a terrible thing it still has its compensations for those who live. What has the war done for me? This—I have traveled in a "far country"; I have partially learned another language; I have met all manners and breeds of men and have learned true human values. I have learned to take my life as

---

*This refers to the Battle of the Piave, June 15–24. The collapse of this final Austrian offensive resulted in the loss of 100,000 men and the demoralization of the Austrian army.

I found it and generally with a smile. I have broadened mentally, am less selfish, have more self confidence initiative and courage and have developed definite and higher ideas of religion. I have seen men suffer, men die and men offer their lives freely within and outside their line of duty. I have seen a "tough" show a yellow streak and a "sissy" show the "Divine Spark" and I am convinced that there a[re] few cowards in the world. I am living in a time when history is being made and am doing my infinitesimal "bit" to help make it. Here I am living a story such as would have held me enthralled as a boy, and—I think nothing of it! The whole business is unromantic, too close at hand for a man of my capacity to grasp the "heroics" of it. It seems that I have never known any other life but this, there are so very, very many here with me doing the same thing that it is just as if we'd been born again in another world and this war was a perfectly natural mode of life. Thus are we able to adapt ourselves and we may thank God who in his infinite wisdom made us as we are. I wouldn't trade this past year for any five other years of my life. Allah be praised! Vive L'Amerique, "Vive La France," "Vive L'Angleterre," "Vive L'Italie" and on with the dance! Are we downhearted? No! No!

Four avions were brought down in flames in sight of the dressing station today. Tho I saw but one fall it was a wonder[ful] sight and one I shall never forget. A French(?) observation plane was attacked by a German(?) chaser. They dipped & manoeuvered for some time but at last the Boche got the Frenchman's tail and we are pretty certain that it was all off with the larger plane. The machine guns were barking away and one could see clearly the chaser's tracer bullets (bullets which smoke in their flight) pouring into the other plane which had turned towards our lines and was evidently endeavoring to out run the other (a hopeless task) or at least reach friendly territory before being brought down. Just as they were about over the lines the middle of the observation plane's fuselage burst out in a sheet of flame. The Frenchman elevated, the flames increased, the machine seemin[g]ly came to a stop commenced to slowly glide down backwards then broke in the middle. The wings twisting smoking, flashing in the sunlight like an autumn leaf fell for 2000 ft bearing the charred bodies of two Frenchmen to a final resting place on their dearly beloved soil which they tried so desperately to reach. The victor circled a bit then flew rapidly in the direction of his own lands. The two Frenchmen lie gloriously horribly dead while the rudder of their machine remains twisting turning flashing in the sun, falling slowly as if loath to admit defeat. Somehow as I watched the rudder which remained so long in the air it seemed to be the soul of the aviator a foolish fancy since the souls of men thus dead for their country rise and do not fall however slowly.

Lieut Abbot came out this afternoon on his inspection of the poste and brought me 19 letters. It never rains but it pours! I had much rather get a letter a day than 19 a month. According to Abbot the Croixs were given in a fitting manner by the "Old Whiskered Man" a ceremony which I am sad to have missed, especially as I could have been one of the main actors and not a "supe." Before Abbot had left Wassom came out to relieve me. From him I learned that Neal Lynch was back again in the Section and of the stupendous "Croix de Guerre" party which had sent poor Deak to the hospital with a broken ankle. Deak's ballast had suddenly shifted while he was attempting to imitated the tree climbing propensities of our Darwinian ancestors. On my way in I picked up Butler at Fleury where two cars are now stationed to supply Gare Ramé and a new advance poste Croix de Vouty. At Maison we waited for a trip which came quickly so that I was permitted to eat an American supper.

Sat. June 29. Most of the day has been spent in listening to the accounts of the citation party. From all reports it was "quelque chose de bonne" [something good] and attracted division-wide attention. There were many humorus happenings, a few narrowly averted catastrophes 2 blessés Deak & Beech and one malade—Kirby who is still recumbent on his couch tearfully demanding from everyone, "Why did I drink so much?"

Sun. June 30. Barracks. The division casket-maker is preparing the Croix de Guerre panels which will be placed on each car as is customary when a unit is cited. They are white ovals bearing a large croix and are decidedly good looking.

Mon. July 1. I decided to have a regular Monday so I washed my clothes or such of them as could be found, after which I was sent to Oigny.

During supper, which we ate outside the grotto in a little ampitheatre we watched a French observation plane attempt to escape from two German chasers. The fight reminded one of two airedales chasing a bear and it was only a question of time before the French plane would go down. Shortly after the two Boches were attacked (or attacked) by a French fighter plane which also went down but accompanied by one of the Germans. About an hour later the "Frenchman" was brought in and proved to be an American from North Carolina. His right leg had been shattered by an explosive bullet and while it was being dressed he told us he was done for and would never live. Kirby & I tried to cheer him up and I drove him in as slowly & as easily as I could but he died (I learned later) during the night and was given a funeral by the Section. He was a brave lad only 21 years old. I should like to write his family telling them how splendidly he died and how well he was cared for but I only know his name "Boughan." Some day perhaps I shall look him up and communicate with his family.

Teus. July 2. Quite and no trips.

Wed. July 3. Still so quite one could imagine that there was no such thing as war. Tonight at supper more aerial entertainment was provided, this time a Boche being fired at by A.A. guns. We soon tired of watching such a common sight and had resumed eating when we heard the nose of an A.A. shell, which by its sound intended joining our little supper party. We immediately scattered for cover, four of us unfortunately picking the same tree which occaisoned a good deal of shoving & hugging as each one endeavored to get next the tree. After we had reseated ourselves the Adjutant remarked "moi foi! s'il est tombé sur la tête je gagnais la medáille militaire" [if it had fallen on my head I would have won the military medal]. The M.M. is usually given when a man is so badly wounded that he is not expected to live, consequently the French are of the opinion that such an honor "coute trop cher" [is too expensive].

Thurs. July 4. Vive L'Amerique! I have been hoping that there would be an evacuation and I would be at Boursonne today but there was not and Kirby and I are doomed to spend the "Grand & Glorious" very quitely.

The Americans in Paris have planned a big "fête" for today and I don't doubt but that the Section will celebrate in a fitting manner. The Lieut & Hub came out about noon bearing a bottle of champagne and two packages of cigarettes. The champagne was the gift of the French as is usual on "les jours de fête." According to Abbot the army is "en alerte" and he cautioned us to be ready for anything which might come up. A general is scheduled to pay a visit to the Section today, an informal review I suppose but I am sorry to miss it. After the Lieut & Hub had left, Kirby and I called nos cammarades les poilus and drank a toast to America & to France. We would have included the other allies but the champagne ran out after America & France had been taken care of so we could not.

Friday. July 5. Boursonne, where I shall probably remain three days unless the Front warms up. We are told that a number of Frenchmen in the trenchs in front of Faverole crawled out beyond the wire the night of the 3rd and after remaining some 20 min. returned minus the small bundles which each had carried. When the morning of the Fourth dawned No Man's Land was dotted with small American flags! The flags didn't remain standing long under the Boche machine gun fire but it was a decided "coupe" for the poilus and they enjoyed it immensely.

[Written in margin here:] Note—since the original was written I have seen this story in a History of the 1st Div.

Mon. July 8. Out to Maison Forestier where there have been small attacks and the Germans have been using considerable quantities of gas. The gas was mostly directed against the batteries in the woods behind us and by the number of artillery men groping blindly about the dressing station at M.F. the gas has had bad results. We make our evacuations via V.C. now and tho there is more shelling than thru the woods the road is better the night driving is easier and we do not have to drive directly under the muzzles of those big 150's.

There appears to be an amassing of troops in this sector which together with the enormous amount of artillery being brought in seems to indicate an attack on a large scale. Today I passed a division of Senegaleze, those great black savages who have been brought from the French province in Africa. They are fierce fellows in an attack tho they are not of great account at holding a line since they has a horror of the noise of the shells. They take few prisoners and have a fancy for the ears, fingers, and even the heads of their victims. The ears and fingers are threaded on string and form a gruesome necklace while the heads are carried in a musette till the odor from them leads to their discovery and the blacks are forced to abandon them. Each Senegaleze carries a long sharp wicked looking knife which is handled in a very expert manner. Their hatred for the German is so great that even when wounded they are never put in the same ambulance with a Boche. Despite their ferocity in battle they are a jolly lot in summer time and a most sorrowful home sick crowd in winter.

Teus. July 9. I have an attack of La Grippe or some sort of ailment so I took the first call which came in at M.F. and am now waiting for Hub to ransack the medicine chest to see what new kind of medicine he can discover. I imagine I will be OK in a day or so if I take his junk & go to bed.

Wed. July 10. Still in bed and am on sick call for about the third time in the army. When a fellow gets sick at the Front & is not evacuated he gets dreadfully "blue" & homesick.

Thurs. July 11. Worked on my car this morning and was sent to Oigny in the afternoon. Neal Lynch is here and as I haven't had a chance to talk with him since he returned to the Section we had a great time kidding each other along. It is very quite here as the Boches have evacuated their old positions in front of Faverole and have installed themselves on higher ground so that in some places their new lines are over a kilometer from the French first line.

Sun. July 14. Vive La France! The Frenchman's Fourth of July. Being impartial I celebrate both our national holiday & the Frenchman's in the same place. We are to be issued 5 "quarts" (not a quart but a cup) of Pinard and one of champagne, otherwise the day will be the same as all others—rain; a few glimpses of the sun; a trip perhaps; a few Boche shells and considerable firing by the French. The Frenchmen are all greatly enthused over the prospect of the holiday ration of Pinard & Champagne tho neither will be more than a drop to their spacious stomachs. I saw a Senegaleze today whose face looked like the crust of a mince pie, all carved up in great shape. This sort of facial decoration is supposed to add greatly to one's beauty and perhaps is not more painful than the methods used by modern women who seek the same end. Whenever we get a trip in to the barracks we are badly misused by the other men who complain because our poste is so quite and the others so rushed with work. Personally I'd rather have a lot to do than to sit around fiddling one's thumb and trying to decide when the war will end. "Perk" is back after having drilled in a concentration camp and narrowly escaped becoming a doughboy. Harper, praise God, has left for Paris or Base Camp where he will attend cooking school. We all pray that he will not be as impervious to instruction as he has been to contumely. The French are somewhat worried by the disappearance of the Boches in this sector. Numerous search patrols have found no trace of them within three kilometers and it is supposed they withdrew fearing that the French were drawing them into an ambush. That blamed Boche offensive is due pretty soon tho I don't believe it will come thru here because they failed here June 1st and if they could not penetrate the Forêt de Villiers Cotterets then the could not hope to do so now. Of course no one can tell what a Boche will do but I believe the attack will be to the South. Each successive attack has been more to the South and they are not yet at the end of their line. I have a "hunch" the attack will start tomorrow I wonder if it will come true.*

August 15. Thursday. It is more than a month since I last entered the "daily doings" and what a month! I'm going back to July 15 to make the daily entries it is of course impossible to be exact as to dates but I have a clear recollection of the sequence of events and will record them under their approximate dates. What a pity I did not enter something each day but it was impossible so here goes and may exactness wait on memory.

Monday July 15. Houlihan came over from Maison early this morning with orders to change postes with me. I had no sooner arrived at M.F. than I was started back to Boursonne with a load of "Yperites" (French name for men gassed with mustard the kind of gas first used by the Germans at Ypres). The Boches are shooting over all kinds of gas and as a consequence I am going day and night.

Teus. July 16. Same stunt of going all day long carrying gas cases. Cunningham and I are the only cars here now and we surely have our hands full. They must be gassing half the men in the divi-

---

*Bowerman's hunch was correct. The Second Battle of the Marne commenced on July 15. The Germans made little progress east of Reims, but to the west, on the edge of Bowerman's sector, they crossed the Marne. On July 18 Marshal Foch ordered a counter-attack. Soissons was retaken on August 2, and the Germans never regained the offensive.

sion and if this keeps up there won't be artillerymen enough to make a crew for one gun. All the other postes are the same even Oigny has "picked up" and Houlihan is cursing his luck as only a Frenchman and an Irishman can. "Old Whiskers" sent me over to Fleury with some chloride of lime for the grave pits. The wounded were lying around thick as flies so I disregarded my orders to return to Maison and took seven of the worst cases into Boursonne. Gassed men can wait better than wounded. The court yard at Boursonne is simply overflowing with blessés. I never saw so many together in my life. Those very badly wounded are operated on at once in the little hospital here, the others are sent to Betz. The flies are hovering in swarms around the wounded men and it is pitiful to watch their efforts to escape them. Some are moaning loudly others cry for water while the rest are either too badly wounded to make a sound or are so slightly wounded that they are only happy that they are being taken away from the front. Betz is so far that the cars doing this evacuation are not able to clear out the wounded as fast as we bring them in. Gil has the large truck going now with "assis" but if this thing keeps up thru the night I don't know where they will put the poor devils. I told Lieut Abbot that I had disobeyed the Medecin Divisionaire's orders and was mightily relieved when he said I had done rightly. That's the beauty of this service, one is generally on his own and surely it is a fine thing that there has been no instance of slacking even tho it could be done easily & go undetected. When I got back to M.F. they told me that Bill had gone out to Vouty for the night and I would relieve him when he came down. A permanent poste at Vouty? Sacré nom de chien! they'll have us driving thru the front line before long. Vouty is about the most unhealthy spot in this neck of the woods, one can only go there at night and every trip the Germans hear the motor and open up with 37's (their equivalent) and machine guns. The place and the road to it are so bad that altho a Frenchman is compelled to ride up with you to show you the road you can't induce him to ride back. When you're in a car 3 or four feet off the ground a shell & a machine gun bullet has a much better chance of killing you and besides you cannot hear them coming and can't throw yourself on the ground. A poste a Vouty? If that's so we may as well write home. I had never been to Vouty so I went down into the dugout and by the flickering (not yet) emanciated candle I poured over a map trying to so fix the turns & twists in my mind that I could not forget them. This was a hopless task for I never saw a war map yet that an ordinary man could make head or tail of. All the time I kept listening for Bill's car coming down the road from Dampleux and if ever I spent a rotten three hours it was then. At last, sleep failing me I went down into the dug out again to ask aid in discovering the road to Vouty when to my great joy & relief they told me Bill had not gone to Vouty to stay but to Croix de Vouty. Now Croix de Vouty is 200 yrds or closer to the lines, but I felt as if a "permission" had been handed me and I was scheduled to go to Nice.

Wed. July 17. Bill didn't come down last night so I got a little sleep but the trips started early and during the day we were swamped with "gassées." I tried to handle all the evacuations myself but the men poured in so fast that I soon saw that I would need help. Three times I told Abbot that if I could take a couple of extra cars out we could bring them all in & clean the poste up, but when we arrived at Maison there was always enough left over to fill two other cars. The men were mostly all blinded and they waited in a mob till a car came and then rushed it darn near overturning it struggling to get in. The cars are meant to carry six with the driver but we had a hard time convincing them that they shouldn't carry fifty. Finally Larkin, Shively and myself left Boursonne on what we were sure would be the last trip. Larkin and Shive were to bring in the men & I was to stay there. We left B at 8. A blacker night I have never seen, the drizzle which had begun seemingly two weeks ago was still falling and the roads were rivers of mud due to the immense traffic which had passed over them. When we came to the cross roads where the big ammo dump was the direct road was jammed with ammo wagons waiting to be loaded and about half of the trucks seemed to be stuck cross wise in the road. Seeing this awful tangle I started (Larkin had gone on ahead and I had Shive) up the other road but a gendarme stopped us and said that that road was impassible since a large truck had overturned & lay side ways in the road. Considering this information authentic we turned around & tried to force a passage thru the mess on the direct road. A gendarme told us that this road also was blocked and when we refused to listen to him a captain or a major (I couldn't distinguish in the dark) came up and also told me it was impassable. I told him that I was driving an ambulance that there were crowds of wounded waiting me at Maison and I was going thru. Again he declared that I should not so I held a council with Shive & told him I thot we could make it by leaving the road & striking out thru the woods. Shive, who was evidently more in awe of the officer's words than I, suggested that we return to the barracks but I refused to listen. He hadn't see those poor blind devils waiting hour after hour in the rain and mud. After some "argufying" Shive agreed to follow tho he was skeptical about ever getting back on the road again. I started ahead again but our friend the officer was there at my elbow declaring vehemently that I *could not* pass. I reiterated that we were "service de santé" and *were* going thru and with that I shoved "Little Eva" in gear dodged behind a camion and out into the woods while he ran after me waving his arms and shouting all sorts of threats after me. The going in the woods was pretty stiff but at last I found a clear place on the road and climbed back on with the help of a few poilus. Once again on the road I turned on my lights as the night was so cloudy they wouldn't be seen and because it was well nigh impossible to advance without them. The road was simply jammed with infantry for 8 kilometers and [we] went by them dodging, yelling, honking and swearing. The lights didn't make any sort of a hit with the Frenchmen, but as I was sure no avions would be over I turned a deaf ear to their cries and curses. Several men struck at Shive with their guns and bayonettes he said and one officer gave him a whack on the arm with a cane but those lights alone got us to Maison. Some shells were landing in V.C. but we went thru comfortably enough and at last turned off from that stream of humanity into a practically deserted road where we were able to go much faster and arrived shortly at M. Larkin was not there (he had gotten stuck in the mud on the round about road) but we did find 17 évacués demanding a ride. After we had fixed a puncture on Shive's car he loaded 8 and I 9 and we are off again for B, I being serenely happy that Maison was at last "cleaned up." The officers told us that we might take the road past the batteries until 2 o'clock when they were to begin firing. This road would permit us to escape that tide of men but we soon found the going too heavy for our overloaded cars so returned the way we had come. In Villiers I stopped to put water in my radiator but one of those blamed Austrian 130's (the

Tommy calls it a "whiz bang" because it travels so fast) came directly overhead and exploded in a square near by so I decided I didn't need water so badly as I had thot. Those 130's are the meanest shell in the war. They are fired (I am told) almost on a flat trajectory & consequently at great speed. One hears the boom of the gun and almost before one can throw himself flat they go "swish-crump." We managed to reach B somehow and crawled in above the morgue at 3 bells having taken 7 hrs to make a 2 hr & ½ trip.

Thurs. July 18. Foch's big counter-attack began early this morning on a forty kilometer front. The plans for the attack were kept secret and altho we could tell that there was to be an attack I'm sure no one knew when it was to start. For two or three weeks we have had continuous rainy & cloudy weather and unless Heinie had spies he never knew what was being "cooked up" for him. Despite the two weeks' rain which allowed all the troops to be brought in & the guns set up unnoticed this morning dawned clear and bright, not a cloud in the sky & the hot sun drying the ground up quickly. Surely the Gods have been with us this time. Our division has been drawn over to Fleury and they attacked Corcy. Divisional fronts have been narrowed down to ⅓ or ¼ their former size and the narrow roads near the Front are simply choked with troops and convoys. As I went up to Corcy the batteries were already getting prepared to move forward. In this war there is very little of batteries swinging into position on a gallop. Now just before the attack they move masked batteries as close to the front lines as is possible. The regular batteries some 3 or 4 kilos to the rear begin the barrage for the infantry. As soon as the attack has advanced beyond the range of the original batteries those close behind the old front line take over the work and continue firing till they too are out of range. Meanwhile the original batteries have been slowly and laboriously moving into a position in front. The little town of Corcy had received the brunt of an opening barrage and the destruction was total. Hardly a stone remained atop another and now it was being shelled by the Boches in order to cut off the supplies & reinforcements. The shells were landing about a hundred yards up from the poste and as I drove up the street looking for a place to turn around a shell fell near me and a man rose up from a crouching position waving an arm with the hand gone. He held it high over his head as he ran towards the poste but the blood pumped out at quite a rate. Just where the man was wounded the infantry is crossing the little stream which flows thru the town. They are getting out near the woods where there are no shells falling as it is crazy to attempt to continue up the main street. As they crouch behind a wall or tree and then run wildly across the open spaces they look like nothing I can think of but it is so unnatural that one cannot help but believe that he is at a movie. The sight of those men scurrying about like wild hunted beasts excited me far more than the shells did but in a strange indescribable fashion. The wounded came in so fast that I did not have long to wait before getting a load. About a half kilometer from Corcy I picked up a Senegalese who had just been wounded. His entire left shoulder had been shot away but the stretchers were filled and I had to put him in front with me. He kept continually falling against me so I put one arm around him and tried to hold him up. Never once did he moan or utter a sound and when I got to Fleury I made them take him out and put him on a stretcher he could never had stood the trip to Boursonne for he would have died of loss of blood since he had only a rough field bandage on his shoulder. I had never supposed that I would like to have my coat stained with a nigger's blood but if I could have eased that fine fellow one jot of pain I would gladly have had my whole uniform wet with it. They were shelling a bit on the Soissons road and there were a number of dead horses and two dead men lying in the ditch.

They say that the attack extends along the entire front from Chateau Thierry where the Americans are to the North Sea where the British & Belgians hold the line. Reports (unofficial) say that the Americans are doing splendidly and are pushing old Jerry back in great style. The prisoners began arriving at Fleury about 6 o'clock. There are large numbers of them, some are very young but they average as well as the French and as far as I can see are well enough fed. Spend the night in the grotto where the prisoners are assembled for examination. One young Boche who did not respond quickly enough to a command to hurry along received a well aimed and powerful kick from a major but otherwise they were well treated. Before censuring the major too severely it would be well to enquire what harm had been done him by the Germans. It surely is splendid to be *attacking* and *advanc-*

ing instead of *being attacked* and *retreating* as we have been doing since last May. Foch has at last sufficient reserves to permit attacks & things will hum from now on.

Friday. July 19. About 8 o'clock Jamon took Bal and I to a poste the other side of Longpont some 10 kilo's in front of Corcy. The whole 10 kilo's are filled with shell holes, in fact they nearly overlap and the roads are barely passable. Several times it was necessary to fill in or bridge over with saplings large holes which filled the road. Everywhere are smashed Boche dug outs, gun positions, wagons, caissons and abandoned shells line the roads. Turned (?) to our left out of Corcy our way lay for some 4 kilo's thru a deep swamp filled valley which runs parallel to the trenchs. The road or what is left of it follows along the hillside nearly to Longpont where the 75's are barking away in great style. At the batteries we turned to cross the floor of the valley, a lake of mud filled with shell holes across which the Geni (engineers) had thrown a log bridge. Crossing the bridge was tedious work since the valley was jammed full of reserves, ammunition, & guns moving up in support. To ascend the opposite side of the valley which is a high and steep bank, the road runs straight for a half kilometer then branches in the form of a "y" and the two forks wind slowly back and forth till they reach the plateau above. If the bridge hindered progress the road up the hill (the right hand fork for ascending traffic) is almost impassable and we are stalled at the fork of the main road for 20 min or a half hour. It was here that our barrage must have caught a roadful of retreating Germans and what a hell-hole it must have been! Dead men, dead horses and demolished wagons & trucks are everywhere. Here is a large truck all burned and broken which was evidently carrying small shells for they are strewn everywhere. Close beside the truck are the charred bodies of two men, beyond at the side of the road the bare leg of a man with a piece of a boot & a sock still around it sticks up from the bushes as if it had become stuck as the man hurried along and had pulled out of the socket. Of all the dead men (10 or 12) none of their faces seem to carry an expression of horror or fear but it is not so with the horses. I remember one white horse in particular, he had a big ragged hole in his side and as he had settled to the ground he had turned his head to bite the wound. Death had frozen him in this position, the nostrils dilated, the lips drawn from the opened teeth and in his eyes was such pain and fear that one could believe he still lived and could hear his scream as the éclat struck him. As we stood there waiting Bal came over, his face somewhat pale and there was no denying the sincerity of his words as he said "God! Bowie but this makes me sick." It isn't pleasant to see these things and know that, but for the mercy of God you might now or may yet be looking like that.

At last the road ahead was cleared and we went up to the broad level plateau where batteries were galloping into position, tanks lumbering along and low flying airplanes hastened toward the ever changing lines to drop their load of bombs upon the fleeing Boches. The plateau seemed like Heaven or at least Purgatory after those hellish sights in the valley below. Here also were evidences of heavy shelling but nothing compared to that of Corcy and Longpont. Being in the open, free from confining villages, trees and hills gave the attack an entirely different aspect, here was war as we had learned to imagine war. The batteries galloping into position in the wheat fields reminded one of the army recruiting posters of pre war days and seemed more natural. It is the unnaturalness of being killed by a huge screaming thundering shell that gives one fear and horror of dying. Not the fear of *death* but the manner of death. Continuing across the valley toward two little villages beyond which the shells were falling we succeeded, after an hour's search, in locating the poste, a ruined farm house at the edge of a village. As the poste was so recently established we had time, while waiting for the wounded to be cared for, to explore the environs somewhat. In a courtyard we found 20 or 30 machine guns which had been captured that morning as well as a nest of other German equipment captured or abandoned. Our desire for souvenirs was considerably abated when a captain cautioned us against touching anything as it was very likely that it might be connected with a bomb placed by the Germans when forced to retreat.

The poste was soon filled with Senegalese and one big hick wore a neck adornment consisting of a German thumb threaded on a piece of string. Getting my load, 3 couchés and two assis (who sat in front with me) I found the return trip a great deal easier except that I was continually in doubt as to the right road. Once my decision to turn left met with remonstrance from the niggers beside me and shortly after I was extremely sorry for my bull-headedness when one of the assis suddenly began shouting Les Boches! Les Boches! Arretez! Arretez! (Germans! Germans! stop! stop!) The cry was immediately taken up by the other men, who knowing their lack of favor in German eyes had no desire to be captured. Looking across the valley in the direction the negro was pointing I saw a bunch of men coming down the hillside. Since I did not know exactly where I was and because the lines in an attack are constantly changing allowing the enemy to filter thru it was entirely plausible that these men *were* Boches tho at their distance I could not distinguish the uniforms. I had no particular desire myself to be captured especially in such bad company so, as it was impossible to turn around where we were, I got out and ran ahead hoping that the road widened beyond the bend ahead. Rounding the bend I saw a French wagon so I knew we were OK and joyfully reported the fact to my blessés who were as pleased as I. In Corcy we met Jamou taking four cars up to the new postes. As each car passed the man asked anxiously "Is there any shelling?" and when I answered no it was worthwhile to see the look of relief that spread over their faces.

Sat. *July 20.* A.M.—They say the Section is to move to Fleury. Wherever we're going at least we're going to move.

P.M.—Our division has been relieved and what is left of them will go on "repose" in some nearby town where they will rest after 50 days' continuous fighting and recruit the division which has suffered heavy losses since June 1. We are going over to help out the Americans near Soissons supposedly to do evacuation work at any rate we hope we're going to do evacuation work. We are stationed in Pierrefonds where we have a good quarters and as a neighbor a magnificent old chateau which looks like a medieaval castle. We are to evacuate from here to Crepy the nearest railroad some 30 kilos distant. I made several trips today and was surprised at the inefficiency of the American Medical Service. There being an insufficiency of ambulances they were using trucks placing 16 wounded men in a springless truck often without even a stretcher and jolting them insufferably for 30 kilos over cobble-stone roads. Arrived at Crepy they were laid in the rain in the railroad yards and left unattended for hours. Thank God for the rain for German bombers would have blown that yard to hell on a clear night. It was in this same town that a month before the Boches had dropped 300 bombs in one night!

and all during the raid poor Neal was cruising up and down the streets trying to find someone who would take his blessé off his hands.

Sun. July 21. Returning about 9 o'clock tonight from Crepy I ran into the worst rain storm I have ever seen. Not only was it almost impossible to see but even to breath[e] was a task and I feared more than once that I would be drowned where I sat. I was drenched when I arrived at Pierrefonds and had to sleep naked as a babe between borrowed blankets while my clothes & blankets dried before the little fire place.

Mon. July 22. Our fears are realized. Our soft snap of evacuation is done and get front line work once more. "As if 50 steady days and nights wasn't enough" Houlihan growled when the orders came. Shive and the Lieut were wounded coming from Chaudun. Shive kept on driving with a broken leg and a wounded arm while the Lieut got an éclat in his knee. Hank came in and I was sent out to relieve him. According to Hank, one has to drive thru a barrage each trip between the regimental & battallion postes and each of these are shelled and mitrailleused by avions. The wounded, he says, are lying at the advance poste pleading to either be taken to a hospital or back to the front line. Lieut Abbot sure showed "guts" by going up with every driver on his first trip. His wound is slight but his leg is stiffening up and he refused to have it attended to. We finally prevailed upon him to have it dressed. Webber had a good deal of luck this afternoon. He and Shively were at Coeuvres when two calls came, one to Chaudun, the other to a farm. As Shive had been going longer than Jim, Jim proposed that he take Shive's call to the farm and that Shive take the Chaudun call. As Chaudun had up to this time been the lesser of the two evils Jim's offer was a fine courageous one and anyone would have bet on his being wounded rather than Shive. Meanwhile however, conditions changed and Jimmy escaped. As I was the last car to arrive at Coeuvres I had no call (there are 3 sections working here) and spent the afternoon rummaging about the ruins of what had formerly been a fine chateau. Tho the evening was cloudy I predicted that we would be visited by Boche aviators and tho my prophecy was not believed further events proved me a second Moses. Shortly after evening mess a Scotch division came up the road to relieve the Second. What a splendid sight they made as they came swinging along in as perfect formation as if they were on the parade ground, singing to the bag-pipes, their equipment and bare knees shining in the moonlight. Neal and I stood watching them at a cross roads but when we heard the syncronised motors of a Boche bomber we decided that the Scotchmen needed no reception committee and we hiked for the drawbridge of the chateau which we crossed and stood under the vault like gateway. Our shelter was neither bomb proof nor éclat proof but we knew of no "better 'ole" and it does give one comfort to have anything over his head. We were joined shortly by 3 others and then the show started as friend Boche released those bombs. How they did drop—swish-zoom! swish-zoom! each one nearer. The third one dropped so close that we all believed that the fourth one would be ours and we pressed into a little two by twice door way which ordinarily wouldn't hold two. We were packed like sardines and yet we cussed because we weren't in tighter. You could feel hearts pounding away on all sides and also the jumping of the man's stomach opposite you (in indication as I have observed of great excitement). After an age of waiting the fourth bomb exploded some 100 yrds from us in the courtyard. I have said before that bursting bombs are beautiful and I wish now to denounce myself as a liar—a monstrous liar. Bursting bombs are the ugliest things on God's green earth and if you doubt me ask any of the five. The Scotch behaved splendidly and I shall never forget hearing the calm even voice of an officer as he called "Hurry along men hurry along." Hurry along indeed! if they weren't bloomin' 'eros they would have been *running along*. Five of them were killed by the 3rd bomb as it fell in the street in front of the drawbridge. During the temporary lull following the fourth bomb I remembered that during the afternoon I had seen an opening in the foundation of the chateau which could be reached via the moat. I informed the others but the question arose how were we to get into the moat and, once there how would we get out? Our "hesitation" on the drawbridge was brought to an abrupt end by the return of the Boche; get back? we should worry and Neal and I dropped simultaneously the 15 ft to the bottom of the moat. We landed on our feet and running nor did we stop despite the trees, wire & what not that blocked our path till we fell breathlessly into a fine vaulted cave. Just as we reached the cave the bombs began falling again—but we were safe. Neal turned and thumbed his nose at the sky.

Teus. July 23. This sector is surely a "mauvaise" [bad] spot for "ambulanciers." 3 or 4 are getting picked off every day. This morning one car came in which had had a narrow escape. A shell had fallen just in front of it and a large éclat had passed between the heads of the driver and the assis seated beside him and had entered the small window in the front panel. Before the shell struck a wounded doughboy's head filled the window as he lay on the top stretcher, after it exploded nothing filled the window the driver and the assis were severely shell shocked and the two men on the bottom stretchers were covered with brains. The two men shell shocked sat huddled up next the wall of the dressing station. They shuddered and trembled like leaves continually and when a gun shot or some one spoke sharply to them [they] jumped as tho pricked with a pin.

The shell that got Shive lighted just under the left hand running board, which was burned with powder and tho the car was riddled with éclat Shive & the lieut were the only ones touched. The second is pulling out and we are relieved at noon. Jamou says that we are going back to our old division, the 128e "Les Loups du Bois le Prêtre." Left Pierrefonds for [Le] Fayel at four towing Lewis. Our road lay thru Compiegne which is badly shot up and a much different place than it was that noon two months ago when I ate lunch in the Hôtel Palais. We reached Fayel about 6 parked our cars under an avenue of trees leading to the gates of a beautiful chateau. After eating we roundly cursed the place for being so small and uninteresting—and went to sleep in our cars.

Wed. July 24. As the cars have not been properly attended to for two months we have lots to do in the repair & overhauling line and time won't hang heavily on our hands for a few days at least. There is a section of English girls living in the chateau. They surely are a hard-looking crowd and I don't blame them for joining up. They are doing evacuation work here tho they say they have been at the Front. This is believable for there are many quite sectors not much more dangerous than one's back yard, but you never see them in an active sector. It would be impossible for them to stand the gaff.

Thurs. July 25. Young Derek Peters has fallen a victim to dysentery and has been evacuated to a hospital. We're all feeling pretty low possibly the reaction from the last two months.

Friday July 27. Bradley and I leave for our "permission." One day in Paris, one night in Lyon, seven days at Aix les Bains, two days in Paris and two days searching for the Section which we finally find at Couloizy [Couloisy] between Compiegne & Soissons.

Sun. Aug. 11. Returned from "permission" today after searching for two days trying to find them. Leaving Paris we went to Fayel from Fayel to Paris from Paris to Crepy by train then 14 miles to Pierrefont via shanks man[?]. Pierrefonds to Hautefontaine by camion but not finding the section there we decided to return to Pierrefonds and wait there till one of our cars came in for ravitaillement the next morning. Leaving Hautefontaine we ran into a Lieut of another section who said he knew where our section was so we drove to his camp where we ate supper and later were taken to Couloizy in one of his cars.

Mon. Aug. 12. Sent to poste Hill 120 where there is not much doing and I learn that one of my brancardier friends has been killed during my absence from the Section.

Thurs. Aug. 15. The shells had been whistling over the top of the dug out where Russel and I slept for about two hours when, about midnight a brancardier called me saying that a man had just been wounded near the crossroad at the bottom of the hill. While I was getting the car ready they brought in another blessé who had also been hit near the crossroads which they are shelling. The men were ready at 1 and as they were being placed in the car the Sergt told me in a low tragic voice that I should go like the devil around the first turn as they were shelling it. I already knew this and had been thinking about it for an hour and my state of mind wasn't calmed any by the Sergt's information. It is about as impossible to take a turn fast as it is to drive thru the eye of a needle, the thing is a perfect hair pin and banked the wrong way at that. I got by the turn unharmed but got lost in Attichy and had the devil of a time getting out. I finally discovered some Frenchman asleep in a cellar who told me the necessary turns. The Section I had been informed had left Couloizy and were now in Jaulzy. I had no idea where Jaulzy was but by making myself a perfect nuisance to every Frenchman abroad or awake I learned that upon reaching the Compiègne-Soissons road I turned left and stopped in the second village. Arriving at the main road I decided to fix my car which was missing badly and was never more surprised in my life when I heard a shell scream and shrapnel burst nearby. I had thot myself in a quite zone but that one shell changed my mind and I left that spot with fitting haste. By 3 I had found the Section and with Perkins as guide we started for Villiers Cotterets. On the way we collided with another ambulance but fortunately my car was not damaged tho the other was put temporarily "hors de combat." Returned to Jaulzy at 7.

Friday. August 16. This afternoon we went swimming in the Aisne which flows just by our barracks. Undisturbed by the occaisonal shells which whizzed over our head to fall in the town we thoroughly enjoyed ourselves and tried to imagine for the time being that we were back in our school boy days (they seem ages back) disporting ourselves in the old swimming hole. They are building a bridge just up the river aways and it is very interesting to watch them driving the piles. The pile driver is quite conventional except in its motive power. In this case the place of the wheezing steam engine has been taken by a rope and pulley arrangement, which permits 50 men to drag the driver to the top of the derrick. The men sing a sort of chanty as they work and it is doubtful whether the steam engine or they wheeze more during the intervals between hauling.

Hap came in from Picardie and I was sent out tho I had only a vague idea where the place was and I could not learn anything from these blamed maps they give you. I scurried around the streets of Vic Sur Aisne for some 30 minutes before I could find anyone who knew any more than I about getting to Picardie. Hap had told me to drive thru a wheat field so I headed Little Eva up a hill thru the only wheatfield I could see and was soundly roasted by an artillery captain for making tracks to his battery which he felt certain would now be spotted by avions and destroyed. I expressed deep regret for having made the tracks and asked him how in something or other I was to know that he had a battery here. This didn't tend to establish cordial relations so I cut him short by driving down the hill again carefully attempting to follow my old path and not make two sets of tracks. I nearly dispaired of ever finding Picardie but I was "getting warm" and was at last directed up a long steep sunken road whose sides are lined with dug outs. It is quite a trick in the day time to keep your wheels out of a dug out parlor and how one can do it at night is a mystery. The poste is in a huge cave at the top of the hill and tho the approach to it is difficult one is paid for his pains by the feeling of absolute security one can enjoy when in the poste. The cave which is immense and will hold a whole division, has been used since 1915 and is fitted up in a luxurious manner. There are several entrances which have been elaborately carved out of the solid rock and look like the entrances to public buildings. The cave itself is cut up into innumerable rooms and passage ways and a stranger to the place could easily become lost.

Evening—Another big attack is coming soon and we are to move our poste to Bery [Berry?], a little village immediately back of the front line. As we were not to move till 10 I lay down to sleep as I have been feeling rotten—grippe I guess. No one seems greatly enthused over moving to Bery and when I got a light from the dentist his hand shook, probably from the cold. As this sector is new to me they gave me a brancardier for a guide. The dentist was going with us but decided that it was better to walk. Somehow we managed to get thru the sunken road without breaking up the car or a happy home (?) but were forced to stop at the bottom of the hill for 10 min. while the Boche poured in shells on the cross roads just in front of us. We lay under a piece of corrugated iron while the show was on and were quite safe from the éclat as long as the shells kept falling where they did. As soon as the shelling stopped we hurried on, which was fortunate as five men of a convoy were killed just after we had passed the cross roads. The brancardier had told me before we left that the road was "mauvaise" and the town of Berry worse and I believed the first part but hoped he was lying about the second. At Bery we unloaded the equipement and were told to return to Picardie. The brancardier returned with me the trip being uneventful except that we were held up for 3 hrs by a jam of two ammunition trains which had attempted to pass. The Boche was shelling with gas but quite far from us and tho we had our masks ready it was needless to put them on. As there seemed no chance of getting the car to the top of the hill we ran it into a little clearning off the road and walked up to the poste about 200 yrds. There being no wounded I managed to get four hours' sleep before I was called at five and told to return to

Bery. A "coup de main" which was intended to give the French a favorable "point de depart" (jumping off place) for the attack, was in progress and all the batteries on the hill were going it full tilt. My brancardier thot we had better wait till the shells were falling less thickly but I found, when I went outside that they were mostly "départs" so we walked down to the car and drove to Bery again. There being no blessés at present and Borden and Larabee having just arrived I was told to return to Picardie where I should wait till a trip came. As the medicin chef of the 167e and I were talking at the door of the dug out a shell struck and exploded on the cave just over the door and directly above our heads, a foot more and we would have been gonners. The captain dove down the stairs and I followed nearly overtaking Borden who, so Ted declares, uttered an "Oh my God!" when the shell struck and staggered down the stairs. The force of the shell had blown out all the candles in the cave but had done no damage due to the extreme solidness of the dugout. I don't like them that close and I can thank God for my escape.

Sat. Aug. 17. After returning to Picardie I waited till noon before a trip came and then went in to Jaulzy. This evening the Medécin Chef of the G.B.D. (Groupe Brancardiers Divisional) tendered us a little champagne party as a delayed July 14 fête. After the customary exchange of toasts we finished the champagne (no great job) listened to the Vic and tried to pull off small talk with the visiting Frenchmen. The Vic tired, the champagne gave out, the small talk dwindled to silence and we went to bed every one agreeing that the only trouble with the party was the lack of sufficient champagne to losen our tongues.

Sun. Aug. 18. We move to Vashe [Vache] Noire near Vic Sur Aisne in order to be nearer to the front for the attack. Vashe Noire (Black Cow) is a "mauvais coin" [bad spot] as it is the center of about 6 objects which the Boche consider worth shelling—and they do justice to them all showing commendable (?) impartiality. Our billet is the Hotel de la Gare which sounds much better than it really is as we inhabit merely two undersized caves not large enough for all of us and no great comfort to any of us. I have been sick for two days and was too ill to drive my car from Jaulzy. I told the Lieut I was sick and he finally took me to the doctor who ordered eggs milk and chicken! There wasn't a chicken or a cow (despite the name of the town) within 20 miles and it is a shame that so much fine American profanity had to be wasted on an incomprehending Frenchman. No eggs, milk or chicken being produced I went again to the Lieut and told him that I didn't want to be evacuated but I was not going to be treated like a dog and wanted some medicine. While waiting for the medicine Sergt. "Pete" came along and seeing my condition told the Lieut that I should be evacuated. Another visit to the doctor diagnosed my case as dysentery, and as Green was also sick they decided to evacuate us for 3 or four days. We left Vashe Noire at 6 just as the barrage for the attack on Noyon commenced. Hub drove us to Villiers and only my condition prevented me from being frightened to death at the way he took corners. I was so weak that I was unable to sit on the little seat but managed to stretch out a bit on the floor. Arrived at the evacuation hospital (a large tent) they tagged us as to our trouble and our destination. I thot I suffered that night but a 20 kilometer jaunt in a camion to another evacuation hospital was so much worse that there was no comparison. I surely thot I would die before we reached the other hospital. We stayed here four hours and were then taken by ambulance to Crepy where they loaded us into a hospital train and we were off on a two day–two night trip to Toulouse, 75 miles from the Spanish border. The hospital train was a string of boxcars fitted with four tiers of three stretchers each. No one came near us except with water which I didn't want and no medical attention at all was given us. I can only thank Heaven that I was no sicker. Near Bordeau[x] we entered the American Zone of the railways and tho it was good to feel that you were being hauled by Americans it was decidedly disturbing when they opened the big Yankee engines up and set the stretches swaying to a dangerous degree. The Frenchmen were particularly alarmed at the speed but two American voices joined the exclamations when we rounded corners. How those dinky toy freight cars stayed on the rails is a mystery. At Toulouse we were taken by a woman ambulance driver to Hôpital Auxiliare No 1 and placed in a ward with 20 doughboys from the 1st and 2nd divisions who had been wounded at Soissons and Chateau Thierry. The two weeks spent at Toulouse were interesting enough and we were soon well and aching to return to the Section. There was absolutely no need of our remaining there longer than a week but the doctors refused to let us go and we passed the second week swapping yarns, playing blackjack and in exploring the town (four afternoons a week). There were three "characters" in the hospital who gave us much pleasure. "Old Issue" a veteran of the Lord knows how many years' service as a regular; "Red" a witty cynical young Irish man from New York who had been drafted, landed in France and wounded within 6 or 8 weeks. Being attached to the 1st before he knew the muzzle of a rifle from the stock or had any idea what a hand grenade was, he was put in a listening poste on the edge of a lake. The German lines lay across the lake and he was cautioned to be constantly on the look out lest a Boche raiding party should skate across & attack his poste! His account of his fears and experiences the first two or three nights was extremely laughable. The third character was a Doctor West, a dentist of Toulouse who had lived in the States years ago and still spoke fair English. He would bring us tobbacco & cigarettes and we would all gather round him in the ward as he told of his life and asked eager questions about America. Later he connived with a Red Cross nurse in establishing a rest room and canteen in the basement of the Red Cross headquarters. The "house-warming" was a great success and old Doc West was in his Seventh Heaven as he served out the doughnuts and lemonade arrayed in a costume which he considered like that of an American barkeep. I shall always remember the Doctor, for tho he was not even well to do he did his best to make life agreeable for us and he succeeded better than he knew.

Teus. Sept. 3. Eight of us left at 8 this evening for Vichy where there is an American Casualty Clearing Camp. The trains were crowded and it was necessary for us to remain standing in the aisle the whole journey. At 2:30 we arrived at Limoge[s] where we changed trains and at 12 the next day we changed again at St. Germain des Rossées [Fossés] where we were fed at a Red Cross canteen. One-thirty found us at Vichy after a seventeen hour trip during 10 hours of which we had stood. 10 hrs on one's feet in a crowded train is no fun by a whole lot. At headquarters we were questioned as to the work we could do and the Adjudant was greatly disgusted when we told him that our pre-army occupation had been "going to college." I greatly feared we would be digging ditches before long but fortunately we were spared and [our] only job was trying to figure out some way to get money to spend at the cafés. The Army has taken over all the hotels here and has spared no money to make this a delightful place to convalesce. As Vichy before the war was "quelque chose" as a resort, the hotels are fine ones tho Kirby and I didn't draw one of the best. There is a very pretty park here and a band is playing away all the time. My bed is in a small ward along side a "nut" he seems harmless but I shall not be surprised to awake some morning and find my throat cut or my head battered in with a bed post.

Sat. Sept. 7. Tho we have made several attempts to be sent away because we are rather "home-sick" and detest getting in bed at 9 every evening and also not having a paltry "sou" to expend for "la biere et d'autres choses" [beer and other things] tho, as I have said, we have tried a number of times to have them discharge us not until today did we meet with any encouragement. We shall leave for Paris at 6 o'clock tonight unless the C.O. in his finite wisdom decrees that we tarry longer within his gates. Vichy is too fine a place to be cooped up in and under the strictess "surveillance."

We left Vichy at 11 only 5 hours later than we expected which is pretty good for the army, to be disappointed 5 hours is nothing when one reflects how easy it is to be disappointed 5 months. Our traveling party consists of two wounded (and pessimistic) Tommies Kirby and me and a Lieut who is detailed to conduct us to Paris and then straight way to our Headquarters. "He's got a job on his hands" Kirby whispered as we pulled out of the station and I nodded assent. The Tommies were evidently "fed-up" on American conversation for they were silent as clams. The Lieut, not having been to the Front, still had the opinion that officers should not be intimate with an enlisted man or perhaps he merely used his rank as an excuse for escaping the sour faces and grumbling of the English lads. Kirby and I attempted to coax the two human crabs from their lairs but met with no success and being tired of talking to each other we fell asleep.

Sun. Sept. 8. Morning found us in Paris and we managed to lose the Lieut by calling a taxi and urging him and the Tommies to enter. When he told us to get in also the cabby raised such a howl (as we had known he would) that we said we would follow in another cab. Reluctantly the Lieut drove away and we joyously climbed into a second taxi whose driver somehow failed to follow the 1st cab and let us down at the University Union where we secured both money & rooms.

Teus. Sept. 10. After two delightful days in Paris during which we mostly annoyed a girl friend of Kirbie's who was living in Paris and doing war work, we climbed into a first class coach at the Gare de l'Est and at 8:30 left for Lizzy sur Orcq [Lizy-sur-Oureq] where, we had been informed at headquarters, we would find the Section. The journey was tiresome except when the conductor came for our tickets. He proved himself a hard hearted scoundrel not properly imbued with the spirit of democracy and tried his best to drive us from the compartment, which he claimed was for officers only. To all of his arguments which reached a climax in a volley of expletives aimed at Americans in general and us two in particular we returned a laconic "comprends pas" [don't understand]. When the official began cursing we nearly forgot the role which we had assumed but restrained our selves preferring to ride first class than to curse him back. At Lizy we were informed that the Section was at Courmelles to which place we proceeded having the good fortune to be taken as far as Villers Cotterets in a general's limousine from which we occaisonly bowed majestically to the populace and returned the salutes of such soldiers as thot us American officers of high rank. At Villers we reverted to our real rank and boarded a "permissionaires" train which ran as far as Vierzy. This part of the trip was decidedly interesting as we passed over the same ground over which we had driven in our ambulances those stirring days in June and July. At Vierzy we found an [illeg.] grotto which was used as an evacuation hospital or "ambulance" as the French term them where we passed the night hoping that one of our cars would come in.

Wed. Sept. 11. If one of our cars came in last night we were not called so we continued to Courmelles on foot being given a bit of a lift by a camion which helped a lot as we are poor hikers. Naturally enough the Section had left Courmelles* but we learned that they had moved toward Soissons to which place we walked and were able, after much questioning, to locate a part of the G.B.D. which had not yet moved up. Here at last were men of

---

*According to the Station List (Appendix 2), the section was never stationed at Courmelles. During Bowerman's absence they had gone from Vache Noire to St. Christophe, Vez, Equiry, Soissons, and finally Crouy.

our own division who told us that the Section was at Crouy some four kilos beyond Soissons on the road which connected with the Chemin des Dames. As a ravitaillement (food supply) cart was going up we hopped aboard grateful to be protected from the rain which was falling heavily. Soissons showed evidence of heavy fighting and of German occupancy. What is left of Crouy is perhaps the most desolate looking village we have seen. Of the 200 houses only one can boast of four walls and a roof and these are so full of shell holes that the house is not fit for occuppancy. We were mightily pleased to be back again with the bunch and had soon installed ourselves in one of the two cellars which the Section has taken over. Just after noon mess Pete brought us back to the reality of things by taking us out to Vauverry where we relieved Hap and Howie. The road ascended a long hill from Crouy, ran along on a plateau from which one could plainly see the shells falling on both lines and finally dipped into a narrow valley which wound nearly to the Front lines. Dead horses line the plateau road and are beginning to smell, in fact, the smell of one dead horse is used as a sign poste. Going from Crouy to Vauverry one is directed to continue straight ahead till you smell a dead horse then turn to the right. One can imagine the possibilities of such directions—suppose a horse is killed nearer to Crouy, than the horse in question or suppose one has a cold in the head. The "poste" at Vauverry is a narrow sap dug in the road embankment just where the road dips down into the little valley. As fifteen men are stationed here sleep is out of the question nor does one feel inclined to remain for any length of time outside the sap for the shelling is promiscous. I have never relished a "one-opening" sap or dug-out being as I fear a victim of claustrophobia but I also have a greater fear of open spaces—when they are shelled so Kirby and I sat with our arms on our knees and reminisced of Toulouse and Paris. Great thing memory I don't know what a man's mind would become if we could live only in this present and a future which will probably be the same. Still there is hope—memory and hope the two things which make this present endurable because they take you out of it. It is appalling the amount of thinking which is being done these days. Deep serious thinking, weighing the value of things and men we have known, casting down some idols and erecting other finer ones in their place. Somewhat the same reaction one gets at a revival meeting and perhaps just as transitory but I think not for our emotions are so much more deeply aroused. About 6:30 Lieut Abbot came out and he changed the poste to a small grotto farther down the valley. As the Boches were shelling the valley he decided to leave the cars near the sap and asked me to walk down with him so that later I could return and direct Kirby to the cave. As we descended the road the shelling stopped and a good wind was blowing which had swept away most of the gas tho it was still quite strong. I began putting on my mask but noticed that the Lieut was not getting his ready and to my question he answered that he had forgotten it and had left it in the car. I was greatly worried about the gas but didn't wish to put on a mask if he didn't so I returned mine to its case and we stalked on thru the gathering darkness, the gas getting stronger as we approached the floor of the valley. The entrance to the cave was blocked by a gas curtain but even inside the doctors and brancardiers were wearing their masks and when they saw that we had none they threw up their hands in consternation and assured us that our foolishness would be the death of us. Coming from a doctor this had great weight with me and I sincerely hoped that the Lieut would accept the mask which they offered him but he refused and we trudged back up the hill—silently for I was, I believed, staring death in the face and even making a grimace. After the Lieut had gone I showed Kirby the cave and we tried to sleep but he got a call about 10 and I one at 11:30. When my call came it was raining and blacker than sin so when I overtook a kitchen going toward Crouy I offered the Sergt a lift as I thot he would know the road. He seemed much surprised when [I told him] that we came up here in the day time. It is rather exposed till one gets in the valley and even then one dare not smoke a cigarette outside the cave. At Crouy I got Deak, who was still sitting up gossiping with Pete to show me the way to Pont Archer. We got back to Crouy about four A.M.

Sat. Sept. 14. Have been in Crouy for the last two days with nothing much to do except help reinforce one of the cellars. We lugged heavy beams for blocks and then tugged and pushed at them till they were in position. Personally I don't believe the work on the Pyramids was any harder but the cave is now "bien solide" and last night bore up bravely under the impact of a shell which struck the corner.

Our division attacked this morning and advanced 3 kilos by hard fighting. They were forced to stop as the division on our right only got 150 yrds. As the division to our left advanced 5 kilos the attack took a pivot movement which is evidently not desired.

Old Jerry is lambasting the roads in his best style clear from [illeg.] to Soissons. I went out to Pont Rouge which is our relay poste and then to the 169th poste but there was little shelling and nothing eventful happened. Later I went out to Vauverry where the Lieut found me and took me again to the 169th. This second visit had plenty of thrills as the big shells were dropping all around the poste and it was a matter of keeping your car ready to go and yourself ready to flatten out in the mud. There were two gray haired Red Cross men at the 169th when I got there who had very recently come from Paris and were on the Front for the first time. They were extremely interested in everything especially the shells and it was difficult to restrain them from poking their heads out of the dug out the moment a shell fell. This is very bad practice as an éclat from a big shell travels a good distance and still retains it[s] killing force. I had a friend who was killed by an éclat from a shell which fell over a 100 yrds away. These old (43 or 45 I should say) are the funniest and the most annoying persons in the world. They load up their Ford with hot chocolate & cigarettes at Crouy and then proceed to make the postes but usually get lost and are found headed straight for the trenchs. It is annoying to have to give directions when a road is being shelled. Ted Larabee who has acquired a violent dislike for the younger of the two recently brought him in from the 169th. The road was being shelled and the man crouched low trying to hide himself behind the tin [illeg.]. Finally he demanded why in blankety blank the cars weren't provided with a steel shield which would protect the driver. Ted assuming what nonchalance he was able replied—"Oh this is nothing but I do hope those birds don't start using their water shells—they're frightful they scald one to death you know." Which yarn was promptly accepted as the truth and I imagine his communique to Homeville spoke of the villainy of the Boche in using "water-shells." Being new to the Front they have not yet acquired that supreme hatred for the Germans that a more experienced man has and they often cause the poilus to criticise them severly for giving so much of their chocolate & cigarettes to the Boches. After ducking shells for a half hour or more at the 169th I finally got my car loaded between shells and I tore down the road for Pont Rouge & Crouy, how that bus did travel.

Sun. Sept. 15. The work is heavy and we are kept going. Pont Rouge (Red Bridge and well named) has developed into a very thrilling place. The small yard of the farm where we park the cars is simply packed with shell holes and big ones at that. It is at this point that the one big road branches into four smaller ones and naturally consistent shelling will hamper all traffic going in four directions. Men and horses are continually being struck just in front of the poste and on a moonlight night it is a rare sight to watch the "charioteers" (men driving small mule carts which carry machine gun ammunition) race their mules across the very dangerous stretch. As they come in flocks and the mules become panicky there is boundless confusion and numerous spills. Four of them were killed (men & mules) on the road today just at the gate of our farm yard. An old white horse who has been wounded sometime[s] roams like a phantom up and down the road and thru the fields. Why he has not been killed is a dark deep mystery but somehow he always decides to change his position just before a shell lands. When the shelling is brisk he needs must be on the jump but despite his wound which has lamed him he is equal to the task. We are betting as to the length of his stay with us and will be sorry indeed to see him go for he has become an institution, a kind of good omen, an albatross if you will and we always call encouraging words to him when we meet him. Thank heaven he's a *white* horse else, I greatly fear, one of us would prove the ancient mariner when he suddenly appears at night blocking the road.

Kirby came in from [illeg.] today greatly excited his heart filled with conflicting emotions—hatred and pride. It seems that Kirby was seen crossing the plateau and the Boche tried their best to get him following him with shells from Vauverry to the very gates of the poste. Naturally enough he is angry for having such continuous scares thrown into him but also he is a bit puffed up to think that he was the sole object of the attention of a hun battery or say two guns. As for me I will readily forego such an honor.

Deak pulled a good one on the Lieut tonight. As Deak was

coming in from 169th today and the road was being heavily shelled and tho Deak collected a puncture in each rear wheel (he *claims* éclats did it), he didn't tarry to fix them but came in on the rims. When the Lieut heard of this he was greatly vexed and wanted to know why it was *Deak* should run the chances of ruining two rear wheels. Deak's reply was, "Lieut I considered stopping and repairing those punctures but I looked at those shells and I said 'Lyman don't be a damn fool Uncle Sam has millions of rear wheels and you have only one life.'" Tho the Lieut had been quite angry Deak's story provoked a smile and nothing more was said. Surely the gift of gab is a rare gift, had I been in Deak's place I would not have known how to so cleverly state that I was *too scared* to stop.

Mon. Sept. 16 In barracks. They have always shelled the town here but lately they have been improving their range and today they scored a bull's eye by placing one full in the road just in front of the GBD. Fortunately the only victim was Abbot's car whose body looks mighty like a potato grater now. The grub is rotten and not even in sufficient quantities. Bill C. when criticised by Abbot for grumbling made the epic remark that if he were fed like a dog he would act like a dog.

Continued in Volume Two

BOOK TWO

Tues. Sept. 17. Due to the increased number of German "visitors" in town I moved my stretcher into the other cave which is stronger being protected by a wall. I believe strongly in the proverb "God helps those who help themselves" and if God pulls me thru this war I'll have the satisfaction of knowing that I helped all I could. At times I am a fatalist but even this does not alter my views except that I believe that Fate needs more help than God does.

They say that the Yanks have met with a reverse but I don't believe it, tho I am uncertain why such a rumor should start unless there is some truth. Still with these Frenchmen who love just to talk one must expect anything. They say also that we are soon to be relieved. I doubt this rumor too but not as much as the American one because I *want* to be relieved. You can make a man believe anything if he wants that thing. Three of our cars are on detached service with the 5th division which is on our right. I do hope we pull out of here soon—then for a long repos and a quite sector. Wouldnt St. Clement seem like Heaven? Besides the physical fatigue of war there is a mental strain which is the most wearing thing in the world.

Wed. Sept. 18. While making an evacuation to Pont Archer my car broke down in Soissons and I had to telephone to Crouy for a car to take my load. It is a very difficult matter to get a call thru to any point as the telephone men are so fearful of spies. It took me three quarters of an hour to convince the officer in charge that I was really what I pretended to be. After I had convinced them the non-coms invited me to eat at their mess an invitation which I eagerly excepted for these men live well and our own food is so rotten. Googins found me just as I finished supper and took my blessés while Beech fixed my car and we returned to Crouy. From Crouy I went to Pont Rouge, then to Vauverry where severe coughing kept me from getting more than 15 minutes' sleep. Out to [illeg.] about four where I couldn't sleep because of cramped quarters.

Thurs. Sept. 19. Some wounded came in at 6 this morning just as the shells started coming over the top of the dug out. Fortunately most of them land in the field the other side of the road but it is remarkable how close they come to the top of the cave. After leaving the poste I had not gone 150 yards when I hit a shell hole and bounced out of that into an abandoned camion. The impact caused my front wheels to stick in their original position and I struck that camion three times before the assis jumped out and gave the wheels a kick which put them straight. After this I had to drive very slowly and keep her carefully "dead ahead" for the steering gear was practically useless. The shells had raked the road and near Vauverry they had caught a convoy of charioteers—what a mess! Arriving at Crouy I was overjoyed to learn that we were being relieved and would start for Soissons in the afternoon. We reached Soissons by 5 and spent the night in the big hospital which is pretty well "shot up."

Note—The following two days were overlooked when copying from my original diary.*

Sun. Sept. 15. The attack isn't going so famously tho there are a considerable number of prisoners. The terrain is quite hilly and the rain makes the tanks useless, besides the Germans are strongly intrenched and our division tired. The prisoners average as well as our men and seem confident that Germany still can make a good fight. Some are cocky enough to maintain that Germany will win yet which is a very impolitic remark for a Boche prisoner to make. The Americans attacked in Lorraine yesterday, all by themselves and are doing splendidly.

Mon. Sept. 16. More attacks but our division is pretty well tired out and we are due for "repose" soon. They are not losing so many men but are simply "fagged out" and this is no sector for a "fagged" division. A Boche brought down a "sausisse" today, it fell in flames making quite a gorgeous sight. At 10 I went out to Pont Rouge which was being shelled quite heavily but it was

---

*This note and the following two entries are inserted in the middle of the September 19 entry in the recopied diary. It is impossible to determine the exact relationship between these entries and the earlier ones for the same dates, as several pages are missing from the original version of the diary at this point. (A number of September entries were given August dates in the original version; Bowerman corrected the dates when he recopied the diary, and apparently he had some difficulty in doing so.)

quite when I got a call to Vauverry and [illeg.]. As the loaded cars go by Pont Rouge they generaly don't stop but merely yell the name of the poste they left. This necessitates having a guard at Pont Rouge who must be where he can hear them yell, a rotten job. When Hub is guard you usually have to stop & go down in the dugout.

Friday. Sept. 20. The Section left early this morning. The destination is unknown but some whisper wisely that it is Flanders. I shall believe it when we get there and not before. As I had an evacuation to make I left before the Section and joined them later at Clermont. Spent the night at Dury.

Sat. Sept. 21. Still in France but are headed north* so perhaps the wiseacres were right. We passed thru Amiens which we had skirted in our trip South last May. Tho we were unable to see the famous cathedral the rest of the city is not badly damaged. Spent night in Bourbourg.

Sun. Sept. 22. An early start for Loon-Plage where our "repose" is to be spent. They had us all keyed up by telling us that we were to live in a huge Casino just 50 yards from the North Sea and only 15 kilos from Dunkirk. Arrived "by the sea" and the cars unloaded, everyone clamored to be shown to their room in the Casino but we had been deceived again. We are to sleep *at* the Casino not in it. If they had said we were going to be billeted in a "chateau" we would not have been "taken in" but that word Casino fooled us. What a dreary, desolate place this is, and there is more sand than the Sahara contains. The sand is everywhere and in everything, our hair, our eyes, our food our beds and so deep in the road that it took the entire Section to get the kitchen trailer any wheres near the shed where we are to sleep. Well any way it's some change from Crouy, and they claim that a change is a fine tonic. Just before we turned in Lieut Abbot told us that no one would be allowed to go to Dunkirk! Gone is another hope and the final one. We went to bed 37 thoroughly disillusioned men.

Mon. Sept. 23; Teus. 24. We pass the time mostly by overhauling the cars but some hardy sons go swimming, others go AWOL to Dunkirk and the rest of us curse the ever present sand.

---

*This movement of troops to the north was in preparation for the last Battle of Ypres, September 28–October 2. Foch hoped to sever the main rail connection between advanced German units in Belgium and their sources of supply.

Wed. Sept. 25. We have orders to leave here tomorrow morning at four. Just our luck three days working all day on our cars and they call it a "repose." We are going up near Ypres.

Thurs. Sept. 26. On the road again at 5. Pass thru Dunkirk a curious old town and spent the night at Rexpoede.

Frid. Sept. 27. Up at 3 bells and on our way by four. They must be in a hurry to get us wherever we're going. We crossed the Belgian frontier at Kroesbeck and spent the night at Beveren. One can buy nearly everything here—chocolate, cigarettes, matches, bread & ginger cookes which taste like honest to goodness American ginger bread. Herbie Hoover sure did relieve Belgium and now these pirates are reciprocating by "relieving" us. This Flemish tongue is the absolute limit and I can't see how they ever understand themselves.

Sat. Sept. 28. At 2 A.M. six of us were called out to take brancardiers and medical equipment to the Front as the Belgians are to attack and our division is to follow in support until the Belgians are through and then we are to take over. Just before dawn we stopped at a cross roads around which the artillery, infantry, and cavalry reserves were gathered. The sausisses were already up and the Belgian and British batteries were laying down a terrific barrage to prepare the way for the attack troops who were to "go over" at dawn. The country is perfectly flat and as we were stopped in the center of a semi-circle of trenches we could see clearly what was perhaps the most awe-inspiring and splendid spectacle which we shall ever be priviledged to see. "Arrivés" & "departs"; red white and green star shells shooting at all angles across the blue-gray horizon; a munition dump burning with a huge dull red glow which was reflected in a patch of high hung pinkish dawn clouds and all these kaleskopic colors blazing forth amongst a terrible, soul shiv[er]ing roar as the thousand guns sent their shells screeching toward the lines where they fell with a terrifying sickening "crump" burned a bright hole in the night, and added their smoke to the haze which made the rising sun blood red. We were rudely awakened from our trance (for such sights as these have rare hypnotic power) by a shell which came screaming towards us and as we threw ourselves flat exploded nearby sending a shower of dirt and small stones upon us. The shells had been going over our heads to explode harmlessly in a field behind us and we had not noticed them but this was a different matter and we moved our cars up the road. There are not many "abris" (dug-outs) in this country and what few there are, are far apart and built of sand bags or cement above the ground. Generally one jumps into a shell hole and prays that nothing else "jumps" in with you. The Lieut, who had gone off to Headquarters to locate our postes, returned and began guiding two cars to each of the three postes. Larkin and I were assigned to the 167th and arrived at their station shortly after daylight where we stayed about an hour glad to be partially sheltered from the rain which was drizzling down miserably and completing the picture of utter desolation which lay around us. The terrain is without doubt the most desolate God forsaken portion of this earth. A vertibale no-man's land 15 miles wide filled with shell holes, water, blackened tree stumps and demolished concrete blockhouses. Across this waste there is but one path—a sickening pretense of a road which winds its shell holed, muddy, splashy way past caved in trenches, water filled gun emplacements and huge mine [?] holes which resemble volcanic lakes. Along this road a whole army was attempting to cross and the mud covered men and wagons bore witness to the difficulties of the passage. No less the dead and dying horses who lined the road having succumbed to the fearful toil. As the division was following in support of the Belgians we soon left the first station and began slowly, tediously picking our way toward the East, where lay the lines and victorious Belgians. We managed at last to outdistance the wagons & artillery of the Division but the roads were almost impassable and by 1:30 we had not yet arrived at the new station. We wondered how we could ever evacuate wounded over this road without killing them. It was the utmost the empty Fords could do to keep going forward and all the other "rolling stock" was mired (seemingly for ever) 3 or four kilometers behind us. Our forward journey was at last stopped by a Belgian medécin-chef who commandeered our two cars for the purpose of carrying some of his wounded back to the Field Hospital which lay on the edge of this no man's Land.

   We discharged our load at the Hospital where we reloaded my wounded including an English aviator who had just been shot down. I saw his pilot who had been killed in the fall and evidently had struck his head on the cowl of his machine. His forehead bulged exactly like a young baby's yet the skin was not broken and his features were natural & peaceful. One might think him asleep until one rolled him over a bit and noticed the brains which spilled out of his close fitting leather helmet. After taking my blessés to an evacuation hospital I returned to Ostveterlin [Oostvleteren] where the Section was then billeted and where I spent the night. From what I hear no Belgian ambulance has been able to operate where we had been and their wounded had mostly died.

Sun. Sept. 29. The Section moved to Langemarke [Langemarck] a spot about half way thru the desolated strip. Even up to this point the going was so heavy that only 7 cars got thru today. Langemarke is a splendid example of what the destruction has been. It was before the war a flourishing little city of 7000 inhabitants today there is not one single stone atop another even the streets have disappeared and the Cathedral, once the toast of the town is now a mere mound of light colored earth filled with small ravines by the ever falling rain. Our billet is a ruined Boche blochouse which is filled with [illeg.] corners which offer good protection from the weather if one can squeeze into them. As I sought my cubby hole in the deepening dusk I stumbled over the leg of a half buried Boche which, when morning came, we buried with considerable exertion and no ceremony. During the latter part of the afternoon we had lent ourselves freely to the work at hand carrying stretchers (a back breaking job), tugging our mired caissons and trying to build up the road. As there was no wood available this last was chiefly accomplished by throwing "duds" (unexploded shells) into the holes. It was intensely interesting to watch the artillery horses as they braced their feet against a "dud" tho usually we watched their efforts from a discreet distance. As the kitchen trailer was struck about 2 kilos behind us it was up to someone to go back after "grub." No one volunteered till 8 when the pangs of hunger began gnawing at our vitals and four of us offered to go. The walk was not exciting but it was hard work for the road was packed with convoys. Arrived at the trailer we rousted out the cooks and managed to get a dixie full of potatoes & meat and a large can of water. On our return I fell into about three water filled shell holes, and walked head on into the rear ends of a thousand horses. By the time we reached the blochouse the dirty water soaked sack which we had spread over the "dixie" had become identified with the meat & potatoes but we were all hungry and this was food.

Hank was stuck in a convoy (or rather *the* convoy) about a hundred yards from the pill box and was so tired that the Lieutenant delegated me to relieve him. When I took his car it was 10:30. He had not moved since 6 o'clock he told me and it was not till 5:30 the next morning that the convoy moved and I was able to pull up a 100 yards and out of the road. Hank had taken 22 hours to make one evacuation and this did not include the seven hours which I spent sitting behind his wheel staring at the leaden sky and wondering when this rotten business would have an end.

Mon. Sept. 30. I managed to get a couple hours' sleep after 5:30 but my cubby hole was so small and I was so wet that I feel a hundred years old today. During the day there was plenty of work to be done and the stiffness soon left my joints. About four P.M. orders came for us to move up but the Lieut decided that we could never get the cars thru so we waited till the next day. We fared better today in the way of food and drink for the truck was at last able to get up with us literally dragging the mud covered kitchen trailer behind it. No one ever praises Gil for being a clever truck driver since it is unnecessary as he praises himself, and our praise would make him insufferable but here in the privacy of this diary I can safely say that he showed remarkable pertinacity, endurance and skill in bringing the big Packard over this road. The only water for the coffee came from shell holes which, when they were half emptied often disclosed rather nauseating sights but the general opinion was that boiling [would] kill the germs and any way a bone or two or a horse's hoof wouldn't make Harper's coffee taste any worse. About seven this morning I was awakened by a terrific yelling and I crawled hurredly to the aperture expecting to find us surrounded by Germans who had counter attacked successfully. The furor proved to be nothing more than half the Frenchmen of the division giving chase to a poor enaemic and emancipated hare. The hare was so bewildered by the vast numbers in the chase that he at last fell prey to the stalwart boot of an artillery sergeant but he died a noble and worthy death since he furnished so much relaxation for depressed men.

Teus. Oct. 1. We started forward this morning on our worst trek and it has been an heroic job to get the cars over this last stretch. During one halt old Jerry, who had at last got up his nerve to come over in the day time, arrived just above us 30 strong and intent upon so ruining the convoy that the war would be over before it was straightened out. Fortunately for us the English and

Belgian air men were on the watch and before Jerry could unload he was engaged by an equal number of the enemy. Every man in the convoy had of course immediately crawled under his wagon or in a shell hole but by considerable craning of the neck one could watch the fight and it was a fight well worth watching! Nearly sixty planes going at it directly overhead their heights varying from 100 to 5000 ft. Such a deal of swooping, swerving twisting turning and firing as there was. We wondered that the whole caboodle did not fall and what was most surprising was that of the thousand or more bullets which were fired directly above us not one fell to earth. Jerry got the best of it for two Belgians went down (in control) and two Germans started machine gunning the road tho those who had crawled out from under scattered and no one was hurt.

I do not know if the Allies were outnumbered or not but I should guess yes since they seem to have absolute control of the air along this Front and one rarely sees a German plane in the day time. Speaking of air supremacy the British are the only ones who can boast it with absolute authenticity. The French divide the honors with the Boche and if we ever saw both German and French in the air at one time it was usually said as a joke that one of the two had their schedules mixed. Of course this is overdrawn and unfair to the French but it is true that the French are not supreme in the air of their sectors. As to the Americans we have never seen an American plane nor an American fighting unit so I am unable to judge them. After the brief interlude we proceeded and strange as it may seem everyone was in much better spirits. We passed numerous batteries which had been drawn away from their positions but had been abandoned before reaching the road. Jerry has lost a large number of cannon in this drive as the swampy nature of the ground has made it impossible for him to remove the light pieces which were close to the lines and the big ones tho farther back presented huge difficulties and were generally abandoned. Nearly every cross roads is heavily mined and tho the engineers are supposed to move just behind the attacking waves and discover them and render them harmless still a number have escaped their search to be exploded later by a horse's hoof, a wagon wheel or a foot causing a number of deaths and leaving huge holes some of which could nearly bury a two storied house. Generally the mines are so laid that a piece of wire when pulled or disturbed will detonate them tho often they are timed to explode after a certain number of hours. We saw many Belgians grouped around horses who had been killed or had died of exhaustion from which they carved off large rump or shoulder steaks. The dead are every where over the fields of mud and I saw one lying on his back his head resting on his knapsack the knees drawn up and both arms raised high in the air. I could picture him as he was struck, his friend stopping a moment to make some crude dressing; to place his head upon the knapsack out of the mud then with a word of encouragement to rush after the victorious line so that he might get his bag of Boches and even up the score for his stricken friend. After his comrade had gone a spasm of pain had seized the wounded man he had raised his clenched fists above his head and death coming suddenly had frozen him in this position. After what seemed miles of mud and hours of back breaking pushing and straining we at last reached the edge of this No Man's Land and were once again on good roads among trees and at least the visible remnants of houses. We have a good billet in a long two story house and nearby is a splendid pill box which will shelter us when Jerry's shells land too near. Our postes are only a short distance away tho I suppose we will continue to evacuate to Oostveterlin.

Wed. Oct. 2. Excepting one hurried visit to the pill box last night we slept well and I am much rested. They are going to try and get the truck and kitchen trailer up today but some are giving odds that they don't. At eleven I got a trip with 3 couchés and one assis. They gave me rations for 24 hours and said they would expect me back when I arrived. Russel left with me and we managed to get down in four hours, tho we gave the wounded a fearful shaking up and had to commandeer Frenchmen every little while to help us out of holes. At Oostveterlin we ate and decided to remain all night as it was senseless to make that trip at night when there were 18 cars still at the Section. Later that night eight more cars joined us so that we had half the Section.

Thurs. Oct. 3. The other six cars left at 5:30 as soon as it was light but I stayed behind to help Wiley whose dash had fallen out due to the fearful strain of the road. His car was repaired by 12 and we left but as luck would have it I lost my way and almost collided with the mail cammion. We had received no mail since Crouy and would probably [have] waited two weeks more before they found us so I was overjoyed. Luckily the mail driver knew me and handed over two sacks of mail. Just at the border of No

Man's Land I met the Medécin Divisionaire who told me to get some wounded at the Belgian Field hospital nearby. After transferring the mail sacks to the Divisionaire's car I picked up three couchés at the hospital and returned by a newly found and better road to Oostveterlin where I arrived about 6 and where I found Bal. The hospital at Oostveterlin being so crowded it was necessary to make a trip to [illeg.] where we spent the night.

Frid. Oct. 4. Bulgaria we learn has signed the peace treaty. If this is so Turkey should be the next and then Austria. An intercepted wireless from Constantinople to Berlin states that while Turkey's spirit is still strong her flesh is weak and she cannot hold out much longer. The English to the south are doing splendidly and as soon as we can get up the artillery in this Front we should go ahead into Belgium forcing the Germans to abandon the coast. Surely peace prospects never looked brighter.

Sat. Oct. 5. "Section 585 last night entertained with a reception for some out of town friends. The receiving line, which was formed in the chic summer house on their estate included all the present members."—Town Topics. Jerry decided to ruin the pill box which he had been forced to leave behind and tho he showered 310s at it a good part of the afternoon and night he never came closer than a hundred yrds. We were, of course, all crowded into the blockhouse and could see the shells landing by looking thru a small window. Those 310's had a nasty explosion, showering the earth 30 ft high and causing our pill box to rock and tremble like a raft on the ocean. The Germans have very cleverly built them thinner in the rear than in front and on the sides this is done so they may not be so impregnable to German fire if captured by the enemy. Lieut Jamou had notions that this abri had [been] built for his own special needs but he soon got over this idea and we even usurped the armchair which he had brought from the house.

"Rumor" says we are to move again but will not say where. This evening we all gathered around a corking fire in one of the less-ventilated rooms in the house and had a good old time "meeting." Songs, stories, reminiscences, prophecies and Deak's own "rip and tear" of songs and stories beguiled away the time and made us forget for the moment the sad reality of war.

Sun. Oct. 6. A battery came in today and took over our house and our pill box so we "shoved off" and brought up in a ruined house with no abri about 100 yrds from the crossing of five roads. We can expect a goodly amount of shelling and bombing in this location. This P.M. there was some desultory firing and Jimmy received a "petite blessure" [little wound] in the shape of a small "éclat" thru his upper arm. Lucky devil that he is for this will mean a month in the hospital. Hank bears a torn sweater and a black and blue shoulder as a result of the same burst and he is grumbling like a gouty old man because he wasn't wounded badly enough to be evacuated or sport a wound stripe. After this episode we commenced work on a dug-out but most of the fellows' enthusiasm for a cave waned as the time elapsed after the shelling so we didn't progress very far. However the rest of us had the affair far enough along that it sheltered us when the avions came over and bombed the surrounding country. When one noticed who used the cave tonight they saw the faces of several who had said during the day that they didn't want a dug out.

Mon. Oct. 7. Germany, Austria and Turkey demand a peace discussion and an armistice so we heard this A.M. from a French dispatch rider. He rode by as we were busy on the abri and stopping told us that there was no need of building a dug out now as an armistice had probably already been signed—and then he told about the three enemy states suing for peace. At his first words we all dropped our various implements and had rushed over to hear all the good news. The rider had just finished his talk when Jerry dropped a shell or two in a field nearby—the rider sadly cranked up and sped away while we silently returned to the abri, and began working again nor did anyone break the silence till Bill C. leaned on his shovel and said quietly, "If an armistice *has* been signed those damned Boches don't know it so let's finish the dug-out." I know we'll not have an armistice and peace won't come for 6 months at least but it shows that Germany knows she's licked and is trying to "git from under." The Kaiser and his crowd are trying to "pass the buck"—Germany I believe knows well that Turkey and Austria are going to quit.

During the first three days after we had crossed the "No man's Land" the division, or at least that part of it which had been able to get up was rationed by airplane. The avions would circle around at a low altitude and would, upon signal, drop sacks containing bread, chocolate, jam and "iron" rations (billy beef). One day, are food being low, we waved a shirt at a low flying Belgian plane which was nearby. Seeing our signal the aviator flew at a very low heigth directly over us. Just as he was above us he stretched his hand out over the fusilage and dropped—not the sack of food we expected—but two young bombs which exploded about 50 yrds from us and among the cars. His miss would have been highly censured by the German military but received nothing but an exclamation of surprise from us. We had heard tell of Germans flying captured planes and here was one as proof. Later he brought down three "saucisses" one after the other and was soon after himself brought down and killed.

Teus. Oct. 8. Worked all day on the abri and completed it. It may be a good place to go when you're being shelled but personally I'd rather stay out of it. There was too many builders each of whom had a different idea as to the scientific way of building a dug out.

Steve and I were on duty at #553 last night and since there were neither trips nor enemy avions we enjoyed a good sleep. The doctors and most of the brancardiers sleep in a large pill box while the s.s.u. and one or two brancardiers sleep in a camouflaged tent. It was while sleeping in this tent that Steve and Bob Larkin heard a bomb falling near them and died several horrible deaths before the thing landed just outside and failed to explode. Harper and Crane have been ousted from their positions as cooks and their places have been taken by Bill C. and Perk. Bill can't boil water but he has set to work with great spirit on the dirty pots and pans and besides he's big enough to "clean up" on any one who is rash enough to criticise Perk's cooking.

Wed. Oct. 9. The avions came over again last night but no one went to the new dug out tho the bomb fell fairly close and they used their machine guns unsparingly on the various encampments [illeg.] around the cross roads. We are all anxiously waiting for the attack after which it is expected that we will leave and go on a long "repos" which has been due us for such a time.

While a bunch of us were sitting around a little open fire in a sort of "lean-to" a young Frenchman came to the door and asked anxiously if we had today's or yesterday's paper. He seemed eager for the news of the reported armistice and expressed the hope that it would be signed at midnight tonight as was rumored. His face was so pale and wore such a worried looked that we should have sensed the pathos of his condition but being young we did not but laughed to scorn his hope that an armistice would be signed. Tho we had no paper he seemed reluctant to leave so we made a place for him among us and listened to his story which he told readily as one wishing sympathy—He had been, he said (he spoke English perfectly) in the war four years during which time he had been in the signal service and three times wounded. He was not yet 26 and was engaged to a beautiful young Parisienne whom he was to marry the moment the war was ended. This very morning in the midst of rumors of peace and an armistice at midnight orders had come for him to report to an infantry battallion which was new in the lines and (as we knew he said) was to attack at four tomorrow morning. Now as you can see he continued if they sign the armistice tonight there will be no attack tomorrow or ever again. This he repeated either because he wished us to grasp the full significance of it or because it held so much for him—life love and happiness. Somehow we all became thotful after he had ceased talking and no one spoke. Each was trying to frame into words the thots of sympathy and encouragement we wished so much to convey to him. Tho he was already overdue at battallion head quarters he seemed loth to leave us sensing as he must have the sympathy of his listeners. Finally however he rose almost painfully to his feet, his face twitched nervously and his hands pecked at his handkerchief as he held it after blowing his nose violently. No one spoke as he stood there trying to master his emotions and regain his self control which he had momentarily lost but as he walked slowly thru the door we called our [illeg.] word to him "Good luck old man." What a pitifully inadequate expression of the emotions we felt as he left us. Here was a real trajedy in the making. He was praying against hope that an armistice would be signed and he was certain of death if it came any time after midnight.

I relieved Bal at the 167 poste near Staden. They have a splendid pill box for an abri so one may quite ignore any shell up to a 210. The Captain of the 167 is a splendid chap—a fatherly sort who treats his men well and is respected and loved in return. Usually when "en poste" we eat with the non-coms but here we eat with the medecin chef and what is more—eat well.

Thurs. Oct. 10. The poste above here was shelled quite a bit last night so I had to take a tire out to Howie as his car was badly broken up by a 77. Another Hun in an Allied plane tonight

[shot] down three more observation balloons. We thot the Boche very clever till we learned that he had used underhanded methods. The air is supposed to be the only element in which warfare remains chivalrous but the Germans are Germans whether in their U Boats or their air craft. I wouldn't swear that the Allies don't employ the same methods but of course it would not be proper to publish the fact among the civilians. It is rumored that the Kaiser has abdicated in favor of his second son.* If he has or does I imagine the war will soon be ended.

Frid. Oct. 11. "Our troops, the communiqué states are successful on all fronts." This is gratifying if true, but one never trusts a communiqué. Foch says that he has not yet had his battle which augurs some more huge attacks which will surpass all previous affairs tho I had thot that we had seen some pretty big "stunts." Foch at last seems to have sufficient reserves and is handling them in a masterful fashion. If every division has been on the go as much as ours it is no wonder that he has been able to attack in such a quick succession. There is to be another attack here soon but I doubt if our division will start the "show."

Sat. Oct. 12. Following a successful "coup de main" in which our division captured a farm to be used later as a "point de départ" ("jumping off place") for the larger attack the Boches shelled the back area violently, putting a young barrage around the poste here (167th) which lasted from 10 P.M. till 5 this morning. From 10 till midnight high explosives were used and from then on a mixture of H.E. and gas. This is done to prevent one hearing the gas shells which have a peculiar explosion. Altho the gas shells were not heard we soon received notice of them via our nostrils and immediately put on our masks. About 2:30 the captain informed me that two men had been gassed and I was to take them in. As I came to the entrance of the pill box I could hear the shells swishing down the street across which I must go to get my car which was parked in a shed across the street. I was reminded at once of the cave at Gare Ramée and did not see how one was going to cross the street with a whole skin but it had to be done so I screwed my courage to the sticking point and dashed madly to my car. It being cold weather I had jacked up the right hand wheel of the car that I might start it more easily and it was neces-

---

*Kaiser Wilhelm II abdicated nearly a month after this entry.

sary to let down the jack after starting the engine. I can only thank Heaven that some things when performed often enough become habits and can be done unconsciously else I never would have gotten the car out of the shed for I was too frightened. I can not remember now starting the car or removing the jack but I some way did and drove across to the door of the pillbox where my two "gasés" were very hurriedly placed in the ambulance. I had discovered in driving across the street that the night was too dark to permit me to see thru my gas mask so I removed it tho the gas was strong and I never expected to reach the hospital alive. The Captain shouted to me as I swung away from the pill box to wear my mask but I was already on my way and going fast. At the top of the hill I missed a gun by a miracle and opened "her" up some more for the shells were falling for a kilometer along the road and I knew my only hope was to get thru quickly. Once a shell (a H.E. fortunately) fell so close to me that I was blinded by the gas and as a consequence I came within an ace of running off the embankment. Arrived at the hospital I told the doctor that I had driven thru a kilometer of gas without a mask and feared that I might be gassed tho I only felt sick at my stomach. The doctor told me to lie down and stay quite but I said that I was expected to return to Station so he advised me to go to our quarters and have another car sent out. On the way back I ran off the road and came a cropper in a "310" hole so I left the car and proceeded on foot to the Section where I awakened Pete and asked for a relief relating what the doctor had said. Pete sent Harp to the hospital to tell Googins to replace me at Staten [Staden] but before he left the Lieut awoke and told me to go with him to look at my car. After considerable exertion we got the car on the road again and I was told to replace Googins at the GBD for there would not be any calls probably and I would be able to rest. Just before Googins left (he did not know the road to Staten and was to follow Wasilik who had come down from the 169th above Staten) a call came in for a car from the hospital so I told Googins that if I had to be on my way anyhow I might as well return whence I had come which I did Wasilik following me. As we approached nearer the poste we saw that the shelling had not abated. About a 100 yrds from the blochouse my car peetered out on me and I couldn't get it to going again. While I was fussing around a bit Was drove up along side and shouted "Good Lord man we can't stop here, it's a regular barrage" and as he started to pull away I jumped on the running board of his car and rode to the pill box where I reported the accident to the car and told the captain that I would repair my car as soon as it got light. I found a poor little hound dog hiding under a house today and because he looked so forlorn and homeless I adopted him. He was evidently left by the Germans since he answers "kommt heir" better than "viens-ici" but he's just a dog and isn't responsible for being owned by a German. Soon after finding my dog I got another trip and went in for relief. My blessé happened to be an artillery man who had been wounded during the night. I was greatly pleased when one of the brancardiers took my arm and introduced me to the artillery man by saying rather proudly "this fellow drove thru that gas last night without a mask." The wounded man made me feel even prouder when he said "yes I saw him go down the road thru that bombardment as I lay in a small dug out next my gun" and he shook his head in a way which told impressively how bad he thot the shelling was. I don't expect to get a croix for this but if I did I wouldn't feel half so please[d] as I did when those two old veterans remarked about my ride. Pete has received notice of his commission and he is leaving tonight accompanied by Pop who is going "en perm." Gil and the Lieut drove to the Parc and I took Larabee's car there for repairs. Gil dropped off at a hospital near the park to have his teeth fixed so the Lieut and I returned in his car. It was raining like the devil, we had no top and to cap the climax we broke our "fish rod" in the middle of "No Man's Land" tho we managed to make it on to L'Etat Major where we spent the night, the lieut inside the pill box with the officers and yours truly outside in an ambulance, one blanket to cover my poor shivering rain soaked body.

Sun. Oct. 13. Lieut Abbot and I hunted over several acres and finally found enough wire to fasten up the "fish rod" temporarily and we started blithely for home. The going however was too heavy and we broke down completely half way to the barracks. Fortunately there was a rail head near the barracks and as we had broken down near the rail road the Lieut jumped an engine telling me to wait till he returned with John Beecher. The Lieut had phoned from the Etat Major to the Parc telling them to send us the needed part by one of our cars and "Crest" Lynch arrived on the scene shortly after the Lieut had left. After a great deal of work under trying circumstances we at last repaired the fish rod and met Beech just as he was leaving the Barracks. Abbot was much pleased as he had not thot that we could repair the car and had believed it necessary to send it to the Parc. There are tanks, big ones, going up tonight so I imagine the attack will come tomorrow. We are on reserve now until after the attack.

Wed. Oct. 16. The Section left Westrosbeck [Westrozebeke] today with Staten as a destination. Three cars (mine included) left before the others as we were to go on poste. At Staten Jamon came to me and said "The 168th poste is somewhere in Staten. Find it." I hunted for the best part of two hours then I ran across Jamon again and he was wild because I had not yet located the regiment's dressing station. After a thousand shrugs and grimaces he ordered me to follow him and *he* would find it soon enough. Another hour passed and Jamon the Great having failed in the quest he evidently decided that it wan't there so he told me to proceed to Hoogled[e] and expend my Holmesque tendencies in locating the 169th. I surely was tickled when "that miserable little worm" (as Ted calls him) couldn't succeed where I had failed. Hooglede is a smaller town and the medecin chef of the 169 hadn't a good chance to hide his poste where no one could find it so I soon located it and began hunting "quelque chose à manger" [something to eat].

The engineers discovered a mine under a crossing in the middle of the town and succeeded in unloading it before it blew half the division to Kindom Come. They had piled the bomb[s] by the side of the road and one look at them is enough to make one darned careful at crossroads. The amount of powder they put in these mines is appalling—from 5 to 10 of the largest airplane bombs and French torpedoes. A young infantryman came in the poste this afternoon. He had entered a dugout and in doing so had stepped on a loose board which exploded a young shell. His face and hands were burned badly and black from the powder and he suffered intense pain as well as great mental anguish to think that God permitted such swinish pigs to live as those Germans are. Bradley came out this evening. Bradley is peculiar—in barracks he is generally disliked but everyone who has ever been on poste with him says he's a very likeable chap.

Thurs. Oct. 17. There was an evacuation to make so I took the call and after taking my man to the hospital rejoined the section as it was moving to a small farm outside of Hooglede. There was a perfectly good unoccupied farm house but we could not sleep in it as the engineers had notified us that the house was undoubtedly mined. No one seemed willing to take a chance after seeing those bombs at Hooglede so we slept in our cars. Everyone went to bed congratulating themselves and each other that at last we could sleep undisturbed by bombs for there was nothing here worth bombing. The moon shone brightly however and a low flying Boche espied our cars parked about the farm and let go a few at us. I was awakened by éclats striking my car but thot at first they were from an anti aircraft gun. When I discovered that they came from an air bomb I hastily climbed out of my car and lay as close to Mother Earth as conditions would permit. Abbot and Jamon had a fortunate escape when an éclat passed thru the small hut they occupied but failed to touch them.

Frid. Oct. 18. Early this morning the Section left for Coolscamp while Emery and I drove off to Gitz [Gits] which is at present our ravitaillement base. After waiting all day we learned that the train had been unavoidably detained by circumstance of the war and would not arrive at Gitz till one A.M. Emery had run across some old friends and was helping them destroy a [illeg.] or two of Pinard so I looked about for a place to sleep. As Gitz had been a German rail head there was considerable booty remaining tho huge quantities of materiel had been destroyed and as the Boches knew that the French would undoubtedly also use this as a rail head I was quite positive that the Hun would come a bombing as soon as night fell and that it would be wise to find a sort of abri. The only abri in town was an "Unterstand" or pill box which the Germans had built near the railroad crossing so I went inside and was none too soon as the floor space was rapidly filling up. The various Frenchmen and myself had finally settled ourselves as comfortably as damp straw on a cement floor would permit when a gendarme stuck a four foot moustache in the door and warned us that we had better vacate as the Germans had mined the place and an incautious step would [be] apt to send us all to Kingdom Come. I should have voted for vacating but before I had time to cast my ballot several poilus began searching the walls and floor with their search lights to discover if possible the wires which set off the mine. I also aided in the search being loath to declare myself afraid to sleep where a Frenchman dared to sleep and gingerly removed the straw upon which I had been lying. Neither the Frenchmen's search nor my own revealed a hidden wire and after dutifully condemning all Germans to eternal damnation we laid down again either to sleep or, as in my case to pretend to sleep. To some the fact that we failed to find a wire might have been soothing but to one of my vivid imagination, the absence of wires proved nothing except that the Germans had timed the bombs and had not meant that they should be exploded by wires. Had I not been so tired this disturbing thot would have kept off sleep till dawn came but as it was I dozed off after an hour or so. It is peculiar how pride helps courage—had I been the lone occupant of the bloc house I should have left immediately but there were 6 or 7 others and no one dared show the others that he was frightened. This is somewhat analogous to the discussion is a suicide a brave man or a coward? Personally I believe he is both or neither rather insane and the truest form of bravery is the courage a man shows when he's frightened to death. I am sure the big fear of all of us was before we got into this thing that we would be afraid. Courage as the world sees it is to my mind an absence of either nerves or a realization of danger, true courage is the force of will begat by pride or an extreme compassion which enables one to do things in which he realizes the danger. We have one man (or had) in the Section who was yellow when it came to a fist fight yet he appeared completely ob[liv]ious to the danger of exploding shells. The Section's only explanation of this paradox was that the man was nutty and all evidence sustained their verdict. I have seen an infantry man who has been over the top a number of times with a company remark on his courage in crossing a shelled area alone, he and countless other unthinking doughboys would give us a lot more credit could they but occupy the front seat of a Ford in our place while driving at night without a single light and totally alone over a badly shelled road.

Sat. Oct. 19. My fears had no foundation for I was still intact when morning came evidently the Boches were too intent on destroying the goods and stores they were abandoning to give a thot to mining the dug out. We secured our quota of ravitaillement after some difficulty and left Gitz at 7. Emery had spent a too riotous night and needed a pick-me-up so we stopped in a little town and after a drink of rum Emery filled the radiator with water while I rummaged around in the houses adjacent to the estaminet. In a narrow dark ill smelling hall way of a little cottage I almost stumbled upon the body of a young Boche. His left leg was severed from his body except for one lone ligament and he had been dead long enough to present a very unwholesome sight. While I stood studying the body trying to reconstruct the scenes which had led to his being wounded and his death three little Belgian children, two boys and a girl all about 7 yrs old, came in the doorway and espied the German. In stead of being frightened or awed by the presence of death in a rather hideous form they laughed clapped their hands and danced about the corpse only stopping occaisonally to exclaim "Ah le sale boche" (Oh the dirty German). I watched in amazement and a realization of what this scene meant. Surely Belgium has suffered when her little children can laugh at a sight like this. As I left the room they scampered out after me doubtless afraid even of a German rendered so impotent by death. Emery and I found the Section at Coolscamp and that afternoon at four we moved to Isgehem [Iseghem] where we found quarters and a generous welcome in a nunnery or convent. On our way to Isgehem we passed through a little town all gaily bedecked with French & Belgian flags where I again witnessed a confirmation of what Belgium has been thru. This time a peasant was wheeling a barrow thru the principal street and in the barrow was the bloated body of a German, dead I should say three or four days. The body was wired in a sitting position by the neck, his arms trailed in the dust and with each side ways tilt of the barrow the bloated head with its pig-eyes lolled from side to side as if in obeisance to the crowds of men women and children who lined the street. Surely, thot I, here is a sight to make a woman shudder and turn away but tho I watched closely not a person gave the least evidence of disgust but laughed and cheered.

Thurs. Oct. 24. Moved from Isgehem to Imelgem [Emelghem] a short distance away. All the towns are decorated as if for a holiday. And indeed it is a holiday for them and everyone seems supremely happy tho just a trifle dazed at the realization of such long felt hopes. As we are the first Americans they have seen they are extremely interested in us and crowd about us as if we were trained bears. At Imelgem we are also quartered in a convent so that we believe we are fated to live in a religious environment.

Sun. Oct. 27. Leave Imelgem for Ostrosbeck [Oostroosebeke]. I go on poste at the G.B.D.

Mon. 28. Had one trip last night and on my way back stopped in Ingelmunster to fix my fan[?]. An M.P. was stationed on the corner where I had stopped and as we chatted it developed that he used to live in St. Anthony tho I had not known him. I was very glad to see him and we spent a long time gossiping about matters of interest. I understand from him that three divisions of Americans are coming up into this sector shortly. Bulgaria has signed an armistice they say and we all believe that Austria and Turkey will soon follow suit.

The G.B.D. moves up to Vive St. Bavon. "Crest" Lynch felt prosperous and bought four hens from an old Belgian for 20 francs. We were all keyed up over a chicken dinner when calls came for all of us and we were forced to leave the "poulets" to the tender mercies of the G.B.D. I was sent out to the 167th poste which "Bal" had previously described as a "mauvais" spot and a place which could only be approached on your belly. Unwittingly I drove my car past the danger line and tho I was instructed to return it to a hiding place down the road and return to the poste on foot, I disproved Bal's statement.

Mon. Oct. 28. . . . There are many wounded civilians coming into the postes these days. As the Germans retreat the Belgians are forced either to retreat with them and remain in safety or stay on their farms and run their chances until the French come up. This is of course more desirable as the Belgians have had enough of Boche rule but each farm is for a time exactly between the lines and catches both fires. The French explain their willingness to stay on their farms by saying that in '14 the Germans advanced so swiftly that they used very little artillery and the Belgians believe the French will advance just as swiftly which of course they do not.

Teus. Oct. 29. Assigned to the Medecin Divisionaire quarters at Ingelmunster in order to "chauffeur" the old man around to the different postes. The old man is such a stoic and so foolhardy that I was quite perturbed today when, as we were driving to the "Colonel" beyond Zult[e] (our newest post) he advised me to drive fast since we were continually in sight of the enemy and this particular road was badly shelled. Needless to say I "stepped on her" for conditions are indeed bad when the M-D will pay any attention to them. Returning from the "Colonel" (Battalion head quarters) the M-D & the medecin chef of the 167th who had accompanied us left me in a little town and after telling me to await them there started on foot for some unknown place. In the middle of Main St. the Germans had exploded a mine, the largest I have ever seen and amply able to hold a large two storied house. Near this mine hole some Frenchmen were rummaging about in a deserted and badly dilapidated estaminet. They called to me to join them in quaffing a discovered liquor so I went over being sure that I would see the M-D returning down the street he had left by as there were no other cross streets. After waiting a considerable time I was startled when the medecin chef ran up excitedly telling me to return to the car at once as the M-D had been looking for me for 10 min. and bellowing his head off all the time. I felt very guilty and did my best to explain that I had thot they must return by the same road they went by, but the old man was badly disgruntled as was natural and it was an hour or more before he softened.

Wed. Oct. 30. Section moves to Vive St. Bavon. I again got in dutch with the M.D. This time at Ishegem. He had left me near the gate of the convent which had formerly been our quarters and as I needed water and knew where it was I entered the convent with my pail. As I came out the gate two you[ng] Poilus were standing there laughing and motioning me to hurry. In answer to my expression of inquiry they pointed up the street where my car was and looking in that direction I saw the old man stamping his feet, waving his arms and crying in a loud angry voice, "Americain, Americain." He was extremely angry when I came up but I explained to him that the radiator leaked and I had gone for water. Instantly his anger died away and with great solicitation he enquired as to the cause and nature of the hole and while I filled the radiator examined it with great minutiae[?] offering suggestions as to a remedy.

Thurs. Oct. 31. The attack started early this morning with two

French divisions on the flanks and one American at the center. The Americans went too fast and got ahead of their barrage which was put up by the French artillery so that there are many wounded and their ambulances don't seem to be able to handle them. At Zult this morning a young Frenchman walked a quarter of a kilometer holding his entrails in with his hands. After being bandaged he asked for a cigarette and when we put him into a car he was smiling as if nothing had happened. I don't suppose he will live but he surely had unlimited nerve. A little later I drove a captain up to an advanced poste a little thatched cottage at the end of a lane. While I was waiting outside I heard a terrible scream from within. I rushed inside but was too late to see the cause of the scream—an amputation without ether of a young Boche's leg. Never in my life have I seen anything which could compare to the pain and anguish in the face and every muscle of the body of that German. As we lifted him into the ambulance his huddled body expressed far better than words his—I know not what—could I describe what I saw there I would be a writer—I only know that I saw something trajic—more than trajic something I cannot put into words.

Mon. Nov. 4. The attack has been very successful and is at last terminated. The Americans added additional glory to their record in France and one may count numbers of kakai bodies lying half concealed by the beat tops of Belgian farms. Some of those young fellows must have felt at home in the beet fields those who came from southern Idaho at any rate and perhaps when they died the homely beet top brought them that much nearer home. The Germans surely did retreat in a hurry tho in good order. At night our postes would be where their artillery had run that morning and each night would find some of it hammering away at our lines. One night the poste was in a little farm house and I slept with the brancardiers in an open shed which faced the lines. Before going to bed I had attempted to light a cigarette but a chorus of poilus discouraged me for they claimed the Boches could see us. Soon afterwards the shells began coming over in our direction but fell a safe distance away. After we had gone to bed a recruit from an infantry battalion joined us and hung his bag of hand grenades on a flimsy shelf directly over my head. Despite the shelling which was close enough to be disconcerting I was deprived of sleep for some time trying to figure out how that shelf kept from falling under its weight.

We were amused one night when an American runner came into a poste considerably winded and some what excited. "My God," said he, "I've just come along that road they're shelling all alone and it's darker than hell." I wonder what our friend would have said if he had *driven* every night over worse roads than that all by himself.

One day I ascended into the tower of a chateau (which had recently been a German headquarters) in order to get a view back of the German lines. The tower had been a Boche observatory and some observer had written in charcoal on the plaster these conciliating words. "Pensez toujours au mot 'c'est la guerre' et pour cette raison pardonnez les hôtes malvenus." (Think always of the expression 'it's the war' and for this reason pardon your unwelcome guests.) A rather decent expression for a German but somehow I am inclined to think that it was conceived and written simultaneously with the author's realization that the Germans were doomed to defeat. But perhaps I am unjust and the man who signed himself "un soldat Allemande" (a German soldier) was merely a gentle, God fearing person who realized that the Germans were unwelcome guests and not God sent over lords of a benighted race.

Teus. Nov. 5. Section moves from Noker[e] to Vive St. Eloi. On our way over we were greatly surprised to be bombed by a German airplane which was flying so high that we never imagined he would try to hit us. We were not only surprised to have him throw his bombs at us but we were utterly astounded when he succeeded in wounding an American officer. The Americans are being relieved and another French Division has taken their place. The L'Escaut has been crossed and from here to the Rhine the going should be easier tho God help us when we get to the Rhine.

Wasilic had a very thrilling time in Audenarde today while driving the Medecin Divisionaire. They both narrowly escaped being killed and the M.D. suffered a slight wound. Wasilic is to receive another citation. I am wagering that the Old Man was tickled to death with his wound and only wishes it more severe. They say he cried during one attack because so many of the "ses enfants" (his children) were being killed. Abbot himself saw him and told us but I would believe it any way. Day after day for the two years we have been with him he has braved every danger. He seemed to have a contempt for life and I'm sure he would be an even more heroic figure in death.

I have a bad cold and I feel like a dog. I hope it's not the Spanish grippe.

Wed. Nov. 6. Not feeling any better today and since we are now on reserve and awaiting orders I can remain in my bunk.

Frid. Nov. 8. Every one is positive that two German generals came across the lines today with a white flag to demand an armistice. Foch has given them 72 hours to accept or refuse his terms and meanwhile preparations for another big attack are being made in this sector.

Sat. Nov. 9. They evacuated poor Bill Flint today. He has a second attack of the Spanish grippe and is a very sick boy. We were afraid he would die before he got to a hospital. Webber Clifford and Chappy all returned from the hospital. Weber and Cliff bribed a French doctor to give them 10 days' convalescence in Nice. 10 days in Nice and all for a 100 cigarettes! The Boches have retreated 25 K beyond the L'Escaut. Bavaria is said to have seceded. Worked all day on my car but feel rotten.

Sun. Nov. 10. 10 P.M. LA PAIX EST SIGNÉE!!

[Written in margin:] They're playing the Marseillaise now. God be praised for His goodness.

All the sky is lighted up with Verey Lights and gun flashes. All the Frenchmen are shouting and shooting and we're so plain *damned* happy we don't know where we are. All the Section is out.

LA GUERRE EST FINIE!

[Undated entry beginning at top of page 55 of recopied diary; (equivalent entry in original diary dated Nov. 17):] Really the entry for Nov. 10 should end on page 54. The make up of the bottom of that page portrays exactly our, or should I say my? feelings but those few lines were written while the daze had not left me. Then all was supreme gladness, un-adulterated, supreme, estatic joy. Joy, pure joy, but thoughtless joy. The entry under Nov. 10 does not explain why our joy was insane nor why, a little later when the spasm had spent itself, we drew within ourselves and went quietly back to our bunks where some of us laid till almost morning, silent, but wide awake. I remember how Rouget the French sergeant threw up his arms and fell limply into his cot exclaiming "Bon Dieu, it is the end of a bad dream." And so it was but like the awakening from a bad dream we were troubled to assure ourselves that the dream had ended, that now we were awake safe from the hideous thing which pursued us in our slumbers. And I remember how Hank looked up into that clear starlit heaven above us and said quite reverently "Do they mean to say that we won't hear again the hum of a Boche bomber and the shrill noise of a falling bomb?" then he shook his head uncomprehendingly. We had heard so many rumors that we thot this but the fabled cry of "wolf." We had hoped so long and passionately for this hour to come and had been so long disappointed that our minds could not grasp the meaning of it when it was here. As I have said before, after our first few months in the war we had so far identified with war that we were as men who have had a lapse of memory. The old life was gone forever and each succeeding day and each succeeding horror drove the peaceful part farther behind us till at last it was gone completely from our ken. Here we were, men made for war, men born to war, men whose life is filled from beginning to end with war and we felt secretly in our hearts that there could be no other life. Then to those of us who had been enough in war to lose our peace identity completely were suddenly, precipitately and unwarned flung into another life, a life of peace. We could have been no more awed, no more bewildered than would the men of Mars could they suddenly find themselves on this planet. Then gradually we came to realize what it all meant tho we walked warily like men fearing ambush fearful of having this new found joy snatched from our grasp. Even, when after a week the guns were still quite, though we outwardly were jovial and carefree, certain of seeing home again yet within ourselves we questioned, doubted nor were we ever sure deep down within us till we got our final pay, took off our uniforms and again sat at our family table.*

---

*A few later entries, describing Bowerman's experiences with the occupation forces, have been omitted as being of less interest than the wartime diary.

Sat. Nov. 9.

are being made in this sector.

They evacuated poor Bill Hunt today. He has a second attack of the Spanish grippe and is a very sick boy. We were afraid he would die before he got to a hospital. Webber Clifford and Chappy all returned from the hospital. Webb and Cliff bribed a French doctor to give them 10 days convalescence in Nice. 10 days in Nice and all for a 100 cigarettes! The Boches have retreated 20 K beyond the L'Escaut. Bavaria is said to have seceded. Worked all day on my car but feel rotten.

Sun. Nov. 10. They're playing the Marseillaise now. God be praised for this goodness.

10 P.M. LA PAIX EST SIGNÉE !!

All the sky is lighted up with Very lights and gun flashes. All the Frenchmen are shouting and shooting and we're so plain <u>damned</u> happy we don't know where we are. All the section is out.

LA GUERRE Est FINIE!

Maps

Map 1. France, 1914–1918.

Brussels
BELGIUM
LUXEMBOURG
Soissons
Compiègne
Reims
Verdun
Metz
Paris
Nancy
GERMANY
Troyes
Dijon
SWITZERLAND
t.-Germain
des Fossées
Vichy
Lyon
Aix-les-Bains
ITALY
Nice
Marseille

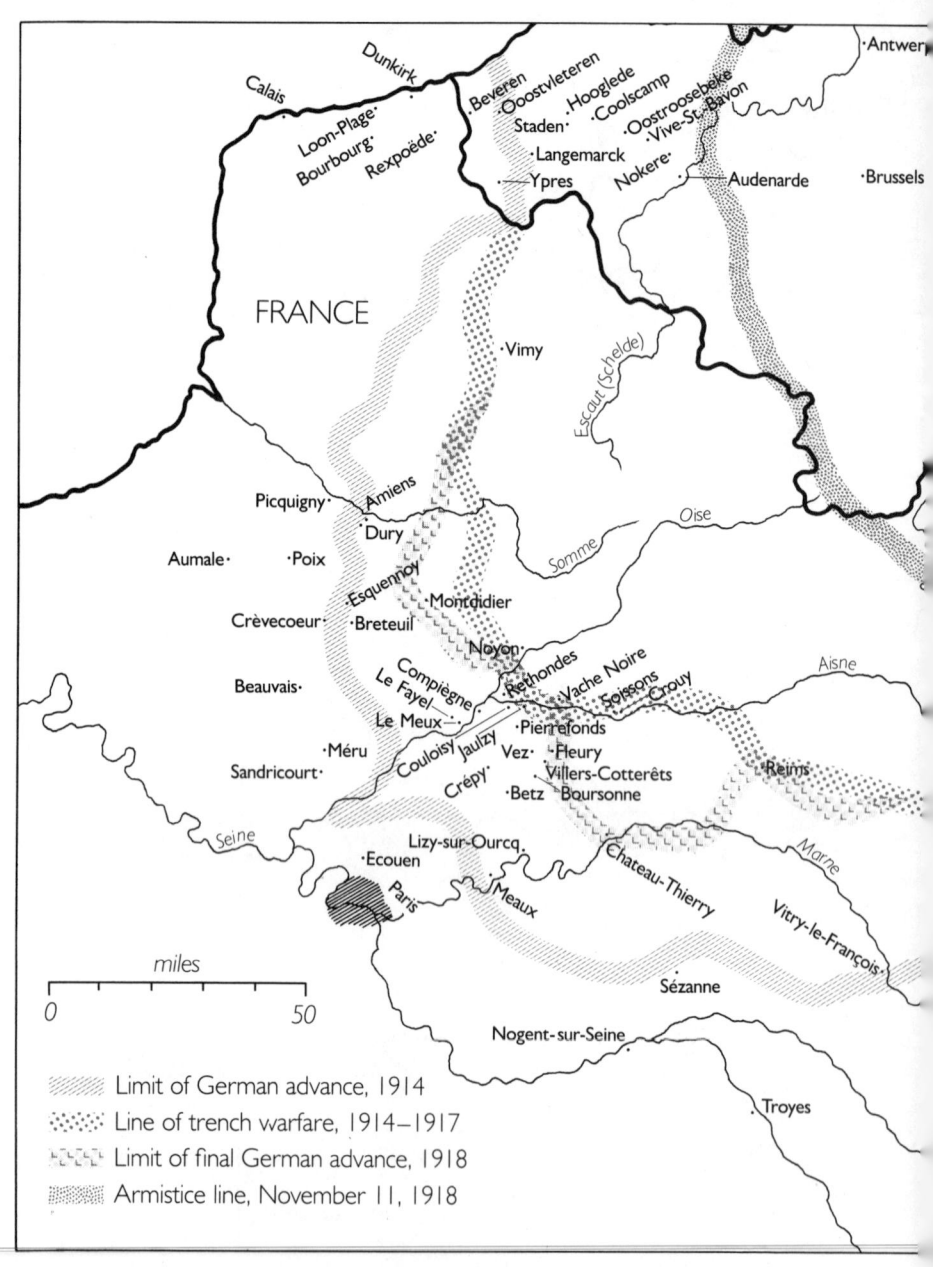

Map 2. The Western Front during World War I. Adapted from *Hammond's*

Historical Atlas (New York: C. S. Hammond & Co., 1954), p. H-33.

Appendix 1

Complete Roster of s.s.u. 585 from
August 7, 1917, to April 23, 1919

* Abbot, John R. (Lieutenant)
  Ballantyne, Aubrey   [Bal?]
** Balmer, Daniel T.
 * Barnes, Henry W., Jr.
** Bates, Alfred E.
  Beecher, J. Wilfred   [Beech]
  Borden, Carlton E.
  Bowerman, Guy E., Jr.   [Bowie]
  Bradley, Clarence I.   [Brad?]
  Butler, George D.
  Campbell, Howard   [Howie, Pop]
  Clifford, Warren T.   [Cliff, Pop]
** Core, Carroll
  Crane, Harold O.
  Cunningham, William   [Wild Bill]
** Durant, Church
  Flint, William A.   [Bill]
  Googins, David S.
  Green, Kirby F.
 * Harper, Lester
** Holbrook, Carl
  Houlihan, Leo J.   [Hap]
  Hubbard, Norman S. (Sergeant)   [Hub]
** Johnstone, Henry W. (Sergeant)   [Sgt. Johnny]
  Larkin, Robert D.   [Bob]
  Larrabee, Lester H.   [Ted]
  Larsen, Yens
  Lewis, Arthur V.
  Lundgren, Erland A. (Sergeant)   [Tony]
  Lyman, Lauren D.   [Deak]
  Lynch, Cornelius A.   [Neal, Crest]
  Marcellus, Gilbert L.   [Gil]
  Perkins, Albert G.   [Perk]
  Peters, Derek C. C.
** Peters, J. Wilton (Sergeant)   [Pete]
 * Potter, Howard P.

*Roberts, Paul (Sergeant)
Russell, Chester
**Shepard, Arthur M. [Shep]
Shively, George J. [Shive]
Sjöstrom, Raymond B.
Stevens, Gordon S. [Steve]
**Thorpe, Harry
Tremaine, Henry C.
**Van Doren, F. C.
Voorhees, Edwin H. [Ed]
Wasem, Louis, Jr.
Wasilik, John
Weber, James M. [Jimmy]
**Wharton, James (Lieutenant) [Myrtle]
*Wylie, Robert S.

Source: George J. Shively, ed., *Record of s.s.u. 585* (N.p.: E. L. Hildreth & Co., 1920). An asterisk indicates that the man joined the section after August 7, 1917; a double asterisk indicates that he left it before April 23, 1919. Brackets indicate nicknames used by Bowerman in the diary. Some of the names he used—e.g., Hank, "Papa Joffre," Chappy—cannot be clearly identified from the information available. Emery, mentioned both in the diary and in the section history, seems to have been omitted from this list.

Appendix 2
Station List, Section 585

Date of Arrival		Nearest Town and Département
1917	Aug. 20	St. Nazaire (Loire[-Atlantique])
	Sept. 29	Angers (Maine-et-Loire)
	Sept. 30	Nogent-le-Rotrou (Eure-et-Loire)
	Oct. 1	Sandricourt (Oise)
	Oct. 9	Génicourt (Meuse)
	Oct. 12	Amanty (Meuse)
	Oct. 16	Burey-en-Vaux (Meuse)
	Nov. 3	Custines (Meurthe-et-Moselle)
	Nov. 23	Nancy (Meurthe-et-Moselle)
	Nov. 25	Sandricourt (Oise)
	Nov. 27	Ecouen (Seine-et-Oise)
	Nov. 28	Sézanne (Marne)
	Nov. 29	Void (Meuse)
	Nov. 30	Nancy (Meurthe-et-Moselle)
	Dec. 23	Baccarat (Meurthe-et-Moselle)
1918	Apr. 1	St. Clément (Meurthe-et-Moselle)
	Apr. 22	Baccarat (Meurthe-et-Moselle)
	Apr. 23	Bazien (Vosges)
	May 3	Charmes (Vosges)
	May 5	Troyes (Aube)
	May 6	Chauconin (Seine-et-Marne)
	May 7	Aumale (Seine[-Maritime])
	May 9	Picquigny (Somme)
	May 20	Esquennoy (Oise)
	May 30	Le Meux (Oise)
	May 31	Rethondes (Oise)
	May 31	Vez (Oise)
	June 1	Villers-Cotterêts (Aisne)
	June 11	Boursonne (Oise)
	July 20	Pierrefonds (Oise)
	July 23	Le Fayel (Oise)
	July 29	Taillefontaine (Aisne)
	July 31	Couloisy (Oise)
	Aug. 13	Jaulzy (Oise)
	Aug. 18	Vache Noire (Aisne)
	Aug. 21	St. Christophe (Aisne)
	Aug. 24	Vez (Oise)

Sept. 4   Equiry (Aisne)
Sept. 5   Soissons (Aisne)
Sept. 8   Crouy (Aisne)
Sept. 19   Soissons (Aisne)
Sept. 20   Dury (Somme)
Sept. 21   Bourbourg (Nord)
Sept. 22   Le Casino (Nord)
Sept. 26   Rexpoëde (Nord)
Sept. 27   Beveren, Belgium
Sept. 28   Oostvleteren, Belgium
Sept. 29   Langemarck, Belgium
Oct. 1   Wifwege, Belgium
Oct. 16   Staden, Belgium
Oct. 17   Hooglede, Belgium
Oct. 18   Coolscamp, Belgium
Oct. 19   Iseghem, Belgium
Oct. 24   Emelghem, Belgium
Oct. 27   Oostroosebeke, Belgium
Oct. 29   Vive-St.-Bavon, Belgium
Nov. 3   Nokere, Belgium
Nov. 5   Vive-St.-Eloi, Belgium

Source: George J. Shively, ed., *Record of s.s.u. 585* (N.p.: E. L. Hildreth & Co., 1920).

Glossary

A.A.: anti-aircraft.
abri: shelter, dugout.
arrivé(e): "arrival," i.e., incoming shell.
assis: sitting, i.e., patient able to sit up in ambulance.
avion: airplane.
blessé: wounded.
Boche: German.
brancardier: stretcher-bearer.
camion: truck.
caserne: permanent barracks.
cave voûtée: cellar with arched roof (stronger than a regular *cave*, or cellar).
couché: recumbent, i.e., patient not able to sit up.
coup de main: sudden attack in force.
départ: "departure," i.e., outgoing shell.
éclat: shell fragment, piece of shrapnel.
gare: railroad station.
G.B.D. (Groupe de Brancardiers Divisionnaire): divisional unit of stretcher-bearers.
H.E.: high explosive.
H.O.E. (Hôpital d'Evacuation): evacuation hospital.
loupé: dud, shell that fails to explode.
malade: sick.
mauvais(e): bad.
M.D. (Médecin Divisionnaire): chief surgeon of a division.
médecin chef: chief surgeon of a regiment, or of a G.B.D.
mitrailleuse: machine gun.
Poilu: French soldier.
poste de secours: dressing station, where wounded were brought by stretcher-bearers and picked up by ambulance drivers.
ravitaillement: food supply.
repos: rest.
rien à faire: nothing to do.
RVF (Ravitaillement de la Viande Fraîche): fresh meat supply train.
saucisse: sausage balloon (captive observation or barrage balloon).
soit: so be it.

s.s.a. (Section Sanitaire Anglaise): English ambulance section.
s.s.u. (Section Sanitaire Unis): U.S. ambulance section.
territorials: soldiers drawn from French colonies or territories, especially from Africa.
tout de suite: right away.